Psychotherapy

A Cognitive Integration of Theory and Practice

Psychotherapy

A Cognitive Integration of Theory and Practice

ANTHONY RYLE

University Health Service
The University of Sussex
Falmer
Brighton

1982

ACADEMIC PRESS London • Toronto • Sydney

GRUNE & STRATTON New York • San Francisco

ACADEMIC PRESS INC. (LONDON) LTD.
24/28 Oval Road
London NW1

U.S. Edition published by
GRUNE & STRATTON INC.
111 Fifth Avenue
New York
New York 10003

British Library Cataloguing in Publication Data

Ryle, A.
Psychotherapy: a cognitive integration of theory and practice.
1. Psychotherapy
I. Title
616.89'14 RC480

ISBN (Academic Press) 0-12-793710-2
ISBN (Grune & Stratton) 0-8089-1488-X

Typeset in Hong Kong by Permanent Typesetting and
printed in Great Britain by St. Edmundsbury Press.

Preface

In this book I have tried to put forward an account of psychotherapy and of the human difficulties it aims to cure, in an accessible language which does not diminish the humanity of those described, and which is consistent with scientific psychology while being capable of assimilating the theories and methods of behavioural, cognitive, and psychoanalytic therapists. In making this somewhat immodest attempt, I shall doubtless be accused of doing less that full justice to some of those whose work I discuss; but I hope the reader will find that the arguments embarked upon are less sterile than the polemics which still characterize so much of the discussion between rival schools, and may discover both a comprehensible restatement of different viewpoints and at least a foundation for a unified theory and approach. Those who are deeply committed to particular paradigms, orthodoxies, or institutions are unlikely to enjoy the book, but I hope the increasing numbers of workers able to appreciate at least some virtues in traditions other than their own will find it helpful; and that there will be some practitioners, trainees and, maybe, some non-professionals prepared to take seriously this attempt to combine, in one approach, both reasonable intellectual rigour and humane flexible practice.

Brighton, February 1982 *Anthony Ryle*

Contents

Preface v

1. Introduction 1

2. The Procedural Sequence Model 7

3. Defences, Dilemmas, Traps, and Snags 21

4. Emotions and Symptoms 41

5. The Self 55

6. Teaching, Learning, and Therapy 68

7. Psychotherapy: Selection, Assessment, and Focus 76

8. Active Methods in Therapy 91

9. Transference: the Metaphoric Relationship between Patient and Therapist 102

10. Instructions, Constructions, Interpretations, and Strategies 119

11. Difficult Patients 130

12. Marking Progress and Ending Treatment 142

13. On Becoming and Being a Therapist 150

14. Aids to Self-scrutiny and Self-help 161

15. Afterword 175

References 177

Appendix: Repertory Grid Contributions to Understanding 183

Author Index 193

Subject Index 195

1
Introduction

This book offers a theoretical and practical account of how people change and, in particular, of how people who are not managing to solve their personal problems can be helped by psychotherapists. That a psychotherapist, in order to be helpful, needs certain human qualities and skills can, I hope, be taken for granted; but he also needs a trained intelligence, an appropriate range of concepts and the ability to share them with his patients. This book especially emphasizes how thinking can be applied to the solution of problems in living and emotional difficulties.

The book is written out of my experience as a psychotherapist; but earlier work in general practice, and some work in psychiatry in hospital settings, has left me very aware of the inadequacy of the provision of this kind of help for the many people who might make use of it. For this reason I am particularly interested in therapy that is brief, in the use of methods that can be shown to be effective, in approaches that enlarge patients' capacities for self-help, and in ideas that are accessible to the lay reader. We all lead complicated lives in a difficult world, and the claim made by psychotherapists that the quality of a person's life can be altered by a few hours spent listening to, talking to, or instructing, is, on the face of it, somewhat outrageous. Not everybody accepts the claim, and sweeping hostile criticisms are still fashionable in some quarters; but evidence, large in volume if mostly poor in quality, points firmly to the conclusion that many different ways of conducting therapy are effective in producing many different kinds of change in many different kinds of person. There is much less agreement as to which methods of treatment are most effective in producing what kinds of change in what kind of person. The clarification of that issue has been much hampered by the fact that psychotherapists resemble the builders of the Tower of Babel, both in the lack of modesty of their ambitions, and in their division into warring groups lacking a common language with which to connect their different ideas and enterprises. In this book I am proposing an approach to psychotherapy which is not confined by the language, concepts, values, or methods of any existing school.

The approach I am proposing is described as far as possible in everyday language, but is based on scientific psychology. The underlying model is of how people perceive, understand, and give meaning to, their experience, and of how they learn to act in the world. The model is a simplified one derived from the study of the growth and development of thinking (developmental psychology), from attempts made to understand thinking by experimental and theoretical work (cognitive psychology), and from the use of computers to carry out functions analogous to those carried out by the mind (artificial intelligence). However, these branches of scientific psychology have only distant contacts with clinical work, and most of the practically based knowledge of use to psychotherapists is available only in the languages of one or other of the rival schools. It is my aim to consider how methods of treatment derived from these different sources can be combined on the basis of the model proposed.

The choice of a model or language with which to describe people inevitably implies an assumption about the nature of man. Psychiatry in Britain has strong medical roots and has concentrated its rather scanty resources upon the care of patients, with serious mental illness, who are not primarily treatable by psychological means. Workers in this tradition tend to think in terms of "man as organism" and to accept only incompletely and uneasily a responsibility for psychologically determined and psychologically treatable distress. Psychologists and social workers have to some extent made up for this bias. In the United States, on the other hand, medical psychiatry has been much more influenced by psychoanalytic thinking, to the extent that some consider that physical and genetic influences have been neglected. In so far as British psychiatry has been influenced by any psychological theory, behaviourism has come to have a larger impact than psychoanalysis; at least, outside the psychoanalytic community in London. In my view, while behaviourism and psychoanalysis have contributed most of the practical understanding that we have of psychotherapy, they are both defective theories. The behaviourists' exclusion of any consideration of self-consciousness and intention and indeed, until recently, of any concern with cognitive function at all, leads to a painfully diminished account of man. Psychoanalytic theory, offering a much more complex model, indeed a chaotic one, is in its own way also humanly reductive in that it seeks to explain man's actions and experiences in terms of the interplay between impersonal forces or entities in the mind. The cognitively based model which I am proposing emphasizes the way in which people actively live their lives on the basis of mental representations of themselves and of the world. A person's system of mental representations places his perceptions, understandings, predictions, and actions within a system of personal meaning. Human life has human, not mechanistic, meanings and issues of learning, feeling, meaning, and choice must be central to any adequate account of it. In emphasizing choice, one does not, of course, deny the limitations imposed upon us by our biology or by external reality. Psychotherapy cannot change many aspects of our natures and it cannot change the world, but it can help us to change how we understand ourselves and our relation to the world. Thinking about changing involves examining how we think, feel, act, and learn, in order to make our experience fuller, and our thinking and acting more effective.

THE VALUES AND SCOPE OF PSYCHOTHERAPY

The central aim and value of psychotherapy, as I see it (and this will become clearer in the course of the book) is that of enlarging people's ability to live their lives by choice. While the removal of symptoms is a worthwhile act, and is sometimes all the patient requests, the nature of psychologically derived symptoms is such that wider aims are nearly always implied. These aims are achieved by enabling patients to acquire a more accurate and fuller experience in place of muted, denied, or distorted experience, and by reducing those aspects of life that are lived by compulsion or evasion, and extending those that are lived by desire and intention.

Those whom we call neurotic may have elaborated recognizably abnormal patterns of thinking or acting, such as obsessions or phobias, but many are distinguishable from their fellows only by the frequency, intensity, or apparent inappropriateness with which they suffer emotional distress. Such distress is related to how their lives are lived and often involves external events of importance, such as problems at work, relationships that go wrong, or bereavements and other losses. In such cases, the external events may appear as causes, but they may also be the result of the individual's own actions. Psychotherapy offers a particular kind of help to these people. Drug therapy may serve to dull emotional pain; political or social action may express an appropriate response to external sources of difficulty; friends may help with affection, material aid, practical assistance, and advice. Distinct from these, psychotherapists will try to help the person in trouble to understand how far his own beliefs, assumptions, attitudes, and strategies of living may have brought about, or maintained, the distress from which he is suffering, and will help him to explore how these ways may be changed.

There are countless ways in which the psychotherapist may attempt to do this: the approach described in this book is a synthesis and extension of some of them. The main sources are the contrasted and conventionally opposed ones of psychoanalysis and of the cognitive and behavioural therapies. From the former is especially derived the view that our personalities are deeply influenced by our particular histories, and the understanding of the subtle use that can be made of the relationship that develops between psychotherapist and patient in encouraging change. From cognitive and behavioural approaches is derived the belief that the therapist who is prepared to direct actively a patient's attention to his need to act differently in discrete situations, or to change habitual actions and thoughts, can enable many people to gain control over important aspects of their lives. To anticipate the discussion of these issues that will recur throughout the book, my overall judgments of the two approaches can be summarized as follows.

Psychoanalysis makes an attempt that is proper in range and ambition, but it has become trapped by theoretical confusion and restricted in its methods by institutional pressures. Cognitive and behavioural approaches, on the other hand, offer effective therapies over a limited range on the basis of theories that attend to only segments of human experience. While I am not seeking to write a comprehensive review of these rival theories, I will indicate their main positions throughout the book, both in the theoretical and applied sections, and describe how the proposed approach resembles and differs from them. My wish to reconcile and combine these opposing viewpoints has rational and intellectual reasons but, as so often in human life, draws some of its energy from less publicly commendable sources and attitudes. This may be illuminated by two incidents that occurred while I was occupied with writing this book. The first was a dream, provoked by a full bladder. I was in a bare, carpeted waiting-room about to see Freud: unable to find a toilet, I lifted up a flap of carpet and discovered a small concealed urinal. Thinking about how to describe this experience to Freud, I considered whether it was appropriate to use the term "Freudian interpretation" to him, and then decided that the main thing was not what I was going to say, but the fact that I had come to the consultation; at which point I woke up. The second incident moves on from the interpretation of dreams to the psychopathology of everyday life. It occurred when I wished to get hold of a book on behaviourism, written by somebody whom I had met and liked. I had walked a mile or so through a very cold Massachusetts winter's day to the bookshop, only to find myself there quite unable to recall the author's name .... I must leave it to my readers to interpret the meaning of these two episodes, and to my text to demonstrate how far my evident ambivaluence in both directions has been satisfactorily resolved.

PLAN OF THE BOOK

Readers who have little background in any psychological theory relevant to psychotherapy may find the comparative and integrated approach of this book a reasonable starting point; whereas those in the field, but mostly familiar with only one approach, may be helped to see more clearly its relation to the views of others. The main text consists of an exposition of my own ideas, using the language and concepts which I consider most appropriate to the task, and it is largely unencumbered by references and quotations. However, each chapter will conclude with a discussion section, which serves to link the ideas put forward in the text to current thought and practice, and to indicate the main published sources.

The book opens with a general account of how we learn about the world and how we act in it, and of neurotic behaviour and experience. In this account I consider how our assumptions, beliefs, and limitations on accurate understanding and experience on the one hand, and how our self-perpetuating, restrictive, or negative ways of acting, on the other, serve to block the effective solutions of our life's problems. The implications of this model for an understanding of symptoms, emotions, and the self are then considered, and the kinds of learning required in therapy or in self-induced change are compared with theories of learning in general. Following this, is an account of the process of therapy, with the main attention being paid to those procedures that are appropriate to relatively brief and time-limited treatment. Finally, consideration is given to how the individual seeking help himself may be guided towards useful ways of thinking about and changing himself.

Throughout the book, I use the term "patient" to describe somebody being treated by a psychotherapist; others might prefer "client" on the reasonable grounds of making a distinction between the psychotherapeutic relationship and that appropriate between a doctor and someone suffering from a physical illness. However, my own familiarity with the term is too great for me to abandon it. "Psychotherapist" can also be taken to include "counsellor" and "caseworker". Similarly, throughout, except where individuals are being discussed, "he" or "his" also implies "she" or "hers".

One important source must be acknowledged. I have made extensive use of case histories, and of the written or tape-recorded words of patients whom I have treated over the past fifteen to twenty years. In all cases, anonymity is ensured by a restriction on the material quoted, and by the alteration of details not central to the argument. Wherever possible I have sought express permission to use these quotations, but in some cases I have no means of contacting the patients concerned; should any such patient recognize his own story or words, I hope he will recognize also my gratitude and debt. I am particularly grateful to "Anne" and "David", the accounts of whose therapies are used as illustrations throughout the book.

DISCUSSION

This discussion will be confined to psychotherapy research, the other issues raised being further considered in the rest of the book. The published literature in the field of psychotherapy research is enormous and is best surveyed through painstaking reviews, such as those of Bergin and Garfield (1971), Bergin and Strupp (1972), and Gurman and Razin (1977). Kazdin and Wilson (1978) offer a coherent partisan review of behaviour therapy; Luborsky *et al*. (1975) take a more general look at the problems involved in comparing different methods of treatment.

Among individual studies, that by Candy *et al*. (1972) describes the failure of an attempt to compare behavioural and psychoanalytic approaches, a failure essentially due to difficulties in defining common terms and criteria, and serving to illustrate the need for a common language and conceptual frame-work. One of the more successful attempts in this field is the work of Sloane *et al.* (1975).

In their study, after special interviews to ascertain suitability, hospital out-patients were randomly allocated, to either a psychodynamic or behavioural programme (each being staffed by experienced clinicians) or to a waiting-list. Progress in these three groups was measured by a wide variety of methods. The study showed that patients in both treatment groups showed higher improvement rates than did the controls, but no clear advantage was shown for either approach over the other, except that the more active behavioural methods had a slight edge over the psychoanalytic ones for more severely disturbed patients.

In general, behavioural treatments are easier to evaluate than psychodynamic ones because their aims are more limited and more explicit, being largely confined to changing observable behaviours. The attempts to define equally explicit and measurable dynamic goals for psychoanalytically derived therapies has been made all too rarely, and seldom with success. The work of Malan (1963; 1976a, 1976b) is one of the more satisfactory in this field. Cognitive therapists (e.g. Beck, 1976) resemble the behaviourists in that they incorporate specific goals in their treatment programmes and, hence, research evaluation is feasible (Rush *et al.* 1977). Workers in the cognitive movement have set a recent trend in psychotherapy research which I personally find somewhat disturbing: in order to standardize the therapeutic "input", treatment manuals are prepared and therapists are trained to operate only in prescribed ways. This apparent simplification of the researcher's task (I say "apparent" for there will still be major variations in the style and personality of therapists) can only be achieved at the cost of crushing the subtlety and flexibility of the therapist, and the whole future of therapy could be distorted if only simple methods, simply evaluated, were blessed with scientific respectability.

In my own view, the development of more appropriate outcome criteria for the more complicated dynamic therapies is the first priority. It is important that we can specify and make measurable the full range of changes sought and, in particular, we must be able to measure the changes in underlying patterns of thinking, as well as the changes in observable behaviours. Small-scale studies of this sort, which demonstrate the achieving of specific cognitive changes indicated as goals at the start of therapy, following the focused, integrated, active therapy as described in this book, have been reported in Ryle (1979a and 1980).

2

The Procedural Sequence Model

In this chapter, the model of human action that is to serve as the focus for the book will be described. A model or theory of something is an account (in a form we are familiar with) to which we can refer when we want to explain or predict the qualities of the thing or process in question. Models can be verbal, pictorial, mathematical, mechanical, or loosely allegorical; their purpose is always to demonstrate or explain only certain selected characteristics, not to reproduce the reality of the thing itself. The same thing or process can be equally truly described by different theories or models. The engineer's model of the physical forces involved in building a bridge, and the physicist's model of the structure of the constituent atoms of iron out of which the bridge is made, are both true, but they serve different purposes. In psychotherapy we need a model of man that is appropriate to the task of understanding neurotic difficulty and informing our attempts to initiate change.

MODELS OF MAN

There is, of course, no shortage of models of man for, once men became self-conscious, they became the object of their own model-building propensities. However, most such models served both to describe and to control: they were expressions of the structure and belief system of the particular culture. Nothing is more effective as a social control device than giving an individual a description of himself that confines his self-understanding to the terms his society allots him. The attempt to build scientific models free from such moral and political influence (while also accounting for the operation of such influence) is of recent origin and has been incompletely successful, and indeed is likely to remain so. Laing (1967) has written with passion against that most general and prevalent distortion which stems from the failure to distinguish the scientific study of persons from the study of natural phenomena. Persons, he argues, must be defined in two ways: "in terms of experience, as a centre of orientation of the objective universe; and in terms of behaviour, as the origin of actions''. On this basis, ''social phenomenology is the science of my own and of others' experience. It is concerned with the relation between my experience of you and your experience of me.'' We can only know people, as we know the rest of our world, by way of our mental representations of them, built up out of our experience. We have an image of a person we know, which is essentially a form of theory, or model, of him. Our aim, humanly and professionally, must therefore be to make that image or theory capable of encompassing the full range of his qualities — qualities which include, among others, his capacity to hold a theory or image of us, and to dispute our account of him.

Failure to build adequate theories of others characterizes all of us in our everyday lives, and are especially characteristic of those we call ''neurotic''. It is often the case in personal life, as in social life, that restrictions on our understanding of others are not just random errors: they serve to convey value and to impose control. Incorporated into a human psychology that claims to be scientific, such distortions of human reality acquire a false authority, while the absence of an explicit, humanly adequate, scientific model of man can lead only to reliance upon unacknowledged, covert models.

While psychological models of man must not be humanly reductive, they are bound to be reductive in a different sense. We must bear in mind the way in which the physicist's and the engineer's models of the bridge differed. A given theory will serve only a particular purpose; in Kelly's terms (Kelly, 1955) it will always have a limited ''range of convenience''. A psychological theory says, implicitly, ''For these purposes it may be useful to conceive of these phenomena in these terms'', and it should not be read as the outrageous, ''Human life is this, and only this.'' To talk about human change, and about the pains and distresses of troubled people, is to touch on experiences which everybody has shared and which everybody knows at first hand to be extraordinarily complex. In considering a theory designed to guide us in understanding and changing the sources of such distress, we should bear in mind that it is a theory for a particular purpose and not an attempt to convey or reproduce the experience.

TWO CASE HISTORIES

In order to anticipate the connection between the theory and the human reality, I will introduce at this stage the stories of two patients, Anne and David, who will be described throughout the book as illustrations. As the account of theory and practice is unfolded we will see how the proposed model can help us understand these two people and their therapies.

Anne

Anne embarked on her professional career at the age of 24. At that time she would have described herself as stable, happy, and competent; and as coming from a close family in which, however, there had been some problems. She had been married for 2 years, and enjoyed a good relationship with her husband. She had recently had minor physical symptoms which left her with a slight nagging anxiety about cancer and, shortly after beginning her new job, she had developed a new habit of compulsively rubbing her eyes. She then had a frightening experience: she took some alcohol while on medication for a physical complaint, not realizing that the pills and the alcohol were incompatible, and she had an experience of light-headedness during which she felt her thoughts were racing and out of control. This made her convinced that she was going to have a nervous breakdown. This fear became an increasing worry and preoccupation, and it was on account of this that she sought psychotherapeutic help.

Anne's life history as told in the first assessment interview was as follows. She was the eldest of three children and her mother had had a psychotic breakdown following the birth of the third, when Anne was aged 5. She had recovered but thereafter had remained moody, difficult, dependent, and morbidly suspicious. Anne, as a child, had taken on the role of "little mother" to her brother and sister, and her father had increasingly delegated to her the responsibility for her mother also. The first few years at primary school, following her mother's breakdown, were marked by slow progress but, at the age of 10, she rapidly caught up, and from that time onwards high achievement was very important to her and she worked somewhat obsessively. Despite this, she had done less well than predicted in all of her major examinations at school and university, in each case underperforming in the subject regarded as her best. From the time of puberty onwards, her mother showed extreme jealousy of Anne's relationship with her father, as a result of which he became rather remote and quite inexpressive physically. Despite this, Anne often accompanied him on social occasions, and when she did so was always cross-examined on their return by her mother about his behaviour. During her adolescent years, both parents drank heavily and there was frequent quarrelling between them.

By the time Anne had completed the first part of her therapy (20 sessions over some 6 months), she had a rather different view of her history. She recognized that she had had a difficult childhood, although it was still hard for her to acknowledge this. Looking back on her family role she could see that she had carried an inappropriate burden through her childhood and adolescence. She recognized how mistrustful she had been of others, and saw how she had tended to structure most of her relationships in such a way that she was in control and offering care to others whom she saw as relatively weak. She recognized that her academic failures had represented a form of self-sabotage, and her husband had pointed out that this was a characteristic pattern in other contexts also. She had almost lost her preoccupation with her fear of a nervous breakdown, and she felt much more in touch with her feelings and much more expressive and open in her marriage. Both she and her husband were pleased with the change in the quality of their relationship. Although she still worked hard and was somewhat over-perfectionist, she allowed herself more time for pleasure. As therapy approached a long interruption, she was able to express openly her feelings about the break, and she was aware of the way in which this experience of directly knowing what she felt was important and unusual for her.

David

David was given an appointment at the request of an occupational guidance counsellor who had recognized his basic sense of not being in control of his life. By the time I saw him for assessment, however, his major preoccupation was the recent, sudden, unpredicted end of a 4-year-long relationship with a girlfriend, Patricia, which had plunged him into a state of disabling depression. He was a 26-year-old student who had left school at 17, soon after his parents had separated — an event which had been a complete surprise to him. He had gone to work as a nursing assistant in an old people's home, a post he held for 4 years. He formed his first serious relationship with a woman when he was 18, and lived with her for the following 4 years. Two months after that relationship ended, he met, and almost immediately began to live with, Patricia, the girl who had recently left him for a mutual friend.

At the interview, David was quietly spoken and self-deprecating. He was angry with himself for feeling needy, and reported that he was now largely avoiding the company of his friends, as he felt they were used to seeing him as a strong person and he could not bear to appear before them in his reduced state. He was not able to get on with his academic work and saw little point in doing so now that he had lost Patricia.

David was an only child and had had a happy childhood, but he had been notably upset at the age of 4, when he suffered a long separation of many months from his mother on account, first of all of his, and later of her, illness. David's first therapy (7 sessions over 3½ months) was concerned partly with supporting him through a period of mourning and with helping him get back to work, and partly with some exploration with him of how far his response to the loss of Patricia was linked with his earlier separation from his mother, and with the more general issues for which he had first sought help. It seemed that he had coped with the insecurity caused by the separation from his mother by "arranging" his later relationships with others in ways that ensured their availability as sources of security; and in this respect, both the professional role of caring for old people and being loved by his two girlfriends had been important. In most of his relationships he had adopted a helpful role which involved submerging his own needs and he now began to see that this had been accompanied by feelings of resentment. At the end of this time David was less depressed and angry, and felt that the experience of being on his own had been an important one. He felt more in control of his life and had begun to work again; he was beginning to be more assertive in general and attempting to be more mutual in his relationships with his friends. He was still markedly sad and lonely and he was aware of, but was resisting, an urge to seek another intense relationship. He had begun to feel more able to claim his life and to make decisions about what he wanted to do, and this was reflected in some firm career plans.

THE PROPOSED MODEL

In considering the model of man most helpful to the understanding of change, we are at once faced with philosophical considerations. The values implicit in a model informing the psychotherapist will have an effect upon the practice of his therapy. In behaviourist theory, the basic assumption is that behaviour is either a response to an environmental event (the stimulus response model), or an act upon the environment which is the result of previous learning about the effects of such acts (the operant model); favourable outcomes reinforce, and unfavourable outcomes extinguish, the tendency to repeat the behaviour. In such a view, change will be achieved by the manipulation of outcomes. In the psychoanalytic view, behaviour represents the expression of biological drives in forms modified by the ego's sense of reality and the superego's prescription of the permissible; with conflicts between these forces taking place largely in the unconscious.

The model proposed here represents a different view, emphasizing the human capacity for exploration and choice, and the human assumption of personal responsibility; it could, in that sense, be considered an existential position, although it is not directly influenced by either Sartre or the existential analysts. It starts from the position that man is in the world and acts upon it, living a life that is aim-directed, purposeful, or intentional. By intentional I mean that our lives are spent, consciously or unconsciously, in the pursuit of goals or in the defence of positions or values, rather than in random activity or in reining in, or giving expression to, instinctual impulses and drives. The satisfaction of basic biological needs such as hunger, thirst, sex, and attachment to others will be included among our intentions, but the way to these and other satisfactions will involve complex social judgements and actions, to be understood in terms of our overall personal understanding of our place in the world, acquired through experience and influenced in particular by our early years. In making aim-directed action the focus of a theory designed to explain and guide change in psychotherapy, I am also countering the assumption of powerlessness and passivity that characterizes many troubled people, by challenging the belief (falsely comforting in the short run) that it is possible *not* to act.

The model is a cognitive one because cognitive psychology offers the best available, and least reductive, account of mental processes. Cognitive psychology is concerned with knowledge, that is to say with how information is received, stored, coded, evaluated, and revised; and with how action is learned, selected, organized, carried through, evaluated, and modified: in brief, with how we know that world and know ourselves. Most of what we know, as information (knowing that), or as skills (knowing how), has been acquired through experience and has been stored in the memory, not as an infinite accumulation of detail, but coded in hierarchically organized systems of mental *schemata* (in Kelly's (1955) terms, *constructs*; in computer language, *programs*). All new experience, from the level of simple perception up to the most complex levels of understanding, is matched with this structured system. We see the world through a template, or grid; we know it by matching it with the distillation of what we already know. Thanks to this system, most situations are easily construed and most acts simply carried out, and survival in a complex world is possible. But the system is not static, for, faced with a new experience that cannot be *assimilated* or with an action that is not adequate to the task, we have the capacity to learn: provided the discrepancy is not too great, our cognitive system *accommodates* itself to take account of the new information, thanks to which we can survive in a complex world that is changing.

DEFINITION OF TERMS

Schemata organizing perception and those organizing action may be separately located, but in practice our understanding of a situation is combined with our plans for dealing with it. These and other combinations of schemata may be called *scripts*. It is not implied, as in transactional analysis, that lives are to be described in terms of a defining script; and scripts as used here may either organize action in the world or be concerned with self-evaluation and self-judgement. Scripts organizing life aims, the most general values, and self-definitions are *self-identity scripts. Strategic scripts* express life concerns as they are manifest in different contexts, determining, for example, sex roles, career choices, political attitudes, and much that is generally called ''personality''. *Tactical scripts* concern small-scale acts or events. In general, lower-order scripts are subservient to, and often expressions of, higher-order scripts. The execution of an aim-directed act involves a series of scripts or schemata, and I propose to call such a series a *procedural sequence* and, hence, the model as a whole is called the *procedural sequence model*, or PSM for short.

A DESCRIPTION OF THE PSM

The basic model describes the sequence of stages involved in aim-directed acts; it can be applied to acts of any degree of complexity. It is a simplified model, leaving out, for example, consideration of short-term versus long-term memory, and not distinguishing the different roles of world and image, or of logical and associative relationships in memory. Any stage of the procedural sequence can occur without involving conscious awareness, and some are not accessible to such awareness. The sequence described involves perception, comprehension, action, and evaluation. It is helpful to distinguish between two forms of evaluation. One is basically concerned with performance, asking the questions: ''Can the sequence be carried through?'' ''Is it being carried through?'' ''Has it been carried through?.'' This is a form of feedback control similar to the postural sense that is required in order to control a physical gesture. A second aspect of evaluation, of particular importance in understanding human conflict and difficulty, is concerned with our judgements of the consequences of our intentions and acts in terms of their compatibility with other aims, especially with those scripts that prescribe what is permissible or desirable (the equivalent of the psychoanalytic superego). We will now consider the basic features of the PSM as it will be applied to the understanding of neurotic phenomena and to the analysis of different theories and methods of treatment. The sequence is summarized in Fig. 2.1. It represents, of course, an ideal and simplified version of the partly conscious, and often illogical, steps and judgements involved in real-life acts.

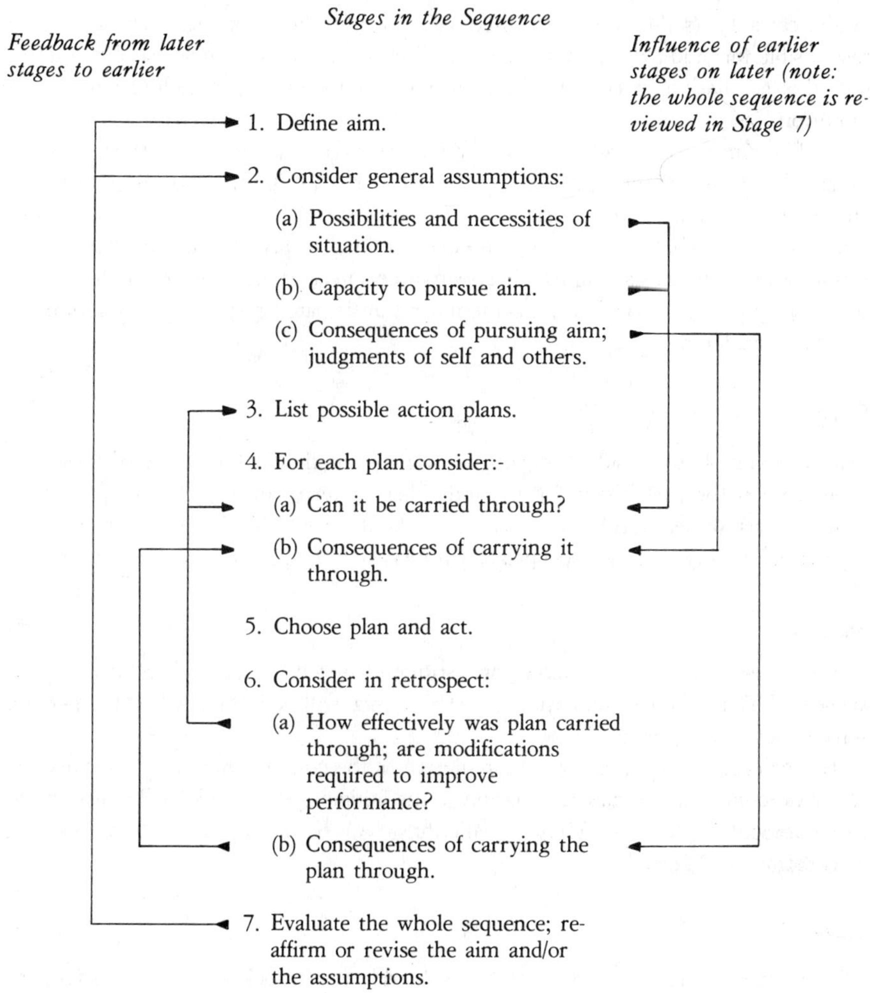

Fig. 2.1 The procedural sequence model

Stage 1

Define the aim or intention.

Stage 2

Consider general assumptions.

(a) The possibilities of the situation must be considered, for an intention can only be followed if circumstances are propitious. People vary in how they see the world as being something they can influence. Some situations necessitate particular acts.

(b) The intention must be considered in relation to one's assumptions about one's capacity (self-efficacy assumptions). People differ in how far they feel responsible for, and able to influence, the course of their lives. Whether accurate or not, this estimation of capacity influences decisions about proceeding with one's intention.

(c) The aim must be related to other intentions and, above all, to those central, salient definitions of self that provide the basis of self-criticism and self-judgement, and that determine the criteria of self-acceptance. Conflict between equivalent intentions, e.g. whether to have a holiday or buy a washing-machine, are not a serious issue in neurosis; conflicts between intentions and these central, judgemental scripts play a large part. The judgements and anticipated responses of others must also be considered.

Stage 3

This stage involves consideration of the available methods. The range of these will depend upon the past history of the individual in terms of his previous pursuit of similar aims under similar circumstances, and upon his ability to extend this repertoire by recognizing appropriate parallels or metaphors from his experience.

Stage 4

(a) For each means considered, an estimate must be made of the likelihood of success. This predictive evaluation of performance will be influenced by the general self-efficacy assumptions.

(b) For each means, similarly, a prediction of the consequences of the means and of the outcome will be made in relation to the anticipated responses of others and to the self-identity criteria. These predictions will be influenced by the general assumptions of Stage 2.

Stage 5.

The option with the best chance of success and lowest associated cost will usually be chosen, and the necessary act proceeded with.

Stage 6

The results of applying the chosen means are retrospectively evaluated in terms of (a) performance, and (b) consequences, judged in relation to self-identity criteria and to the effects on others. These retrospective judgements will be fed back to modify Stage 4, and possibly modify plans (Stage 3).

Stage 7

Finally, the degree to which the script was effectively carried through is evaluated, and where the results are discrepant with the aim, then either the assumptions will be modified or the aim or purpose revised.

At this point, we will return to the two patients whose case-histories were briefly presented earlier, in order to see how their stories may be understood in these terms. We will consider at this stage aims we infer to have been operating before the experiences that led them to consult.

Anne

In the case of Anne, we will consider two self-identity scripts: one serving the aim of preserving self-esteem, and the other the aim of being sane. As regards the first, Anne saw herself as a strong and lovable person and felt capable of sustaining this image. There were two situations relevant to this, and hence two sub-scripts. In the situation of the family, she ensured that she was seen as strong and that she was loved by acting consistently within the terms required by her ascribed role of helpful, thoughful, uncomplaining person. Acting in this way (which she did in most other relationships as well), she felt good about herself and gained the love of others and she had felt no reason to revise the script. In the situation of school, university, and work, Anne saw herself as intelligent, effective and capable of extracting confirmation of this by high achievement. Here, too, her actions were largely successful. The inconsistency of her history of incomplete success in examinations with this aim had not led to any serious questioning of central assumptions or strategies.

Anne also aimed to be sane. She perceived herself as being unusually stable, and she used two main strategies to maintain this view. In the first place, support of her mother and her siblings, and her generally sustaining, helpful, and resourceful role in relation to most others, gave her continuing evidence of her stability. In the second place, in her acts and in her self-descriptions, she maximized the differences between herself and her mother, demonstrating the degree to which she was in control by almost never acknowledging or giving expression to angry or suspicious feelings, and avoiding any dependency on others on terms which might indicate weakness. These strategies had been largely successful and she had not felt any need to reconsider them, although the recent minor compulsive habit and anxieties about her health (which preceded the episode induced by the medication) were discrepant with this aim.

David

David's aim of feeling worthwhile in the world had been pursued in the past on the basis of negative assumptions about both his capacity and his worth, although he was not entirely aware of this. His strategy in the face of these assumptions was to make sense of his actions in terms of their meaning for others, e.g. in his work with old people, and in his seeing university as being justified by its relevance to his anticipated future with Patricia. In general, these strategies of proving self-worth by being helpful to, or loved by, others had worked well, but they had contributed to the sense of not being in real control of his life, which had prompted him to seek the occupational counsellor's help, and were the basis of the sadness and pointlessness which persisted after his recovery from his mourning for Patricia.

THE ISSUE OF CONSCIOUSNESS

We have no more direct experience of most mental processes than we do of the functioning of our kidneys, lungs, or intestines. The mental operations involved in carrying out a procedural sequence can all occur without our being aware of them. Some processes, such as the way in which we make sense of primary sensory data in the act of perception, can never be made conscious. Other parts of the sequence, however, are accessible. In Bartlett's (1954) words, our schemata can "turn round" upon themselves. While consciousness is neither possible nor necessary for most mental processes, by allowing us to reflect upon our intentions and upon the assumptions and acts involved in carrying them out, it offers another level of experience and a further opportunity for learning. When we can reflect on what we assume, and on how we act, we can modify our assumptions and our actions. The extension of accurate self-awareness is an important aspect of psychotherapy. At any given moment, we are conscious of what is in our short-term memory. This represents only a fraction of what we can consciously know, however, and we can be led by external events, unbidden thoughts or images, or by our own intention, into extensive and intricate systems of memory and knowledge. Most of what we remember is codified and reduced, as Bartlett's (1954) early experiments on memory demonstrated; but some aspects of memory, experienced in the form of images, seem more like direct re-experience. Codified, schematized, "word-thought" memory is organized by reason and inference, while images are linked more by being associated with common personal meanings and emotions. Such images may be of particular interest to the psychotherapist in so far as they give access to systems of personal meaning that may be discrepant with the more logically ordered, verbally mediated communication of the patient. Encouraging associative thinking, using guided imagery or imaginary rehearsal, and the consideration of dreams are examples of the therapeutic use of this mode of thinking.

A great deal of what is stored in memory is inaccessible to us, and much of our action is therefore based upon scripts that we cannot describe to ourselves. One of the functions of a psychotherapist is to infer the nature of such scripts and make them available to the patient. There are two main forms of not knowing. In many cases, the patient can describe quite clearly his tactical scripts, but is unaware of how they are patterned by higher-order strategic or self-identity scripts. This is evident in clinical work, and is also very clearly demonstrated by research with the repertory grid (Ryle, 1975). In completing a grid, patients record in a paper and pencil test their conscious discriminations between people or relationships. Analysis of these ratings often reveals patterns of discrimination and judgement of which they were not aware; that is to say, their tactical judgements prove to be manifestations of strategic assumptions which had not been recognized. The other form of not knowing is the result of defence mechanisms, these will be considered in detail in later chapters. They operate as if, at various points in the script, another script, serving the aim of reducing mental conflict, intervenes with the instruction not to "access" certain perceptions, memories, or plans of action. Psychotherapists need to be interested in making both forms of unconscious mental activity conscious, for only then can poorly functioning scripts be considered, challenged, and altered.

DISCUSSION

The model of the procedural sequence proposed here is based upon current thinking in cognitive psychology. Major sources include the work of Bartlett (1954), of Miller *et al.* (1960), and of Neisser (1967). Keith Oatley, both personally and in his writings (Oatley 1978), persuaded me of the contribution of artificial intelligence and of the value of the computational metaphor as a basis for a theory of human psychology. My acceptance of a basically cognitive approach, and my understanding of how such an approach illuminated rather than denied the role of emotions, owes much to Kelly (1955) and to my work with the repertory grid, a mode of psychological investigation derived from Kelly's theory. Working clinically in a way largely influenced by psychoanalytic theory, and at the same time investigating my patients with the repertory grid, forced me to consider over and over again the connection between the two very discrepant accounts I was giving of the same patients (Ryle, 1975).

Kelly's personal construct theory, however, has remained strangely insulated from the rest of cognitive psychology, and neither Kelly nor his followers have given serious consideration to its relation to behavioural or psychoanalytic approaches. Moreover, personal construct theory, as its title suggests, has been concerned with the understanding and prediction of the world (the second stage of the PSM), but has paid relatively little attention to the organization of action.

The comparison of the PSM with other theories will unfold during subsequent chapters, but at this point some preliminary issues need to be discussed. To relate the model to behavioural/cognitive approaches is relatively simple, as the majority of those can be subsumed directly within it. I see their deficiencies as being those of incompleteness and, in particular of their neglect, in varying degrees, of cognitive processes, of an adequately subtle consideration of the self, of self-evaluation and self-judgement, and of conflict between aims and self-judgements. Psychoanalysis, on the other hand, while dealing with these issues, and while taking subtle account of the problems arising from early stages in cognitive development, does so in a language and a theory that at first sight seem to bear no relation whatever to the model proposed here.

As regards the cognitive/behavioural approaches, I find it hard to take simple behaviourism seriously as an account of man, or even of behaviour therapy; but in recent years the growing attention paid to central cognitive processes (e.g. Lazarus, 1971: Singer, 1974) and the concern with issues such as the sense of efficacy (Bandura, 1977b) and of expectancy (Rotter, 1978) have changed the picture considerably. Such work, and the parallel emergence of cognitive/behavioural methods (Meichenbaum, 1977; Goldfried and Goldfried, 1975; Goldfried, 1979) and of cognitive therapy (Beck, 1977) have produced an array of treatment methods which are clearly effective for a range of problems, and mark the emergence of a more coherent theoretical base. Bower (1978) has argued persuasively that the marriage between social learning theory and cognitive psychology is overdue, seeing social learning theory as "a form of cognitive psychology that has been applied ingeniously to issues of socialisation, to personality development, psychopathology, and behaviour modification." He thinks "it is time for people to see that behaviour modification technology could just as well rest on cognitive psychology as on S–R theory."

In the case of psychoanalysis, it is necessary to offer a brief review of the evolution and nature of the theory. The history of Freud's thought is a vivid illustration of the process of model-building through the use of multiple metaphors chosen from diverse origins (see, for example, Amacher, 1974). The abandoned "project" represented an attempt to base the understanding of mind on a study of brain: if the engineer resorted to the physicist's models of the atom in designing his bridge, he would be a victim of the same fallacy of failing to see that things in combination are governed by laws determined by their combinations, not by the laws governing their constituent parts. Although soon abandoning this attempt, Freud incorporated some metaphors derived from it in his theory, and added to these others drawn from the physical sciences, in particular in his description of mental processes in terms of the distribution, flow, or binding of energy. To these he added a geographical model of the mind in terms of regions separated by frontiers with border guards, later partly replaced by the structural theory which is a social metaphor of competing mental institutions. This latter can be seen to parallel the Judeo-Christian view of man (ego) suspended between demonic forces (id) and a judgemental deity (superego). Meanwhile, Freud was elaborating a developmental psychology which recognized how the bodily and social experience of the infant were inextricably linked, and which explained the heavy symbolic weight carried by bodily experience. This understanding of a particular content of mind became confused with a theory of mind, and these bodily metaphors were incorporated as further theoretical constructs (Schafer, 1975, 1978). Later in life, Freud gave more recognition to the model-building function of the mind in his increasing attention to the activities of the ego in mediating between the inner world and outer reality.

In the subsequent evolution of psychoanalytic theory, different schools have emphasized different metaphors. The primitive concepts of the body and its boundaries, and the distorted perceptions met in psychosis, which are assumed to reproduce some of the characteristics of infantile thinking, are made cornerstones of the Kleinian theory of mental processes. The object-relations school (Fairbairn, 1952; Guntrip, 1961, 1968) extended the structural theory by emphasizing the importance of the child's earliest mental representations of his relationships with others and by studying the effects of these earlier representations on later patterns of relationships. The growth of ego psychology (Hartmann, 1950) and the work of Sandler (Sandler and Joffe, 1970) signified an increased interest in perception and cognitive functions. As a result of these developments, there are few voices left within psychoanalysis wholeheartedly defending the full metaphoric jungle that grew in Freud's fertile mind; but none, it seems, prepared to transform it radically.

In psychoanalytic theory, the source of action is seen to lie in drives originating in the id, whose expression is allowed, modified, or disallowed, according to the ego's appreciation of outer reality, and the opposing forces of the superego. This superego is seen to originate as the internalization of parental authority; its operation is conscious to a varying degree, while the id is seen as more or less synonymous with the unconscious. The equivalent issues are conceived of differently in the proposed PSM. While intentions may include the expression of "drives", such aims are pursued by reference to complex models of the self and of the relationship of the self to others, organized in the personal self theory. Moreover, the exploration of reality and the "drive" to gain cognitive mastery of it are seen as very important sources of action, as suggested by White (1963) but still largely neglected in psychoanalysis. Issues described as id–superego conflicts in psychoanalysis are reconceptualized in terms of dissonance between aims and self-identity scripts.

The distinction between timeless non-logical associative primary process thought, said to be characteristic of the unconscious, and the secondary process thought associated with the conscious ego, is sustained in the cognitive view in the distinction between thinking in imagery and thought-word thinking. This distinction may be related to the different functions of the dominant and non-dominant cerebral hemispheres. Noy (1979) has offered a revision of psychoanalytic thinking, arguing that the two are inextricably related and of equal status. In his view, primary process thought organizes *experience*, with personal meaning incorporated in that which is known and remembered; whereas secondary process thinking organizes *knowledge* through representations of outer reality. In this paper, Noy also provides an example of the unsatisfactory nature of psychoanalytic theory, observing that primary process thought occurs in the unconscious id, ego, and superego, and hence that the primary–secondary distinction bears no relation to the structural theory at all; he says: "I would simply approach the two groups of concepts . . . as two different models, describing the mental apparatus from two points of view, and therefore stop bothering about the possible relationship . . .".

The differences between psychoanalytic and cognitive descriptions are all aspects of the fundamental one: psychoanalysis offers a set of compounded metaphors of energy, location and conflicting entities, while cognitive psychology describes the storage, retrieval, organization, and putting into operation of information. The PSM offers a very simple account, but should not be taken to constitute an invitation to accept a naive simplification of human experience. At each stage of the sequence, procedures may be coherent or contradictory, and any aspect of the process may be consciously recognized and under conscious control; consciously recognized but not under control; not consciously recognized but capable of being made so; or unconscious and inaccessible either inevitably or as the result of unconscious, conflict-reducing, cognitive strategies. Each procedure is shaped by the particular past history of the individual, and many will be limited by the persistence of assumptions or strategies rooted in earlier life stages. In the general assumptions of Stage 2, and the range of methods considered in Stage 3, will be found the results of the whole personal and cultural history of the individual. The simple PSM serves to locate these complex influences in relation to the individual's life; any understanding we may have of them, from whatever source, will serve to flesh out the bones of the model.

As regards the cognitive view of unconscious mental processes, Oatley (1981) suggests a six-fold classification, as follows.

(1) The unconsciousness of unconscious inferences. The perceptual processes whereby we make sense of our perceived world may be understood, but we do not have introspective access to them and cannot alter them.

(2) Unconsciousness as confusing inner and outer — as in dreams, hallucinations or misattributions due to using schemata to structure experience inappropriately.

(3) Unconsciousness as being without an appropriate schema.

(4) Unconsciousness as being unaware of the origin of our interpretation, due to the persistence of "implicit theories" based on forgotten (often infantile) learning.

(5) Unconsciousness of other people's meanings, usually due to false assumptions of similarity to one's own.

(6) Unconsciousness as being stuck within some too rigid theory.

3
Defences, Dilemmas, Traps, and Snags

In the ordinary course of life, most of us develop a reasonably accurate view of ourselves and others, a realistic range of purposes, and a repertoire of effective means; but for all of us sometimes, and for some of us always, our means prove ineffective and our aims unattainable in important ways. In order to overcome our failures to solve potentially soluble problems, we need to know about the ways in which our normal problem-solving and aim-fulfilling scripts work and about how the processes can go wrong.

The emphasis on aims in the PSM should not be taken to imply that only conscious logical action is important, or that only deliberate thought and action can produce change. An important part of psychotherapy for some people is that it provides permission for, and the opportunity for, non-logical thought, e.g. through dreams or the exploration of fantasy. Indeed, one aim of therapy may be a richer contact with those aspects of thought and feeling that can be called non-rational, mystical, or creative. In guiding patients through such experiences, however, the therapist needs to have a clear model of what kind of process he is intervening in. Many patients are out of touch with their feelings and confused about the personal meanings of their experience, and are hence unable to recognize and pursue the full range of potential human aims. Their state represents one of the end results of restrictions imposed on the self by the self, or by the terms of relationships with others. In this and ensuing chapters we shall be considering common ways in which personal meanings become confused and intentional scripts "go wrong".

The procedural sequence is a sequence of mental operations, each one of which must be completed satisfactorily if the aim is to be achieved. Abandonment of an aim may take place appropriately if it is seen to be incompatible with other aims or if it is judged correctly to be beyond one's powers to attain, or if the situation is recognized accurately as being unpropitious. In the same way, the absence of an available means or plan of action, or the correct evaluation that the proposed means would be — or, after execution, have been — ineffective, undesirable, or costly, will lead either to the modification of the various judgements made and procedures used, or to the abandonment of the aim. The last step in the procedural sequence (the stage of reviewing evaluations and modifying assumptions and purposes) represents the learning process, whereby more accurate perceptions, more appropriate assumptions, and more effective actions, may be developed.

In considering why intentions are inappropriately abandoned or modified, and why the problems in the way of their attainment are not solved, we must consider all the ways in which the procedural sequence might be interrupted or diverted. If there is no realistic reason for abandoning an aim (and this is the defining criterion for neurosis and for the sort of problem that we are considering), then there must be a false reason; and if there is a false reason which is not corrected, there must be a factor at work which makes the error self-perpetuating: understanding these self-perpetuating processes is essential if we are to interrupt them.

In considering this issue of failed or abandoned procedural sequences, we are not concerned with isolated acts or events, but rather with those that recur. We need, therefore, to look at every stage of the sequences, including the last, at which learning does, or does not, take place. We will start by looking at each stage in the sequence in turn, in order to consider how it might contribute to difficulty, before moving on to the various forms of self-perpetuating problem that are clinically important and which usually involve several stages in the script.

CAUSES OF INAPPROPRIATE AIM ABANDONMENT AT DIFFERENT STAGES

Stage 2

(a) At the stage of considering assumptions, the understanding of the possibilities of the situation may be subject to specific, systematic distortion e.g. through a negative, depressive bias or through the denial of the meanings of particular aspects of reality.

(b) As regards self-efficacy, negative beliefs about one's capacity to influence events, or the assumption that the "locus of control" is largely in others, will inhibit effective action. Unrealistically positive self-evaluation can also lead to inappropriate acts.

(c) The criteria which define and judge the self may prescribe limits to the roles and capacities available to the individual, or may apply harsh, unrealistic, critical conditions for the maintenance of self-esteem. Specific aspects of the self, in the form of certain acts, attitudes, or qualities, may be undeveloped or forbidden expression. Negative responses to self-assertions from others may be anticipated consciously or unconsciously (see below: Snags).

Stage 3

At the stage of the listing of possible action plans, an individual may possess only a narrow range because of restrictive past experience, or because his ability to draw on analogous experience may be limited, or possible acts may be conceived of in terms of two contrasted, polarized alternatives (see below: Dilemmas).

Stage 4

(a) At the stage of the anticipation of performance, there may be a systematic over- or underprediction of the likelihood of success by the available means; this will be influenced by the general assumptions about self-efficacy and about the situation.

(b) At the point of considering the consequences of a plan, either the outcome or the means may be seen to conflict with basic assumptions and values; or there may be a realistically or unrealistically based anticipation of negative responses from others.

Stage 5

At the point of deciding on the means and operating them, the performance, for whatever reason, may fail to achieve the desired end.

Stage 6

(a) During the process of retrospective evaluation of performance, the effectiveness of the act as performed may be underestimated or overestimated.

(b) In the same way, the retrospective evaluation of the consequences of the act may be distorted by bias of a positive or negative sort.

Stage 7

Finally, in reviewing and evaluating the procedural sequence, the aim, or the process, whether realistically understood or seen in a biased way, may be judged in such a way that basic assumptions about the self and the situation may be revised in ways diminishing the likelihood that the attempt will be made to pusue the aim again.

THE DEFENCE OF DENIAL AND REPRESSION

We will now consider two of the classical defence mechanisms as described in psychoanalysis, namely denial and repression. The function of these defence mechanisms is to reduce anxiety and conflict. (In psychoanalytic terms, they serve to defend the ego against unmanageable aspects of reality or against id–superego conflicts.) Denial represents the failure to acknowledge the meaning and implications of a situation; it can operate with varying intensity from minor distortions due to idiosyncratic interpretations, through the editing out of the most uncomfortable aspects, to an extreme inability to face obvious meanings. In terms of the PSM, denial represents the reduction of conflict between an aim and the perceptions and assumptions reviewed in Stage 2 by means of distorting or selectively ignoring aspects of the latter. In repression, the aim or the means available for its attainment are not acknowledged.

Rosa

An example of denial is provided in the account of Rosa, a 30-year-old Italian woman who had described, in her first psychotherapy assessment session, two events in her life which would be expected to be very distressing, but which she had met, it seemed, with calm indifference. These events were her premarital pregnancy and her husband's suicide. During the (tape-recorded) second session she returned to these issues, and I asked her, "What happens to the feelings?". She replied:

> I've thought about it; I wonder why. I must explain something: I was passing through the churchyard and there were graves there and I could see them. I didn't feel anything but crossing the road was very difficult because my eyes were sore and tears were coming down. I thought that my eyes had something sensitive to the sun, though it wasn't very sunny. Once I visited the cemetery again at visiting time for about 1½ hours; my tears was coming down, I didn't cry. Again I thought the marbles were white and there was snow on the ground and because of the white my eyes were irritable. Then these sorts of things happened always related to death in some way, and then I thought, "it is a real tear".

Denial is located in the situation-scanning stage of the PSM. The original aim is made subservient to a more dominant aim — that of preserving a manageable degree of conflict or discomfort. In repression, the meaning of the situation is similarly distorted, with an additional "forgetting" of the aim or with the exclusion from the repertoire of possible means of certain actions that might achieve "forbidden" outcomes. Here, too, there is a continuum from minor blocks on memory and action through to the quite specific exclusion of certain situation–action procedural scripts.

The more general statement about denial and repression is that they represent extreme ends of a spectrum of restriction on, or distortion of, aspects of the procedural script. As Haan (1977) points out, the healthy equivalents representing coping strategies rather than defensive ones, are concentration for denial, and suppression for repression. These modes are healthy because they represent adaptive, consciously reversible behaviours which heighten the capacity to pursue aims, whereas the defences of denial and repression achieve the aim of anxiety-reduction only at the cost of reduced accuracy in the understanding of the situation and a reduced range of available action.

We will now consider three classes of self-perpetuating difficulty, which I have described under the heading of traps, dilemmas, and snags (Ryle, 1979a).

TRAPS

The concept of the trap is intended to suggest circularity or self-perpetuation. The basic sequence of a trap is that an unwanted or inappropriate belief leads to a form of action intended to correct it but, in fact, serving to maintain or reinforce it. The circularity of traps derives from the feedback to the early stages of the PSM of judgements from the later stages. Simple traps involve only feedback from Stage 6 to Stage 4, whereby the prediction of an unsuccessful act, based on the judgement that earlier acts were unsuccessful or disallowed, leads to poor subsequent performance or to avoidance. However, more general considerations (Stage 2) may influence, or be influenced by, these detailed procedures, and actions may be further impaired or diverted by revisions (Stage 7) of the basic judgements about the possibility and permissibility of desired acts.

A clinically familiar example of the trap is a phobia. A simple model of phobic behaviour is that the false perception of danger in the situation or object for which the phobia is felt (PSM 2a), linked with the sense that there are no means adequate to cope with it (PSM 2b), leads to the abandonment of aims involving facing the situation. If an attempt is made to overcome the fear but the execution fails (PSM 6a) or leads to symptoms of fear or panic (PSM 6b), the assumptions of danger and of incompetence (PSM 2) are heightened, reinforcing the initial perception of danger. Repeated experiences of this sort have the further effect of redefining the self as a phobic person, and this can lead to the abandonment of further attempts to confront the feared situation (PSM 7). The identity of the self as phobic, once established, may colour a number of the strategic relationship scripts enacted by the individual; this can be seen as a form of secondary gain from the symptom, to use the psychoanalytic term. Primary gain, in the psychoanalytic view, lies in the fact that the original avoidance served a purpose in that it prevented the carrying out of some other, often unacknowledged, forbidden intention (PSM 2c); e.g. the phobic, housebound wife, according to some psychoanalysts, avoids exposure to men other than her husband, and achieves the primary gain of avoiding the (often unconscious) temptation to infidelity. The initial cause is often less hidden, however: feelings of incompetence, an incompletely developed sense of autonomy (PSM 2b), and the example of inappropriate fears in other family members may all play a part in the initiation of symptoms. The sequence: experienced fear— anticipated fear— fear on exposure but fear relief on avoidance— avoidance, is a trap sequence maintained by the experience of symptoms whenever exposure is attempted.

Obsessive–compulsive phenomena may be similarly understood. The aim of the compulsive act or thought is to avert danger; in so far as the danger is unreal, the act is a magical one. The simple model involves a false perception of danger, as in the phobia. The intention to confront the anxiety and avoid the obsessive act, which is what recovery demands, is difficult or impossible to pursue because of the knowledge, based on repeated experience, that to do the act is possible and is effective in relieving anxiety. If the danger feared carries symbolic ''moral'' meaning to it, its control by means of the magical compulsive act serves as a protection against the external danger (PSM 2a) or against the forbidden act (PSM 2c) which it might otherwise call forth. The identity of compulsive person is in due course acquired, and may acquire secondary meanings, as in the case of phobias. The fact that compulsions to do with cleanliness (which, according to tradition, is next to godliness) are common, suggests that the primary gain of obsessive–compulsive states includes the magical control of guilt-provoking thoughts or wishes. In psychoanalytic terms, the compulsive act is a reaction formation, that is to say, it is an act repeatedly performed as being the reliable alternative to other forbidden (id) acts. In terms of the PSM this represents a restriction at the third stage, based on a false dichotomy or dilemma (see below).

Robert

This may be illustrated by a case history. Robert, aged 21, had suffered from panic attacks, a marked travel phobia, and extensive, severely restricting, obsessional–compulsive symptoms for the past 5 years. Medication had eased but not abolished his symptoms. He was the only child of highly achieving, controlling, perfectionist parents. His symptoms began soon after he had defied his parents by refusing to stay on at school at the age of 17. At about the same time, both his grandfather and his aunt had had surgery for intestinal obstruction and both had been left with colostomies, whereby the bowel empties through a surgically constructed opening in the abdomen wall. The colostomies seemed to have become symbols of loss of control, and were associated in some way with his own sense that his assertion of his independence had been a "shitty thing to do". He developed extensive rituals, including counting, special ways of going through doors, up and down stairs, getting dressed, and washing, and he became obsessively preoccupied in public places with the possibility that the people he saw there might have colostomies. At times he became concerned with the fate of his garbage, becoming unable to part with it, so that at those times his room was lined with plastic containers full of waste paper and kitchen refuse. Along with this, he began to have the feeling that he did not really exist, and would have to look repeatedly in the mirror to reassure himself. Robert had left home at 18 to live with a girlfriend and in that relationship his symptoms enabled him to be highly controlling. He was unable to travel or spend a night without his girlfriend's presence, and, if she were away for more than a few hours, she was required to telephone. Robert's symptom, therefore, continued to punish him for, or prevent him from, repeating self-assertions, while sustaining him in a controllingly dependent role with the girlfriend.

Some forms of depression can be regarded as a trap. The basic depressive vicious circle may be summarised as follows. Harsh self-identity criteria, a low estimation of self-efficacy, and a negative evaluation of the situation together determine negative predictive evaluations and negative judgements about the consequences of particular acts. This can lead to the abandonment of the intention, or to unconfident, diminished performance. In so far as performance is diminished or absent, the sense of reduced self-efficacy is further reinforced; alternatively, some success may be achieved but success may seem forbidden, conflicting with self-identity judgemental scripts, so that the self-criticism is reinforced. This cycle may be initiated in a number of ways, for example: by the experience of repeated failure, for which responsibility is taken; by the impairment of performance due to illness; by exposure to unfamiliar and more difficult tasks; by an increase in the harshness of the conditions set for the maintenance of self-esteem as a result of guilt for some act, either committed or anticipated; or by physiological changes affecting energy levels and concentration, as a result of physical illness or of manic-depressive illness.

It is important to understand the relation of this psychological model of depression to endogenous depression (unipolar in bipolar manic-depressive illness). It is assumed that, in such illnesses, which may be apparently spontaneous or provoked by childbirth, the primary disturbance is physiological. This affects the organization and execution of tasks and these changes are experienced subjectively as a loss of energy and concentration, without in every case an accompanying depressed mood. The experience of incompetence, however, can lead to depression by lowering the sense of self-efficacy in general, and by leading to the progressive abandonment of aims, as failure is increasingly predicted. Moreover, as self-esteem is normally rooted to some extent in the perception of the self as competent, guilt will be added to the picture; in some cases, denial may operate and lead to the making of quite unrealistic, grandiose (hypomanic) claims.

In the treatment of this kind of depression, therefore, it is important to relieve the physiological changes with drugs, where this is possible, and to try to protect the patients from unreasonable self-blame for their diminished performances. At the same time, as soon as any physical recovery begins, the depressive spiral of hopelessness and predicted helplessness needs to be challenged by the encouragement of appropriate activity, by the imposition of accurate estimations of achievement, and by teaching patients to monitor and block their depressive thinking, along with any other appropriate psychotherapeutic methods.

The differential diagnosis of neurotic and endogenous depression is not easy because severe neurotic depression may provoke physiological changes of the kind associated with endogenous depression, whereas endogenous depression may make longer term neurotic problems manifest. In practice, any depressed person, who is not physically ill from some other cause, who is showing marked impairment of concentration or energy, alterations in appetite or major changes in sleep rhythm, especially where early morning waking is a feature, should be considered for anti-depressant medication. If there are strong reasons to suppose that life events have provoked the depression, for example, by exposing the ineffectiveness of some procedural script, or by exacerbating a conflict between aims and self-judging scripts, then the effects of supportive, explanatory, and interpretive therapy, and the use of some active methods may be tried as the first therapeutic methods, and in some cases these will give rapid relief. It is important to exclude physical illness as a cause of depression. Once this is done, mild cases, not apparently explicable psychologically, or anyone who is severely depressed, with retardation of thinking and talking, agitation, and marked self-blame, may be helped by anti-depressant medication. This should be given in adequate dosage for an adequate time, and not in the small, unsustained regime all too frequently prescribed. Psychotherapists whose patients become depressed during treatment will be reluctant to use medication, as the depression will often be seen to arise as a result of dealing with important issues in the therapy; but transference emotions may serve to trigger mood swings in manic-depressive patients, and during such swings patients may be inaccessible to psychological methods. It is clear that non-medical psychotherapists will need to treat depressed patients in co-operation with doctors.

David

In the case of David, although there was a family history of depression in his father which might suggest a predisposition to manic-depressive illness, the onset of his depression was closely related to Patricia's departure and was clearly a reaction to it. As a result of the upset caused by this, by the time I saw him he was some weeks in arrears with his work, and had failed in a minor examination. He had therefore suffered a reduction in academic performance as a result of depression from another source. In discussing his situation, he showed a pessimistic and unrealistic estimation of his chances of catching up; that is to say, his predictive evaluation of performance was biased by his mood. Moreover, in discussing his past academic record, he reported several assessments and comments from his tutors which suggested a quite satisfactory situation but he discounted these as being based on kindness rather than judgement. In this it seems likely that David's retrospective evaluations of performance were also negatively biased due to his depressed mood.

In another form of trap, related to the defence of regression (in psychoanalytic terms), anxiety about long-term goals, e.g. about being sexually attractive, may lead to short-term strategies, such as comfort-eating, that replace those actions needed to solve the problem or achieve more important aims. Often, these actions actually hamper the achievement of the more important aims, e.g. overeating causing obesity. Regressive behaviours of this sort represent the pursuit of diminished goals, usually goals related to the satisfaction of basic (childish) needs. In "bulimia nervosa", which is marked by cycles of binge-eating followed by self-induced vomiting, this regressive satisfaction is followed by the ritual emptying out that is at once relieving of guilt and productive of shame and self-disgust, paving the way for further depression and further resorting to regressive comfort-eating.

Another important group of trap behaviours are those in which the undesired state of the self, or assumptions about the self, are maintained by the reactions provoked from others. At the level of strategic scripts concerned with relationships, these traps are usually the manifestation of negative assumptions about the self, typically as being weak or dangerous or without value, and of unrealistic judgements of the other, typically as being critical, rejecting, or harsh. Restrictive beliefs about what constitutes permissible behaviour or negative predictions about the likely responses of others to what one wants to do may also play a part. A common example is the belief that to be self-assertive will inevitably provoke rejection. These beliefs can lead to forms of relating to others which serve only to heighten or sustain them.

Two common examples are the social isolation trap and the placation trap. In the former, the shy person feels boring and expects rejection; in company, he avoids eye contact and responds brusquely and awkwardly to conversational approaches. He is then perceived as aloof or hostile, and people tend to avoid him, from which he concludes that his initial poor sense of himself is clearly shared by others. In the placation trap, a person who fears that his assertion will lead to rejection tries to please everybody, only to find that this leads to his own needs being ignored, so he comes to feel misused and resentful, and may end up by acting in childish ways with ineffective forms of aggression in inappropriate circumstances, behaviours which both he and others may indeed find unacceptable. These judgements, in turn, can reinforce both the lack of confidence in the self and the sense that assertion does not pay.

Other traps are acted out upon the body. Scratching the skin, which makes it itch, and causes further scratching, or compulsive hair-pulling, are examples of physical acts which are also expressive of self-attitudes. Such acts are often associated with issues of guilt and self-punishment, although this may not be known consciously. Self-cutting, for example, often produces relief; it would seem to represent the enactment of self-punishment which eases or obviates guilt. Many other symptoms, some of which will be considered in the next chapter, serve to maintain the individual in an unsatisfactory state that combines some gratification with restriction or punishment.

DILEMMAS

A dilemma operates at Stage 3 of the procedural sequence. It puts restrictions upon action by defining the possibilities narrowly: typically, as lying between equally undesirable alternatives, thus preventing the individual from freeing himself to try out a range of other possible courses. Two situations can be envisaged: in the first (a false dichotomy), the choice is restricted, seeming to lie between two courses. Sometimes either may be pursued, sometimes one is chosen, although it is unsatisfactory, because the only apparent option is even less desirable or more frightening. In the second, the dilemma is seen in the form of "if, then" (a dilemma of false association) so that the course which is desired is seen as unattainable because it is felt that to pursue it has negative connotations for the self-description. Reaction formation, which is part of the obsessive-compulsive syndrome, can be seen as an example of a false dichotomization of possibilities between the compulsive act and the feared alternative.

At the strategic level, dilemmas are concerned with the terms of relationships and with their associated costs. Such dilemmas can usually be seen to be derived from childhood and family roles; they are manifest in adult relationships, where mutuality would be appropriate, often representing the imposition of roles appropriate to parent–child interactions. Common examples may be summarized as follows. *If* dependent, *then* submissive; *either* dependent *or* in control; *if* caring, *then* submissive. Issues of this sort frequently link up with cultural notions about the appropriate male and female differentiations. For example, a woman brought up in the old tradition, which could be summarized as "*if* feminine, *then* passive" will have difficulty in feeling feminine while being assertive. People restricted by such dilemmas often select partners prepared to play reciprocal roles or they will endeavour to mould their relationships within their familiar terms.

At the level of the self, dilemmas are expressive of conflicted self-attitudes; here too, issues of control are common, notably the "*either* in control of feelings *or* risking going crazy" dilemma, in its various forms; but particular histories can generate highly individual and complicated dilemmas. A list of common ones is given in Chapter 14. For a psychoanalytic discussion of these issues see Kris (1977).

It is clear that everyone is faced with dilemmas; life presents them inevitably and few of us can find easy resolutions to them. The brief descriptions given later of neurotic patients' dilemmas in these terms do not necessarily imply that is by virtue of having such dilemmas that these individuals are neurotic. What is true is that neurotic individuals seem to have such dilemmas in more extreme forms, or it may be that they have been forced to face some of the painful consequences of them due to the breakdown of previously matching or collusive relationships (Ryle, in press). In therapy, or problem-solving, the important task is to identify these dilemmas that are serving to restrict the capacity of the individual to solve his particular problems. Having identified such dilemmas, one can proceed to generate alternatives beyond those possible within the terms of the dilemma. To put this differently, the concept of the dilemma is a way of describing explicitly the premises (at PSM Stage 3) from which the problem-solver is addressing his problem. These premises seem self-evident to the person with the problem because they are his familiar terms, but they will usually turn out to be idiosyncratic and narrow, and to recognize this can lead to a fruitful redefinition.

Anne

Anne exhibited a relationship dilemma, in which the alternatives were seen to be between being *either* helpful, controlling, and sane, *or* dependent, weak, and potentially crazy. This dilemma did not dominate all her relationships, however; with her husband, one friend and, in time, with me, she was able to accept that a dependent role could be safe. Anne showed a second dilemma in relation to work, in which the choice had always seemed to be between *either* stressful striving for perfection *or* guilty failure, alternatives which left out the possibility of working from interest, ambition or pleasure towards realistic ends.

David

In the case of David, there seemed to be a similar underlying relationship dilemma, probably related to his early separation from his mother, which could be expressed as "*if* dependent, *then* not in control", and in most of his relationships he aimed to be in a position of amiable control.

SNAGS

The word "snag" implies complications and difficulties, and it can also be seen to stand for Subtle Negative Aspects of Goals. Here, we are concerned with the individual who fails to pursue what he wants to do or be, as if the outcome would be dangerous, forbidden, or otherwise undesirable (PSM 2c and 4b). This prediction is seldom conscious and (unlike traps) is not maintained by symptoms or by the responses of others; often, the abandoned aim is forgotten. To the extent that the "as if" is false, a person can be freed to act more as he wishes by being helped to recognize his "snag". At the tactical level, such predictions are manifest in countless acts of self-diminution, but the understanding of them comes from studying the strategic and self-identity levels. In external snags, the predicted consequence of pursuing desired life aims is of adverse responses from others.

The whole of family and marital therapy, and the application of systems theory approaches to such therapies, has grown out of the very well-validated observation that the problem or sickness of one is often — perhaps nearly always — an aspect of the emotionally significant group of which he is a member. The individual who does not live his life fully may do so because he believes that another, or others, cannot permit it. Sometimes he has directly experienced the adverse responses of others, or has had more or less direct prohibitions issued by them; but such knowings are usually concealed within family or interpersonal confusions or myths. Individual psychotherapy in the psychoanalytic tradition, with its preoccupation with history and the "inner world" and the transference, has often underestimated the importance of such current emotional forces. The way in which the other indicates prohibitions may be through direct threats of abandonment, rejection, or punishment; or through illness, either physical or psychiatric, or through attributions. In such cases, the individual cannot change until such relationships have been clarified, revised, or broken. In many cases, however, it turns out that the extent of the adverse response anticipated from the other has been exaggerated and, in reality, the other accommodates to the changes in the individual without too much difficulty. Here, patients in individual therapy need to be helped to test out realistically what responses their changes do evoke, and to deal with the effects of such changes upon others.

Internal snags are the consequences of self-identity judgemental scripts that deny one the right to pursue one's aims or be oneself. Their effects are often manifest in widespread prohibitions on success or enjoyment, and their existence is seldom recognized by the individual restricted by them. It may take time for a therapist to discern the operation of internal snags: this recognition may be through seeing the way in which the patient dismantles, or arranges to pay for, or be punished for, the gains made in therapy. (This is the negative therapeutic reaction of psychoanalysis). The existence of snags of this sort should be looked for where such dismantlings, punishments, or restrictions are seen to recur. There are common antecedents of such snags in the patient's history which can alert the therapist to look out for them. Many are derived from the child's omnipotence, which can lead him to assume unrealistic responsibility for illnesses, deaths, or failures of other family members. The case of Peter in Chapter 9 is an example of this. Another common source can be the exposure in childhood to the active envy of a parent, brother, or sister.

It is as if the person with the snag is saying to himself: "All that I might have, do, or become, will be at the cost of . . . I can avoid this or I must pay for it by failing, by not enjoying my life, by undoing achievement, or being ill . . ."; but he is not conscious of this process of guilt and expiation.

Because such self-prohibitions are seldom fully conscious, the recognition of their patterns is an important step in reducing their force. Once recognized, patients will often name the snag; for example, Win, described at the end of Chapter 9, called hers her "gaoler". The recognition of the debate that is going on between such irrationally determined negative voices and the ordinary assertions of the self, and the clarification of the way in which the restrictions of the self may have been falsely attributed to others, opens the way for a challenge, but the change may be slow because, like everything else positive, the understandings and the gains of therapy may also have to be or paid for dismantled. In terms of the PSM, the experiences of adverse outcomes (Stage 6) and the experiences that such outcomes are avoided by abandoning the aim, leads to the elimination or "forgetting" of the aim (Stage 1).

David

In David's case, I was alerted to the possibility of a snag by his self-deprecation and depressive thinking about his academic work, and at the end of the first session the following interchange took place.

AR: I don't know how far the issue of success was an issue before your father's breakdown, as the issue of dependency obviously was; but I do know it's very common for people who have a family catastrophe at that time of entering the adult world to feel guilty. The coincidence in time of one's growth and the illness, death, or whatever, of a parent gets some kind of magical connection in one's mind. As if your entering into manhood was at the price of your parents' marriage and of your father's severe mental illness.

DAVID: Which isn't true.

AR: Which isn't true, but if you feel that, then one way of paying is never to have the life you might have.

DAVID: Yes, I can see that.

This somewhat brusque introduction of the notion of the snag was returned to and discussed more extensively in later sessions; later in therapy David recognized another source (see Chapter 5).

Anne

In the case of Anne, throughout childhood and adolescence a snag was imposed by the family, although the avoidance of plain speaking and the family myth of mother's immense vulnerability meant that it was difficult for Anne to see her role and her yielding to mother's alleged needs as being other than normal and appropriate. Mother's illness was always described as being due to biochemical disorders, by the father. Anne was only allowed to pursue those aspects of her own intentions which did not conflict with this set of assumptions, and these ''rules'' had become part of her own self-identity script.

DISCUSSION

The PSM is compatible with a number of behavioural and cognitive/behavioural models. The relation of some of these models (of depression, of attribution, of learned helplessness, of self-efficacy, of cognitive therapy, and of generalized expectancies) to the procedural script model is summarized in Table 3.1 a, b, c. These models, in turn, are similar to the various behavioural and cognitive/behavioural models reviewed by Whitehead (1979) in which she showed that attention was focused on four issues: depression as behaviour; depressed behaviour as maintained by the absence of positive reinforcement; depression as reflecting the absence of a sense of being able to control the environment; and depression as reflecting a negative view of the self and of circumstances. Beck's (1976) work on depressive thinking, and its control by monitoring, represents the recognition and correction of negative evaluations of performance. The model of depression proposed by Rehm (1977) and of learned helplessness by Roth (1980) are more systematic studies of the same area, which are fully compatible with the model proposed here. Roth, for example, writes as follows, in discussing her refinement of the theory of learned helplessness:

> The current model is also unique in its consideration of influential factors at each of three stages of a subject's movement, from objective contingency to learned helplessness deficit. 1. Objective non-contingency— perception of non-contingency. 2. Perception of non-contingency— further expectancy of non-contingency. 3. Expectancy of non-contingency— learned helplessness . . .

In simpler terms, a failure to control or influence events is correctly perceived (Stage 6) but overgeneralization from this means that future attempts are expected to fail (Stage 4); this may be further generalized to the general assumption of 'learned helplessness' (Stage 2).

The PSM can also take account of the work on the locus of control and

Table 3.1a Six theories in relation to the Procedural Sequence Model

Procedural Sequence Model	*Rehm (1977) (Depression)*	*Roth (1980) (Learned helplessness)*
1. Define aim.		
2. Consider general assumptions about:		
a) possibilities for pursuit of aim;	Selective monitoring of negative aspects;	
b) capacity to pursue aim;	negative evaluation of efficacy;	
c) permissibility of pursuing aim (judgments of self and (others)	self-derogation; failure to self-reward.	
3. List possible action plans		
4. For each plan, consider:		
a) can it be carried through?		Prediction of non-contingency;
b) What consequences will follow carrying it through?	Selective monitoring of immediate over delayed consequences.	
5. Choose preferred plan, and act.		Ineffective action
6. Consider:		
a) how effectively plan was carried through. b) what were the consequences of carrying it through?	Inaccurate attribution of responsibility for outcome. Overgeneralisation of failure.	Objective non-contingency resulting in perception of non-contingency (attribution and over generalization)
7. Evaluate the sequence; reaffirm or revise the aim and/or the assumptions.		Prediction of future non-contingency.

Table 3.1b

Procedural Sequence Model	*Beck (1976) (Cognitive therapy)*	*Rotter (1978) (Generalized expectancies)*
1. Define aim.		
2. Consider general assumptions about:		
a) possibilities for pursuit of aim;	Selective monitoring of negative aspects;	Understanding, trusting; discriminating between others reduced;
b) capacity to pursue aim;	negative evaluation of efficacy;	ability to control, especially in long-term, reduced;
c) permissibility of pursuing aim (judgments of self and others)	Self-derogation, stringent criteria.	
3. List possible action plans.		Limited view of range of possible actions.
4. For each plan, consider:		
a) can it be carried through?	Capacity to influence events underrated.	
b) what consequences will follow carrying it through?		
5. Choose preferred plan, and act.		
6. Consider:		
a) how effectively plan was carried through;	Overgeneralization from failure.	
b) what were the consequences of carrying it through?		
7. Evaluate the sequence; reaffirm or revise the aim and/or the assumptions.	Failure increases negative assumptions about situation and efficacy.	

Table 3.1c

Procedural Sequence Model	*Försterling (1980) (Attribution)*	*Bandura (1977) (Self-efficacy)*
1. Define aim		
2. Consider general assumptions about:		
a) possibilities for pursuit of aim;	External locus of control assumed;	
b) capacity to pursue aim;	effects of acts on outcomes under-estimated.	Self-efficacy influenced by performance, vicarious experience, persuasion.
c) permissibility of pursuing aim (judgments of self and others).		
3. List possible action plans.		
4. For each plan, consider:		
a) can it be carried through?	Effectiveness of own acts underestimated.	Efficacy assumptions determine prediction and influence performance.
b) what consequences will follow carrying it through?		
5. Choose preferred plan, and act.		
6. Consider:		
a) how effectively plan was carried through;	Faulty deductions from outcome; underestimate responsibility for outcome.	Failure reinforces low self-efficacy; success enhances self-efficacy.
b) what were the consequences of carrying it through?		
7. Evaluate the sequence; reatfirm or revise the aim and/or the assumptions.	Belief in external locus of control reinforced.	Level of self-efficacy as perceived influences Stage 2.

expectancy (Rotter, 1966, 1978) and of Bandura's (1977b) recent writing on self-efficacy.

While they are compatible with the procedural sequence model, these cognitive and behavioural approaches are incomplete. In so far as self-evaluative processes are considered in them, they are largely concerned with performance and only marginally with personal meanings and judgments. While Rehm (1977) does discuss the issue of self-punishment and self-reward, she considers these only in terms of "maladaptive modelling or reinforcement schedules". Here, as in the other works, the self appears variously as the object of negative behaviours, the object of negative evaluations, as the more or less effective executor of acts, or as a proper object of monitoring and control; but no serious attention is paid to the structure of the self or to who, or what, it is that rewards, punishes, measures the power of, or controls, this self. The issue of the self will be considered more fully in Chapter 5, but at this point it must be said that many phenomena, including several of the clinical states discussed in this chapter, cannot be explained adequately unless it is assumed that the self includes both an executive and a conceptualizing and judging aspect. This is most notably true when there is a conflict between aims and judgements, or where the avoidance or relief of guilt by expiation of self-punishment becomes a salient aim. The understanding of these issues is one of the important contributions of psychoanalysis.

Another inadequacy of these approaches is in their neglect of defences and of the influence of early psychological development. Beck (1976), for example, who is probably the most influential clinically, avoids any discussion of guilt or conflict. He considers that emotional difficulties arise from the individual's "distortions of reality based on erroneous premises and assumptions" and does not consider the role of denial or repression, despite the fact that satisfactory accounts of them are available in cognitive terms, e.g. in the writings of Loevinger (1976) and of Haan (1977).

Because of the circularity of trap phenomena (including depression, phobias, and obsessive—compulsive behaviours), intervention in any part of the trap circle may be therapeutically effective, and therapies based on these incomplete models may therefore work by modifying either behavioural or cognitive stages in the circular sequence. Moreover, the therapeutic situation also serves indirectly to relieve guilt and accord positive value to the individual. There will, however, be a proportion of cases in whom the full understanding of the more complex circular processes in terms of the PSM will be needed for therapy to be effective.

Some of the ideas presented in this chapter deal with phenomena familiar to many in psychoanalytic terms as repression, denial, regression, and reaction formation (Anna Freud, 1936). What is proposed, however, is not a simple translation of these terms, but rather a more general consideration of how intentions, including those seeking "outlets" for "drives", may be blocked, modified or diverted; how the meaning of experience may be idiosyncratic, narrowed, distorted; and how choices of action may be restricted. The psychoanalytic concept of the dynamic unconscious, whereby unacceptable memories, ideas, or impulses are actively denied access to consciousness, is re-described in these terms as cognitive strategies involving selective forgetting, schematic isolation, or replacement of action plans by alternative plans. These strategies serve to reduce conflict between competing plans and values, to reduce the distance between desire and possibility, and to avoid challenging the conditions imposed by self-evaluative criteria. They are therefore the adult internal equivalents of devices used visibly by children to cope with unpleasantness or conflict. (For example, my grandson, not quite 3, brought home a note from his nursery school, announcing its intended closure; he put the note in the cupboard and shut the door, announcing, "Now you can't see my broken school." On another occasion, he wanted to bite his sister; he was prevented and was reminded of how his wish was unkind, given that she had recently given him a piggyback; he dealt with this discrepant fact by saying, "Can't 'member.").

In psychoanalytic terms, it is the conflict between the primitive urges of the infant and parental authority, as internalized, that sets the tone for how subsequent "drive–defence conflicts" are resolved. As a corollary of such a view it is claimed that interpretation of the regressive transference offers the only real key to cure in neurotic problems. In contradistinction to this view, the PSM allows one to see how the effectiveness of intentional scripts can vary in a number of ways, and how the scripts an individual operates with will always show some degree of simplification, distortion, or restriction. Moreover, although some areas of exploration or development may be blocked because of early conflict-reducing strategies, it is by no means clear from clinical work that this occurs to a total extent, and there is very often evidence that the later experiences of childhood and adolescence have served to shape the individual scripts. This later distortion can occur, both through the definition of certain thoughts or behaviours as "no go" areas (e.g. Anne was brought up never to argue with the definition of her mother's behaviour as due to illness) and, perhaps more importantly, by leading to the development of scripts that are perfectly effective and sensible strategies for dealing with the family situation, but which prove inflexible and restrictive in the larger world. These successful but restrictive strategies are often obvious to the therapist but have not been recognized fully by the person; or they may be seen by him as self-evident, or as an aspect of personality rather than as constituting a limitation on possibility. The recognition that such strategies are operating can often lead to their revision, without the need for prolonged, extensive interpretive work.

There are important clinical implications in the different account offered by the cognitive model. Are the detailed "not-knowings" which characterize repression and denial, the *causes* of the deformation of self-identity scripts, or are these defensive devices made necessary by ineffective higher-order scripts? In the classical psychoanalytic view, it is by the analysis of ego-defences against forbidden impulses, dating back to childhood and seen as presenting in the transference, that recovery takes place, implying the former version. However, there is evidence, including some from psychoanalytic sources, that memories so recovered during the treatment process may bear little relation to the actual early experience (e.g. Kris, 1965;

Kennedy, 1971; Gill, 1978). In practice, psychoanalysts are divided in how far they attempt to reconstruct childhood, as Gill (loc. sit.) discusses, but the trend is towards a focus on the here-and-now, and most writers seem to agree that the understandings gained in the transference and the safety offered by therapy permit the de-repression of (or, more probably, the construction or reconstruction of) memories, more often than the recovery of memories promotes a new understanding.

If this is the case, it seems likely that *any* extension of the patient's self-understanding and self-control (i.e. any increase in his ego-strength) would have a similar effect in reducing his need for defences, and analytical approaches for treatment are clearly not the only means of achieving these. Behavioural and cognitive treatments are often effective in this regard, but I believe that a more elaborated cognitive approach is better.

The most effective way to reduce defensiveness is to improve the patient's control over his life, and here, while successful behavioural change or cognitive modification can be helpful, I believe that the sharing of explanatory concepts upon which these and other treatment methods are based is valuable. The concepts of the trap, dilemma, and snag (first proposed in Ryle, 1979b) are descriptive of important malfunctionings of the procedural script; their purpose is not only to guide the therapist, they also direct the patient's attention to the essential nature of his difficulty. In teaching a person a way of understanding his processes, one is enabling him to overcome the obstacles to learning. Minsky and Pappert (1972), in urging the usefulness of computer analogues for thinking, wrote that "learning to learn is very much like debugging complex computer programs. To be good at it requires one to know a lot about describing processes, and manipulating such descriptions." In sharing with a patient a suitably complex model of how his procedures are faulty, we make it clear to him that the point of our various therapeutic methods, whether behavioural, cognitive, interpretive, or whatever, is precisely to help him develop more satisfactory procedures, and we at once alter his experience of his difficulties in ways that increase his sense of possibility and responsibility.

The relation of cognitive control styles to therapy (Klein, 1970), in particular with children, is discussed from a psychoanalytic viewpoint by Santostefano (1980) in ways that have some bearing on this chapter. The function of cognitive controls is to integrate inner information about feelings, drives, and fantasies with information about the outer world (in terms of the PSM, to integrate aims with the perception of the situation and self-identity criteria). Individuals differ, for example, in being undifferentiated or distinct in their body and ego tempo regulations, narrow or wide in their intentions, relevant or random in the selectivity of their attention, global or complex in their discriminations and crude or elaborate in their categorizations. Santostefano reports the relationship of these aspects of functioning to psychological difficulty in childhood, arguing that personality development requires satisfactorily established cognitive controls. Where these are absent in a child in therapy, development of more satisfactory ones may require successive working through of the issues in the modes, first of physical activity, then of fantasy, and only finally in language. He suggests therefore that "cognitive control therapy" may need to precede defence analysis, and notes that problems in cognitive control are quite extensive and not confined only to issues which are the subject of drive/defence conflict.

Extending this view to the field of adult psychotherapy, it would seem equally important to pay attention to cognitive features in all cases, and particularly helpful to develop as quickly as possible a discriminating, well-focused, and adequately complex way of thinking about the problem being dealt with. The dilemma, trap, and snag formulation put forward in this chapter serves precisely to mobilize better cognitive understanding in this way. For some people, however, action and fantasy work may be especially useful in modifying maladaptive processes, and the active methods of therapy to be discussed later (teaching self-monitoring, rehearsal in imagination, graded exposure) may be more accessible than more verbal or conceptual approaches.

4

Emotions and Symptoms

In the last two chapters the essential features of the PSM have been described, and some ways in which it serves to describe common neurotic difficulties have been considered. We need now to consider further the sources of aims (the question of motivation), the nature of the emotions, and the nature of the symptoms that so frequently accompany neurotic difficulties in living.

Many colloquial descriptions of human activity, and some psychological ones, offer a dualistic model whereby we are "motivated" by some force which is separate from, but in some degree controlled by, us. Such accounts are unhelpful because they contribute to what Schafer (1975) called "disclaimed action" or what, in the vernacular, might be called "copping out". It is easier to say, "I want to get on with my work but somehow I lack motivation" than it is to say, "I choose not to work". In psychotherapy, where one is concerned above all to extend the patient's sense of his capacity to choose and act, the challenging of this kind of conceptualization is important. In terms of cognitive theory, the idea of motivating forces is redundant once we accept that human activity is, essentially, meaningful, that is to say that man is inevitably and always concerned with the extension of his cognitive understanding and control of experience, and with the active exploration of his world. We bring to the world our curiosity, our biological drives for food, drink, and sex, our innate need for attachment to others, and we learn from the world, above all from the social world, how to satisfy these and how to pursue our complex, culturally determined desires and intentions.

A COGNITIVE THEORY OF EMOTION

If we are to pursue our aims, we must be able to recognize how far, at any given time, our state and situation correspond with, or conflict with, these aims. Emotions are understood in cognitive terms in relation to this issue; they are the subjective accompaniment of our recognition of the current match between how we see ourselves and our situation, and how we would like to see them. When we perceive a discrepancy between our reality and what we want, we experience one of the emotions such as sadness, anxiety, anger, or sexual desire, which rouse us to action. When such action successfully closes the gap between what we want and our reality, by the revision of one or the other, or when our perception is of a satisfactory match, we experience positive emotions such as contentment or joy (see Katz, 1980; further discussed at the end of this chapter).

Positive emotions signal no mismatch; they are not accompanied by obvious physical sensation indicating the need for action, while mental functioning is experienced as fluent. Negative emotions, on the other hand, represent a call to action, and are accompanied by the physical changes that prepare the body for action and by mental changes in the direction of concentration or restriction, or sometimes disruption.

The power, or impact, of a script-reality discrepancy will obviously depend upon its place in the hierarchy of our life aims A mismatch at the self-identity level of the PSM (e.g. "my life is out of control") is clearly more powerful as a source of emotion than one at the strategic level (e.g. "I cannot manage my relationship with my employer.") and much more powerful than one at the tactical level (e.g. "I cannot mend my typewriter."). Generalizations up and down the hierarchy can occur, however, so that one may be cheered up by getting the typewriter to work on the one hand, or too depressed to do a simple repair job on it on the other. These generalizations represent the revisions of self-efficacy assumptions.

The physiological changes accompanying emotion are to some degree specific to the emotions, but the recognition of emotional states is also dependent on one's understanding of the situation and its meaning. Cultural differences in the sorts of discrimination made between emotional states are considerable and, within cultures, particular families may develop idiosyncratic rules for the naming and expression of feelings. In some cases, the physical symptoms accompanying emotion may be mislabelled, e.g. as hunger, and their personal meaning may not be realized. Non-recognition of feeling states in this way is a common attribute of patients with anorexia nervosa and other serious eating disorders (Bruch, 1973). A reverse instance is the mislabelling of physical symptoms as emotion: the pallor and rapid pulse following drinking too much coffee can make one feel anxious, unless one remembers how much coffee one has drunk (see Schachter and Singer, 1962).

ABNORMAL EMOTIONAL STATES

We have considered so far emotions as being the result of schematic mismatches between reality as perceived and as desired, and have noted their function in initiating appropriate action. The persistent failure to resolve such perceived mismatches is one source of dysphoric mood states, notably depression and anxiety. Another important and common source of persistent mood states is the unresolved conflict between aims and self-judgements: in terms of the PSM, schematic discrepancies between aim scripts and self-identity criteria. Harshly critical self-evaluations, unrealistically high criteria for self-acceptance, or the sense that success is forbidden or must be paid for are all potent sources of persistent negative mood states. These long-term emotional states derived from internal conflict can become a further source of difficulty by impairing cognitive functioning and provoking feelings of self-doubt or incapacity. In other cases, the avoidance of conflict is achieved by the abandonment of important life aims with a consequent restriction of experience and possibility, as in the snags described in the last chapter. The sense of emptiness or purposelessness which follows such abandonment of important aims becomes a further source of despair.

The importance of such conflict is recognized fully only within psychoanalysis, but in some respects the psychoanalytic view of emotion is a narrow one. Emotion, identified with the id and regarded as being concerned with the primitive "pleasure principle", is regarded as actually or potentially disruptive, to be controlled by the ego. Schachtel (1959), in an important critique of this position, saw Freud's pleasure principle as being a reductive account of emotion in both infant and adult. To the tension-relieving "pleasure principle" affects described by Freud (more properly labelled as effects of the "unpleasure principle") which he labelled as "embeddedness affects", and equated with the torpor of the infant after a feed, Schachtel proposed the addition of another class: the activity affects, related to the experience of achieving mastery over the world, and manifest in the infant's eager exploration of his environment. In terms of the PSM, Schachtel's "embeddedness" affects repressent mismatches solved by the actual or fantasized reliance on external sources, rather than upon action. Many emotional states in adults, especially the usually neglected positive affects, can be seen to exist in two forms, discriminated along this embeddedness/activity distinction. Thus, Schachtel contrasts the magical joy of fantasy wish-fulfilment, which is often accompanied by the fear of envy, with joy reflecting an active turning towards the world, and he makes a similar distinction between magical hope and the active exploration of reality. Among negative affects, he regards anxiety, especially in the established mood state of angst, as the classical example of an embedded affect, representing the passive expectation of incapacity in the face of reality, as opposed to the active mobilization of resource. These views of Schachtel represent an important revision of psychoanalytic thought, and, in the emphasis on activity and on the positive integrating effect of emotion, are in line with the cognitive model proposed here.

We will conclude this theoretical account of emotion by considering once more the cases of Anne and David.

David

In the case of David, the original impulse to consult the Careers Adviser had come from his uncertainty about his future plans, and from a sense of not being sufficiently in control of his own decisions. In effect, therefore, he was mildly unhappy to recognize a mismatch between a perception of himself as he was and as he would like to be, namely, competently in charge of his life. He acted appropriately to try to resolve that. Patricia's departure, however, presented him with an abrupt and disruptive mismatch between his expectations and reality. His sense of the purpose of his life and of where it was centred had been taken for granted for a long time. When Patricia left, he felt lost, without purpose, sad, and angry. These emotions came and went according to how he thought about the situation: despair or depression at the though of a future that now seemed meaningless, grief at the loss of his closest relationship, self-reproach that he had not cared for the relationship better, anger at Patricia's act and at the way in which she had done it. Attempts to win her back were soon abandoned and he was left, therefore, with the task either of replacing her, which was the solution he had adopted at the end of his previous relationship, or of forming his purposes and definitions upon some other base.

Anne

Anne's experience of her thoughts being out of control confronted her with a version of herself that was contradictory to a very important basic aim, namely to remain sane, stable, under control, and unlike her mother in every way. Although the original symptom, which was probably chemically induced, was short-lived, uncontrolled rumination about possible brain-damage, or about the probability that her symptoms (or the fact of worrying about them) might be a harbinger of, or a cause of, a future breakdown, served as continuing reminders that she was *not* under control; and the anxiety that flooded her when she had that thought was itself a further contradiction to the stable self-definition she had successfully defended up until that point in time. Anxiety erupted whenever she was confronted with this discrepancy between her experience and this centrally important self-definition.

PHYSICAL SYMPTOMS OF EMOTIONAL ORIGIN

The physical symptoms accompanying psychological and emotional difficulty can be divided into three groups differing in origin and significance: arousal symptoms, hysterical symptoms, and psychosomatic symptoms.

Arousal symptoms arise when schematic mismatches elicit the physiological changes that occur in nature, either in preparation for fight or flight, or as signals (such as the raised hair that frightens off the enemy). These symptoms include changes due to autonomic nervous system activity such as pallor or flushing, palpitations or sweating, and changes in muscle tone leading to weakness or tremor or, if persistent, to fatigue or tension symptoms. When these changes occur inappropriately, due to one's misconstruction of the situation (PSM 2a) or of one's own state (PSM 2b, 2c), or when the arousal is appropriate but the response that might alter the situation (e.g. by dealing with the threat) is not proceeded with, then awareness of the symptoms (PSM 6b) can lead to secondary anxiety, such as the fear of collapse or the fear of loss of control. With repetitions, this secondary fear, which may be associated with a particular situation, or which may be evoked by particular thoughts or images, becomes a sufficient cause of the symptoms. In understanding such symptoms, attention must be paid to the circumstances of their origin, the situations in which they occur, and the thoughts that precede or accompany them, so that one can identify the nature of the abandoned act and consider the accuracy with which the self and situation have been construed.

Hysterical symptoms (which have become increasingly rare in western cultures) represent the translation of an idea or wish, that is not acceptable, into a physical symptom, such as loss of voice, writer's cramp, or the paralysis of a limb. The unacceptability of the idea of wish may relate to the anticipated responses of others, or, more frequently, to one's own self-judgements. In essence, rather than the person saying "I will not", the symptoms announce that "he cannot"; in terms of the PSM the aim is not abandoned, but the means is, unconsciously, inhibited.

Eileen

Eileen sought a psychiatric opinion a year after the onset of her symptoms, which consisted of headache, panicky feelings, and attacks of cramp and numbness of the right hand. She was a highly achieving postgraduate student who said she felt like "an exhausted dog chasing an inexhaustible electric hare". In recent months, her ability to produce written work had diminished and she was now entirely blocked, and feeling depressed and ashamed. During the previous year she had had a full neurological investigation which had proved negative, and she was currently attempting to arrange endocrinological investigations, still seeking an organic explanation for her troubles. From childhood onwards, Eileen had been her teacher's golden girl, working frenetically and achieving high grades up to the end of her undergraduate career. Her angrily critical self-judgements, as I saw it, were based upon her early perception that only achievement could win her father's respect and then only at the cost of her being seen as unfeminine. Failure, unless justified by illness, was therefore unthinkable, and the desire to give up could only be expressed through the symptoms, just as her rejection of this explanation was initially expressed by "forgetting" to get off the train to come to her third appointment.

Psychosomatic symptoms, with varying degrees of complexity, combine the symbolic expression of denied feelings with forms of self-restriction or self-punishment, and with ways of obtaining or justifying care from self or others. The symbolic nature of symptoms is often apparent from the way in which popular speech incorporates them in expressive phrases such as: "It sticks in my gullet"; "I can't stomach it"; "You make me sick"; "You are a pain in the neck (or elsewhere)"; "Why don't you piss off". Many of these metaphors suggest a bodily image of taking something in, refusing something, or expelling something, and they serve to support the psychoanalytic notions about the child's early cognitive development in which the experiences of taking in and rejecting food, and of retaining and expelling urine or faeces, are linked with, or become the coin of, a developing sense of himself in his relationship with his mother.

In addition to serving this symbolic function, symptoms of this sort can also be seen as the expression of a substitute aim. In terms of the procedural script, symptoms can represent the abandonment of an intention at the stage of judging the anticipated consequences, and its replacement by a revised aim. This revised aim, as Freud pointed out, represents a compromise combining elements of gratification and elements of punishment. The punishment lies in the abandonment of the first aim and in the discomfort of the symptoms. Some symptoms seem to occur primarily as punishment, e.g. Saturday morning migraine that deprives the obsessionally driven person of a well-earned weekend. But some gratification usually accompanies symptoms of this sort, commonly in that they are the occasion for "deserving" care from oneself or from others, or sometimes simply that they represent payment, and therefore serve to relieve guilt.

James

James, a 36-year-old solicitor, consulted on the advice of his doctor when full audiological investigation had failed to demonstrate any physical cause for a constant whistling in his ears. The symptoms had started one day, six months before, and on enquiry it seemed that the day in question was one in which he had had an angry exchange with his adolescent stepdaughter at breakfast followed by an awkward and unsatisfactory meeting with colleagues during the day. He was the middle of three sons of a judge; his eldest brother was a successful barrister, and his younger one was a "charming alcoholic". James described himself as a quiet, unassertive person. He felt satisfied with his career, though he felt he would not equal his father's or elder brother's achievements. James was unwilling to acknowledge the psychosomatic nature of his symptom until he kept a diary on my suggestion, which showed a consistent pattern. Over a brief period, his symptoms became worse in relation to an interview with an awkward client, seeing a film about the crushing of a slave revolt in which he identified strongly with the slaves, having an unsuccessful argument with his wife, and being unable to refuse an invitation from the firm's senior colleagues to a social occasion he did not want to attend. On the basis of this, and only after a further consultation with an ear, nose, and throat specialist, he was finally able to acknowledge that the noise, which had become a signal of his wish for quiet and care, should really be regarded as a call to action and assertion. In this way he was helped to recapture the appropriate arousal function of the unacknowledged emotion that was concealed by his symptom. The underlying dilemma here was between being *either* assertive, nasty, and liable to provoke rejection *or* being placatory and nice. The aim to be nice, however, was incompatible with the aim of getting his own way. The evolution of the symptoms in terms of the PSM is given in Table 4.1. After some therapy, James became more assertive and less anxious, at which point his wife, who had chosen him for his niceness, became depressed; this snag was eventually resolved through conjoint therapy.

Psychosomatic symptoms can become incorporated into very complex systems of self- and other-control, often combined with magical thinking of the type we have

Table 4.1 Symptom as "compromise formation" between incompatible aims

Stages			Compromise aim
1.	(i) *To get my own way*	(ii) *To be nice*	*To be looked after* (because I have a buzzing in my ears and deserve care and can't be expected to be assertive).
2a b c	Other people are stronger than me. Being assertive is like my (envied, disliked) father and brother.	People like it. I know how. It is like I prefer to be.	
3.	Tentative plans to assert.	Placate.	
4a b	Unlikely to be effective. Will provoke dislike, rejection, and I'll feel bad.	It will work. Others will like me.	
5.	Incompetent performance.	Placatory act.	
6a b	Failure. People don't like me being pushy, anyway I failed.	I was nice, but I did not get my own way.	
7.	I've a buzzing in my ears.	I've a buzzing in my ears.	

Stages

1. Define aim.
2. Consider general assumptions about
   a) possibilities for pursuit of aim,
   b) capacity to pursue aim,
   c) permissibility of pursuing aim (judgements of self and others).
3. List possible action plans.
4. For each plan, consider
   a) can it be carried through?
   b) what consequences will follow carrying it through?
5. Choose preferred plan, and act.
6. Consider
   a) how effectively plan was carried through,
   b) what were the consequences of carrying it through?
7. Evaluate the sequence; reaffirm or reverse the aim and/or the assumptions.

considered in relation to obsessions; e.g. anorexia and bulimia can combine the ritual repetition of the experience of self-deprivation or of greed and punishment with a controlling dependency cn, and defiance of, concerned others.

In the smooth course of an untroubled life, unpleasant emotions initiate acts that resolve the discrepancies that gave rise to them, and pleasant emotions provide a secure base from which to respond to new events or develop new aims. As lives are not untroubled for long, the unavoidable pains and difficulties we encounter usually test out, and in some way find wanting, our capacities to pursue our purposes and solve our problems. To conclude this chapter, we will consider two major sources of long-term emotional difficulty: the experience of loss and the experience of sexual intimacy.

LOSS

Losses occur inevitably through the course of life. One may lose important other people; one may lose one's place or one's prospects in the social world, one may lose one's skills and resilience due to illness or age and, with the passage of time, whether or not these other losses occur, one feels one's future inexorably shrinking and one loses one's illusions. Some of these losses occur at transitions which also mark new departures, which can make the element of loss difficult to acknowledge. Perhaps this is most marked in the case of parenthood for women: the birth of the first child, especially for working-class women, often involves a massive restriction of the social world, and an end to financial independence. The effect of this may only be overcome by the time a second loss is faced as the children leave home. The most severe loss, however, and the one most thoroughly studied, is that of bereavement.

Of the negative emotions, sadness about loss is the most difficult one to cope with because there is no act that can serve to close the gap between the desired and actual situation: the schematic discrepancy is permanent. In the case of bereavement, replacement is impossible, even though certain roles or functions can be repeated. What is called for in the bereaved individual is acceptance, which involves the revision of all those aims and purposes of life which concerned the lost person. The end of the 4-year relationship with Patricia presented David with such a task, as we have seen, although this was clearly a less severe experience than bereavement by death after longer-term attachments.

The fact that sadness cannot provoke effective action in most cases, probably accounts for some of the characteristic features of normal mourning in its early stages, notably the searching and restlessness and the almost universal use of denial in the form of continuing thoughts, images, or even hallucinations implying that the dead person still lives. Other features of mourning reflect the fact that sadness is not the only emotion felt; we seek always to attribute causality, and most deaths are, unless seen in a religious light, random and meaningless events. Rather than accept this, it is common to attribute blame to oneself, to the dead person who has abandoned one, or to the doctors and nurses who failed to care or cure. The attribution of blame to self or other will be a larger feature where hostility, acknowledged or denied, was a part of the relationship, and is particularly liable to cause trouble in the case of the deaths or disasters of parents during late childhood and adolescence. In these instances, the normal angers and assertions of the child (which, in the psychoanalytic view, are seen to carry over some of the child's omnipotent assumptions from infancy) can be interpreted, often unconsciously, as having contributed to, or caused, the death or illness of the parent. This may result in incomplete mourning, because the death cannot be fully acknowledged, or in expiatory self-punishing or self-restricting acts (PSM 2c), a common source of the snags described in the last chapter.

The completion of mourning involves both the recognition that the death has occurred, and the revision of life plans acknowledging that fact. Where the dead person has been a central source of external validation, completion of mourning allows one, in some sense, to take into oneself the values that were accorded by the other. If one cannot let the death be true, which is more likely to be the case where guilt and hostility are active but not acknowledged, this process cannot be completed, and the external source may be located in objects linking one with the dead or in a shrinking world of memories, which effectively closes off the possibility of further change or growth.

Loss will be an issue in most therapies, most obviously where past loss is the source of difficulty. These losses may be of people or of illusions, or may follow from the recognition of past restrictions; such mourning for the self is both painful and freeing. The therapist's job is to guide the process of ending therapy in such a way that that loss, and, symbolically, past losses, can be acknowledged and mourning completed.

Not only therapists are involved in the issue of loss. Doctors, nurses, social workers, ministers, and others likely to be in contact with the bereaved, need to be aware of the ordinary mourning process. Our society offers impoverished rituals and many social pressures reinforce the unhelpful prolongation of denial. Those in touch with the bereaved, or with those coping with other losses, such as physical disability, need to know how to allow the expression of grief and anger, how to support the process of acceptance, how to encourage the development of new aims, and they need to recognize those who need psychotherapy to overcome the effects of incomplete mourning.

PROBLEMS RELATED TO SEXUAL INTIMACY

It sounds cynical, but it is probably true to say that if you see somebody weeping it is as likely that the cause is love as that it is loss. The reason for this is to be found in the unresolvable paradoxes involved in our simultaneous wish to be both free and dependent, both separate and joined, and to the fact that how we deal with that paradox is deeply coloured by the particular history of our own slow growth from the total dependency of infancy to the precarious autonomy of adulthood. That autonomy is most at risk where we are most exposed, and it is in our sexual relationships where exposure is most possible, most desired, and most feared, and where our sense of self and other is expressed in physical language as was our first experience of ourselves and of the other in infancy. It is not surprising that our primitive strategies for self-definition and defence, our primitive needs to control the other and fears of being controlled by the other, find their expression in sexual relationships, where schematic discrepancies between consciously desired aims and unrecognized wishes and prohibitions are common.

Such issues are present throughout adult life, but the main concerns vary with age. In late adolescence and early adult life, self-proof may be a larger concern than intimacy, and sexuality may be a game, involving little personal exposure. This unconcern serves as a defence against the threat posed by intimacy in someone whose sense of self is still uncertain or largely other-dependent. An alternative adolescent pattern is that of total immersion, or fusion with the other. Through this, the normal late adolescent separation conflicts with parents, which are defining of personal identity, are evaded by reconstituting dependence on, and definition by, a peer. David's first involvement, shortly after leaving home at 17, which lasted for 4 years and was rapidly replaced by his relationship with Patricia, may have contained some aspect of this.

Once intimacy is sought, and some committed relationship is made, the implications of dependency become a major preoccupation. The forms in which these issues are manifest will reflect the way in which dependency and autonomy were experienced in childhood and upon the resulting central self-identity scripts, and upon how far the self is stably constituted. To the extent that autonomy is felt to be threatened, efforts to control the other, directly or by withdrawal, will be exercised. In many instances, the conflicts arising from these issues are not faced; the craving for, and the conventional myth of, easy positive relationships in which each person sustains his life while caring for, and being cared for by, the other, makes it hard to acknowledge the almost inevitable experience of disillusion and disappointment, competitiveness, hostility, or envy. The denial of these feelings, and hence the avoidance of the acts that might resolve the issues, can contribute to depression, combining elements of sadness and anger, and to psychosomatic symptoms. The psychotherapy of these conditions in adults leads on to the consideration of self-identity and relationships scripts and, hence, to disturbing the patterns of existing relationships.

If the myth is not sustained, and if mixed feelings are acknowledged, then the battle-lines will be drawn up, sometimes in ways determined by sex-role stereotypes, sometimes in ways clearly repeating the issues of the individual's own child-parent experiences. A common spiral that can develop in this is that, under stress, both partners feel more childlike and hence seek more care, while becoming less parent-like and hence giving less care. To endure such conflict involves a capacity to acknowledge negative feelings that our culture does not support, and the retreat into mood states or symptoms may seem preferable. For the therapist involved in helping such struggles, the task is both to recognize this, and to understand the mutual projections which are normally built into such relationships. Joint therapy, based upon an object-relations approach, is probably the best solution.

The conflicts of later life, whose frequency is reflected in the soaring divorce rates, are partly the final surfacings of these earlier issues, and partly the expression of the firmer individuality and autonomy of the partners. This healthier process is accompanied by the reassertion of aspects that have been denied in the service of the relationship (and often, also of parenthood) or that have been recognized in the other but effaced in the self. Issues of this sort may arise at an earlier stage now than was the case in the past, as the impact of feminism upon marriage has encouraged greater self-awareness and greater reluctance to accept self-abnegating definitions. Once conflict is acknowledged, the choice lies between a return to collusion and denial, or a progression, bound to be painful, to the fullest possible acknowledgement of the reality and individuality of the self and of the other; sometimes only at the cost of the relationship.

Common sexual difficulties, in my view, are nearly always expressions of these personal (self-identity) and relationship (strategic) difficulties, rather than being either causes of, or independent of, these higher-order issues. The most severe sexual problems such as fetishism, perversions, and major confusions of sexual identity, reflect radical problems of self-identity, and the understanding of these owes much to the developmental aspects of psychoanalytic theory. The common problems of absent or incomplete sexual capacity (erectile impotence, premature ejaculation in the male; varying degrees of frigidity and orgasmic failure in women) are statements about how the self or the other is seen. Problems present from the first sexual experience are likely to reflect combinations of ignorance and of negative self-evaluations and judgements. Problems arising in the course of a relationship are likely to express feelings about the relationship. (In older subjects in particular, physical disorders such as neurological disorders and diabetes need to be excluded.)

Behavioural approaches to the treatment of sexual problems are based upon the simple premise of reinforcement strategies. Some, which to me seem humanly and ethically very undesirable, make sexual availability contingent upon other behaviours, such as work about the house, or time spent together. Others serve more simply and more positively to remedy ignorance and overcome inhibition by encouraging plain speaking and providing a vocabulary for it, by teaching how to give, and ask for, pleasure, and by breaking the failure-anxiety-failure cycle by a regime of slowly increasing sexual activity short of intercourse. Ostensibly, such approaches operate, in terms of the procedural sequence model, at the tactical level, by extending the repertoire of means and by replacing negative predictive evaluations with positive ones. In fact, however, such programmes include, implicitly or explicitly, the modification of self-identity scripts by challenging such self-statements as "I am not, and may not be, a sexual person".

Because sexuality is an expressive act of considerable symbolic weight, development of a more satisfying, more self- and other-regarding, sexual relationship may influence favourably other aspects of the relationship; but, by the same token, unresolved interpersonal issues may make such a solution unattainable, in which case sexual difficulties will persist until the other problems are resolved. These other difficulties often include fundamental issues about identity, related to particular family experiences, and represented in conflicts between sexual aims (PSM 1) and self-judging scripts (PSM 2c). Sexual guilt may be less prevalent now than it was in Freud's Vienna but it can hardly be said to have been eliminated. Sexual difficulties which develop in the course of a relationship are expressive acts; although the patient will often say, "I cannot", the impotence, frigidity, or other symptom, is saying in effect, "I will not". The real task for the couple, which they will often fall back from, is to understand and remedy the reason for this negative statement. The long-term negative emotional states commonly accompanying unsuccessful marriages represent, for each of the couple, a mismatch between the desired and perceived other. This is often complicated by contradictions (mismatches) between different aims in relation to the other who therefore, in fulfilling one aim, inevitably frustrates another. To understand the complexity and persistence of these problems, the phenomenon of projective identification, to be discussed in the next chapter, is an important concept.

DISCUSSION

The paper by Schachter and Singer (1962) on the "Cognitive, Social and Physiological Determinants of Emotional States" provides experimental evidence on the relation between physiological changes and emotion, and concludes that the labelling of the physiological changes accompanying emotion is determined largely by the accompanying cognitions (see also Schachter, 1964). Attempts to develop more comprehensive theories of emotions in cognitive terms have been made by a number of writers. Kelly (1955) and, among Kellians, McCoy (1977) have attempted to develop a systematic account of emotions on a cognitive basis. I find the definitions emerging from this work to be unsatisfactory. To a man about to be run over by a steam-roller, the description of fear as "awareness of imminent incidental change in one's core structure" (core structure referring to the construct system) would not adequately cover the situation. However, Kelly usefully defines the often neglected form of anxiety which accompanies the loss, or threat of loss, of cognitive control. In Kelly's terms, anxiety is the awareness that the events with which one is confronted lie outside the range of convenience of one's construct system.

Beck (1976) discusses emotion in terms of his concept of the "personal domain", by which he means the self and those things, people, and values, identified with the self. In his somewhat entrepreneurial view, for example, euphoria implies expansion, and sadness implies loss to the domain. Anxiety is a response to the prospect of loss, anger arises out of a sense of the domain being deliberately attacked by another. Beck does not consider the relation of intrapsychic conflict to emotion at all and, to a greater or lesser extent, this restriction is true of most other cognitive and behavioural writers.

Plutchik (1980) offers an account of emotion, drawing on ethology, and emphasizing the importance of cognition. In his view, an emotion is a chain, starting with the cognition of an event which evokes a feeling leading to a behaviour having some appropriate biological goal. The objectives of emotionally provoked behaviours are variously to seek protection, to remove obstacles, to incorporate, accept, or reject, reproduction, to recall or replace a needed other, to orient, and to explore. His view therefore links emotions explicitly to aims. This author also offers a useful circumflex model of primary emotional terms and of mixed emotions, based upon studies with the semantic differential.

The fullest account of emotions from a cognitive viewpoint is that provided by Katz (1980) whose paper was a major source for this chapter. Emotions, as we have discussed, signal a schematic matching or discrepancy; they are cognitive and biological events, labelled in ways determined by our personal and cultural histories.

The importance of bereavement and loss has long been recognized in the psychoanalytic literature and their influence on morbidity has been extensively researched by epidemiological means. The experience of bereavement and the indications for professional help are lucidly described by Parkes (1975).

There is an extensive behaviourist literature on the treatment of "sexual dysfunction" and associated marital problems, much of it stemming from the work of Masters and Johnson (1966) (e.g. Gurman and Rice, 1975; Bancroft, 1975; Crowe, 1979). Kaplan (1974) combines behavioural and interpretive methods, and Skynner (1976) presents a humane eclectic account based in particular on psychoanalytic and systems theory concepts.

5
The Self

We have considered in the previous chapters the PSM as a basis for understanding how our aims are achieved, diverted, or blocked; how our system of understanding and procedures are developed; and how emotions and symptoms may be understood. At this point we need to look back on the life of the individual to consider the ways in which his repertoire of scripts bears traces of its earliest origins in infancy, and to describe how the self can be understood in these terms.

The adult whom we have been describing bears traces of his earlier history, both in the structure of his thought, as Piaget in particular demonstrated, and in the content of his thoughts, as Freud argued. The contrast of content with structure is not ideal: the ''what'' of experience and the ''how'' of the thought processes are to be comprehended only in terms of their relation to each other. What is common to psychoanalysis and developmental psychology is the recognition of the fact that later structures of thought grow out of the thought of the child, being built upon a basis of primitive knowledge and skills acquired before consciousness and beyond the possibility of recall. Traces of this origin may be apparent in how the adult thinks and acts.

In the self the conclusion drawn from our lifetime experiences are organized, in the form of processes that determine how we conduct our lives. The self can be conceived of as the highest and most general set of memories, understandings, and procedures. The meanings of situations and events are understood, and the selection and evaluation of lower-order aims and actions occur, through reference to this overall cognitive structure. There is more to the self, however, than this: the self is also self-observing. We have described how, in carrying out any procedural script, we elaborate schemata to evaluate the effectiveness of our performances and the meanings of the outcomes of our acts. In the case of the overall ''life-script'' we elaborate similar evaluative schemata; these form our conscious self-awareness, and are concerned with providing feedback on our performance and on the personal meanings and values of what we do.

Our judgement of the meaning of our life is considered by relating our perceived qualities and actions to a personal theory of values or, to put it more generally, by matching the self as perceived with the ideal self. How we feel about ourselves reflects discrepancies (schematic mismatches) between the self as perceived and the ideal self. This ideal self represents those values we personally identify with; but how we view ourselves and how we would like to be viewed are based historically upon the perceived responses of others, notably of those who cared for us before we could talk and before we can remember. In this way, our first mirror, providing the foundations of our self-awareness, was held up to us long before we were aware of self.

Although there can be no recollection from these earliest times, learning then takes place, and schemata organizing our knowledge of ourselves and others, and our interactions with others are being developed from the earliest days. That the terms of these interactions are not always admirable from the adult point of view was well understood by St. Augustine (1971) when he set about retracing his own moral development in his Confessions.

> It can hardly be right for a child . . . to cry for everything, including things that would harm him, to work himself into a tantrum against people older than himself and not required to obey him, to try his best to strike and hurt others . . . including his own parents . . . This shows that, if babies are innocent, it is not for the lack of will to do harm but for the lack of strength. I myself have seen jealousy in a baby and know what it means; he was not old enough to talk, but whenever he saw his foster-brother at the breast he would grow pale with envy. This much is common knowledge. Mothers and nurses say that they can work such things out of the system by one means or another, but surely it cannot be called innocence.

Infant experience is of importance in understanding the adult, for three reasons. In the first place, one has to recognize the persistence into adult life of elements of these unrespectable feelings, more or less imperfectly concealed beneath the later acquired, more "civilized" values. In the second place, particular experiences at these early stages, such as privation, the failure of the mother or mother-substitute to respond sensitively to needs, or the failure of parents to acknowledge and encourage the child's growing capacity for autonomy may be embedded as unspoken, unrecognized basic assumptions in the subsequent scripts organizing the self and relationships. This can lead to restrictions on, or distortions of, the means available for the pursuit of ordinary and appropriate life aims. The third reason concerns our understanding of the history of cognitive development. There is an inevitable sequence to cognitive growth, dictated by physical maturation and by the growth of conceptual ability. This progress, and the accompanying successive modifications in our relationships with others, provide us all with a universal history, a common source for our concepts of the world and of ourselves on which our later experience will elaborate. Any issue in later adult life which is related to early basic themes first encountered before consciousness, may be construed as a version of the earlier situation through primitive thought processes shaped at the time of the first encounter with the issue. The persistence of these primitive processes appears writ large in the disorganized thoughts of the psychotic patient, some of which clearly bear traces of — although clearly do not simply reproduce — the primitive thought of the infant. In the neurotic, or ordinary troubled person, on the other hand, the manifestations of these early processes is likely to be more subtle in the form of restrictions, oversimplifications, or overgeneralizations. To understand ourselves and how we can change we need, therefore, to be able to recognize the manifestations, in thought or action, of these early forms of thinking, and to be alert to the possible later effects of events occurring in these early formative years.

We will now consider what the important issues are that can colour our basic theory of ourselves and of our relationships with others, by discussing in turn the origins of the basic sense of the self as separate and of trust in others, the growth of autonomy, issues of rivalry and of sex-identity, and the relations of the structure of the self, of self-control and of self-judgement, to the structure of self-other relationships.

SENSE OF SELF AND OF TRUST IN OTHERS

Uncertainty about the strength and integrity of the self can be manifest in various ways, notably by the need to withdraw or retain emotional distance from others, in the experience of confusion or pain if closeness is achieved, in patterns of relationship marked by manipulative dependency upon others, or in the need for others to provide an idealizing or reassuring mirror to the self by presenting a seeming admiring similarity. Some such states were summarized by Horney (1937) as the four "mottoes": "if you love me you will not hurt me"; "if I give in, I shall not be hurt"; "if I have power, no-one can hurt me"; and "if I withdraw nothing can hurt me". (These mottoes could be rephrased in terms of the PSM in the form of interpersonal dilemmas concerned with basic security). In seeing the other as powerful and as need-supplying one can see references back, or parallels, to those issues faced in the first years of life, during which a child's total dependency and necessary attachment to his parents is modified. The child gradually recognizes that he is separate from the other, learns that the other exists even when not present (this requires the ability to form stable mental representations), and engages in an increasingly active exploration of the world. As he achieves this understanding, this trust in the other, and this capacity for action, he is establishing the basis for his sense of his individual self.

One can see that this process inevitably, involves, the exchange of forms of restrictive safety for risky extensions of the independence of the self. This choice between safety and freedom persists throughout life, the need for safety surfacing when the sense of self is diminished as in depression, illness, or failure. This fact makes the issue of dependency of importance in most psychotherapies. The seeds for an unsatisfactory resolution of the debate may be sown during the child's first experiences; for example, by a mother who unduly prolongs physical closeness and the child's dependency; by one who provides too abrupt and early an experience of separation; or by parents whose response to the child's exploration and emerging individuation is to emphasize closeness and similarity rather than differentiation. We must also note that these same themes are enacted, and with the same parents, throughout childhood, and are revisited sharply at the time of adolescence, and that these later periods can remedy or further distort the growth of the child's individual sense of self. We will now look at these issues as they presented in our two patients.

Anne

Anne showed an incomplete separation from her parents, as was shown both by the extent of her continuing responsibility for providing practical and emotional care for her mother, and in the form of her self-definitions which were still based very much upon her family role. Her self-respect was dependent upon seeing herself as the healthy daughter of a dependent mother. Moreover, on the basis of quite specific parental injunctions which had been given throughout childhood and adolescence, she acted as if she had to set limits on her own life in order to protect her mother (her snag), although she was not consciously aware how extensively this rule was operating. However, Anne's identity, though not separate from that attributed by her parents, had positive qualities (those of being strong and stable) and was at least based upon a differentiation from, rather than a merging with, her parents. The disruption of this identity by her symptoms led to panic and, in the short run, to a sense of the self as falling apart, but her qualities of strength were of service to her in her recovery.

David

In the case of David, his early separation from his mother at the age of 4 was a remembered traumatic event, which he described in the first interview as follows:

AR: Was your physical health OK as a child?
DAVID: When I was 4 I got pneumonia but I got over that.
AR: Were you in hospital?
DAVID: Yes.
AR: Do you know for how long?
DAVID: Let me get this right. I think it was a week. I was taken in with suspected meningitis, but in fact it was tonsillitis, and I just had a cough. Then my mum had TB which was a bit difficult.
AR: Were you with her at that time?
DAVID: No. She wanted to stay at home but had to go to hospital. She did convalesce for a long time at home afterwards.
AR: How old were you?
DAVID: Well, this all happened at the same time; it happened in one go.
AR: Ah, I see, so there was probably quite a gap in that year?
DAVID: Yes, I was away from mum for some time.
AR: Do you recall the mood of that time at all?
DAVID: Well, I recall the desperation of course. I remember — I don't get these dreams

> any more — but I remember odd little snippets of dreams from childhood — you know, the one about distance — like you're asleep in bed and you're having a nightmare of some kind, and your parents came in the door and and they say, "That's alright" and the point is that they're about 200 yards away; but you know they're actually touching you and you know they're there and it's going to be OK, but you can see them so far away. I don't know whether that happened before or after — I guess that's the kind of mood of that year.

Soon after David left home at the age of seventeen, when his parents separated, he was deeply involved in his first serious sexual relationship, and when, 4 years later, this broke up it was only a few weeks before he became involved with Patricia. In discussing Patricia's loss, it became clear that his decision to go to University was understood by him as being, in part at least, an expression of his relationship to Patricia, and in this it was linked with a more general sense of being unjustified in his own terms. It seems that, at the age of four, David had concluded that those you cared for were liable to leave you, and he had tended to seek binding relationships which were central to his sense of self to overcome the insecurity, but the pain of loss was correspondingly profound.

AUTONOMY AND SEXUAL IDENTITY

In the psychoanalytic view, basic trust in others is acquired in the earliest months of life (the oral phase). The fact that feeding plays a large part in the first exchange between child and mother accounts for the later equivalence between feeding and the giving or withholding, and accepting or rejection of affection or care. As the child matures and becomes capable of independent movement and of control of bowel and bladder functions, the issue of autonomy and of interpersonal control are similarly encountered with the immediate care-givers for the first time. This is what constitutes the anal stage in Freud's original classification. To the bodily metaphors of taking in or refusing good or bad milk are added the metaphors of letting go or holding on to good or bad urine and faeces. Parental overcontrol at his stage may deny the child the experience of appropriately extending his self-management and self-control, and may impose upon him the choice between compliance or defiance. Even in the absence of overcontrol in infancy, later situations that involve coping with the demands of others, where free giving does not come easily, may be conceived of in the primitive terms of angry holding on to or angry letting go.

In the oedipal stage as described by Freud, the relationship of the child to both parents, his conception of their relationship with each other, and the loosening of his passionate physical attachment to the mother, bring to the fore issues of rivalry, of authority, of guilt, and of sex-role identification. Difficulties at this stage will usually occur in the wake of earlier failures in the process of separation and the establishment of autonomy.

We acquire the "grammar" of our sexual identity in this first three-person situation. This "grammar" will include traces of the far-from-innocent child's attempts to make sense of his feelings and experiences. For healthy development to be possible, two main distinctions have to be established at this time: that between the generations and that between the sexes. The recognition of the parents' relationship and the exclusion of the child from it provides the necessary basis of the child's freedom from overprolonged attachment. The definitions and implications of sex-roles are derived from the way these roles are established in the family. They vary greatly between cultures, and have historically included rules and assumptions which have served to maintain a diminished status for women. The current challenging of these rules leads to much conflict in the present generation of young people, many of whom have been unconsciously shaped by family experiences based on traditional sex-role definitions which they have come to consciously reject. The Women's Movement offers an important external validation for revised assumptions during this period of transition, but men lack an equivalent supportive resource.

THE SELF AND SELF-TO-OTHER RELATIONSHIPS

The object-relations school of psychoanalysis modified the traditional psychoanalytic account of infancy by emphasizing the importance of the way in which the child first of all conceptualizes his relationships with others. In this view, the providing, frustrating, exciting, and prohibiting aspects of the mother are initially construed as being separate by the child. The polarization of good and bad figures, and exaggerated, over-simple discriminations made between people in later life are seen to result from the persistence of these early "splitting" mechanisms. One can appreciate this theory by considering its relation to some aspects of commonsense psychology, which point to similar conclusions. This discussion will lead on to a consideration of the processes of projection and projective identification, and to an understanding of how the structure of the self and the structure of relationships with others are connected.

Everyday accounts of others are full of phrases such as: "He is hard on himself", "He is sorry for himself", "He drives himself", "He neglects himself". Such descriptions, which relate to the self identity criteria of the PSM, have far-reaching implications for our understanding of the person. If we know how someone views or treats himself, we are often nearer to understanding how he is likely to engage with others. We are faced here with the way in which commonsense psychology conceives of the self as being in some way divided: part of the self is seen as doing something to another part of it, such as caring for it, neglecting it, and so on. Further consideration suggests that the first of these parts has parental, and the second, childlike attributes.

The connection between this relationship between these two aspects of the self, on the one hand, and the relationships the person has with others, on the other hand, is often fairly clear. A man who neglects or disregards himself allows others to do likewise; a man who drives himself is liable to drive others; a man who admires himself is likely to try to extract similar admiration from others. In some cases, however, the connection between these self-to-self and self-to-other relationships is less obvious because of two complicating issues. In the first place, the inner relationship of parent-self to child-self can be reflected in the relationships with others in one of two ways: the other may be elected to play either the parental role (e.g. as neglecting or caring) or the child role (as neglected or cared for), with the self playing the reciprocal part. In the second place, the fact that a particular kind of self-parenting may be apparent may conceal the existence of a contrasting parental image, which is the result of the splitting mechanism described above. Thus, the self-neglecting person, who was uncared for as a child, and seems now unable to care for himself, may have built up, on the basis of what care he did receive, a compensatory image of an idealized and caring parent. In his relationship with others, whom he elects to play parental roles, such a person may either "arrange" a repetition of neglect, or he may seek recompense by electing another to be an ideally caring person to him. This retention of dual parental images, representing in psychoanalytic object-relations theory the effect of the splitting of internal objects, is manifest in the wicked uncles, stepmothers, and fairy godmothers of traditional childhood stories.

Once we understand these two complicating factors, we can see that the effect of poorly integrated self-to-self attitudes on interpersonal behaviour is a complex one. Relationships with emotionally significant others will not represent simple recapitulation of the original experience of the person as a child, and will not necessarily be a simple parallel of his parentlike-self to childlike-self internal relationship. They will, however, be limited to a relatively restricted repertoire, and the repertoire of means available for self-care and other-care, or self-control or other-control, will have common features. In the example we have considered of the childhood-deprived, self-neglecting person, the choice of the role for the self would lie between one or other pole of a neglecting parent-neglected child relationship, or one or other pole of a dependable adult-dependent child relationship.

Much stress and interpersonal difficulty arises from our attempts to force others to play one or other of these reciprocal roles with us, although we are also quite adept at finding people prepared to play the "bit" parts for which we are rehearsed (such "bit" parts represent what object-relations theory calls "part object-relation"). In terms of the PSM this phenomena will be manifest in relationship dilemmas. As will be discussed in more detail later, one important gift of a therapist (or a good friend) is to resist this invitation to participate in such repetitions.

PROJECTION AND PROJECTIVE-IDENTIFICATION, AND THE INTEGRATION OF THE SELF

One source of inner conflict can be the warring between the parentlike and childlike aspects of the self; often in this conflict any self-expressive aim may be judged as childlike. One way of reducing such conflict is by the disavowal of one or other of the aspects. One sees sometimes grim and humourless people who seem to be all parent, and other feckless, irresponsible ones who seem all child. However, the relationship patterns of such people will often show that the disavowed part has been located in another. A fight between the rebellious child aspect and the harsh, parental aspect of the self, for example, can in some sense be relieved if aspects of one or other of the inner protagonists can be attributed to ("projected into") another person. The process of projection represents the misattribution to others of what arises from, or is an aspect of, the self; we are intolerant of our faults in others. Projective-identification represents the more elaborate process of structuring relationships in such a way that the internal relationship between parts of the self is repeated in the reciprocal role with the other. Many adult relationships, particularly in marriage, have, beneath the adult-adult relationship, a collusive system of such mutual projective identification, which can be a potent source of trouble. Interpersonal dilemmas where issues of power and affection are confused may represent the outcome of projective identification.

In cognitive terms, the process of projective identification involves the following:

(a) The script for self-control and self-judgement is based upon the child's conceptualization of the control and judgement initially exercised over him by his parents.

(b) The script determining self-other relationships in adult life may show persistence of features based on this early relationship of self-parent, either repeating the recalled relationship or a polarized, compensatory alternative version of it.

(c) In such recapitulations in adult relationships, the self may occupy either the child or the parents pole of the reciprocal relationship.

Projective identification represents conceptual confusion in so far as self-other discrimination is blurred. This is self-maintaining inasmuch as the projected aspect of the self is not consciously acknowledged, at least as long as the other is prepared to play the reciprocal role. The element of confusion involved might suggest that the origin of projective identification is at the early developmental stage of individuation and separation, whereas self-control and self-evaluative scripts would probably be elaborated later in childhood, when parental control and judgement in response to autonomous activity are encountered. As with the other issues we have considered in relation to early childhood, however, the parents whose behaviour can cause problems in development in this respect are likely to be present throughout infancy and childhood, and in most patients seem to have provided problematic situations for their children right through to adolescence. Conversely, recoveries and resolutions of difficulty are also apparent during this time.

David

David's insistence that his tutors' previous positive accounts of his work had been based on friendliness rather than on sound judgement represented his projection of his own self-doubting judgements. In his relationship with Patricia, he sought justification for his life, specifically for his degree course; this could be seen as the projection of a compensatory, ideal source of approval into another, as a balance to his more basic and permanent self-doubting attitude.

Anne

Anne's preference for the care-giving role represented the projection into others of the needy, potentially crazy aspects of herself; the origins of this in her caretaking of her mother, and her need to deny in herself the frightening connotations of dependency, are clear.

THE PERSISTENT INFLUENCE OF INFANTILE THINKING

Given that all adult cognition develops from the thought of the child, and that learning continues throughout life, it is not always obvious what traits or problems in the adult represent the maladaptive persistence of unintegrated infantile patterns of thought, particularly as some degree of personal inconsistency is normal. Many adolescents, and some adults, apply different criteria of self-control and self-judgement in different contexts. These separate criteria may reflect their acceptance of the attributions of different external sources (e.g. conflicting values of parents and peer groups) and can in some cases be manifest in the form of markedly different alternative personalities. More commonly, there is some sense of a dominant and central identity which can recognize the operation of "sub-personalities"; these sub-personalities may be more or less comfortably allotted expression in particular contexts, but in some cases may jostle uncomfortably for control, a state which will be experienced as conflicted or discontinuous, and which is marked in the identity diffusion sometimes experienced in late adolescence. The more or less mature adult achieves a secure sense of a central identity and a relatively binding set of assumptions and values through the process of integrating or abandoning dissonant elements of his personality; in the neurotic personality this integration may only be achieved at the cost of restriction.

All adult thought bears, to a greater or lesser degree, traces of the primitive conceptualizations of the child. This is evident in the patterns of relationships sought, in the nature of discriminations made, in the range of means available to pursue aims, and in the metaphors of speech and symptoms. What is important about the past is reflected in what is done or not done, known or not known, in the present. Later experiences through childhood and adolescence may continue to heal old, or cause new, troubles, and it is often impossible and unnecessary to estimate the influence of the earliest experiences as against those that occur later and are accessible to memory. To end this discussion, we will further consider how traces from infancy and childhood were manifest in the cases of Anne and David.

Anne

Issues of trust and mistrust, and of rivalry were prominent in Anne's history. Her actively paranoid mother was constantly suspicious of others, and had directly intervened, out of explicit jealousy, to keep father and Anne apart after Anne's puberty. This active intervention was probably helpful to Anne, serving to protect her from too close a relationship with her father, despite the fact that mother's incapacity had forced her into the role of co-parent and (in some social circumstances) wife-replacement. However, mother's illness posed other problems: the normal generational issue faced by the adolescent, of who is king or queen of the castle, is best resolved through the ordinary forms of adolescent struggle, in which, in the end, the child can become, and the parent can remain, effective adults. For Anne, however, her growth and achievement were always in the context of her mother's decline and incapacity. Her mother, if a rival, was already defeated; and, if a model, one to be avoided. Anne did not see herself as a mistrustful person, because to do so was contrary to her procedural script that defined how to be sane but, living in a family in which so much mistrust was voiced, it was inevitable that to some extent she should share that characteristic. The extent of her mistrust was only made evident to her through her relationship with me, manifest firstly in the third session in the form of an unfounded suspicion that I had spoken without her permission to her mother's psychiatrist and, more complexly, after the fourth session. At that meeting she had struggled with many of the issues which had been raised in the course of the assessment; at the end of the session, I remarked how strenuous her efforts were and suggested that perhaps she need not work so hard and might allow herself to experience things as well, suggesting in particular that she might feel sadness or anger in relation to a forthcoming break in treatment. As she was leaving my office, I put my hand on her shoulder and said, encouragingly as I thought, that I felt she would manage alright, and I liked her for the way in which she was struggling with her problems. Early the next day she telephoned, requesting an extra session, having felt furious with me from the time she left the room. She had felt invaded and abused, and linked these feelings with past episodes with older men, including being molested at the age of 9 by a family friend, and also with a feeling that tutors at University to whom she had gone with work difficulties had, on two or three occasions, responded by making sexual advances. I apologised for having upset her, and suggested that perhaps her mother's explicit forbidding of any physical contact between her and her father had contributed to the extremity of her reaction. I also wondered if, in the previous episodes she reported, she might have in some way conveyed a wish for comfort or affirmation, or for a sexual response, as well as a refusal of it, expressing in this way the same mixture of feeling that she must have felt in relation to her father.

Much later on, when I had obtained Anne's agreement to her case history being included in this book, her husband commented that it was typical of her to gain a "special" response for herself by being chosen for the book. Other things emerged later that provided some confirmation for the view that Anne in part elicited responses she did not always like, due to oedipal issues. She had, as a child, sought older friends and, as an adolescent, had had largely older boyfriends, including in one case an ex-school-teacher. More recently, a friend had commented on the way in which she made immediate and quick contact with men and then withdrew abruptly. Later in treatment Anne had one explicit ''oedipal'' dream (see Chapter 10.)

Anne's mistrust and anger with me was therefore related to a complex set of feelings, rooted in the triangular relations between herself, her mother, and her father. The result of their surfacing in treatment was helpful in that she was able to appreciate and begin to overcome her mistrust, and recognize her own actions more clearly.

A second issue in Anne's history could be related in psychoanalytic terms to the ''anal'' issues of withholding. At every major academic assessment, Anne had underperformed in one part of the examination, commonly in her best subject. She described herself as preferring to do very well or really badly, and spoke with some glee of her father's writing to one examination board when he was unable to believe her failure, although she knew it was deserved. In psychoanalytic terms, one could see this as a pattern of perfectionist offerings (good faeces) alternating with making a real mess (bad faeces). Here, too, however, there seems no need to suspect specifically infantile *origins* for this pattern. Her work history was one of underachievement between the ages of 5 and 9, when she was suffering from the effects of her mother's first breakdown. Thereafter she recovered rapidly and subsequently her usual pattern was of high performance, and she enjoyed the approval she won for such success. School achievement was especially pleasing to father, who was himself a teacher. Conversely, failure can be seen as a way of disappointing him. In terms of Anne's procedural scripts and their implications, to succeed was a means of securing approval and love, but to be loved also involved putting her own needs second to those of her mother. The very conditional nature of the love she was offered by her father, and his failure to protect her from mother's enormous demands, would be likely to evoke anger towards him. However, to feel or show anger directly was, for Anne, equated with being crazy; it seems likely, therefore, that the aim of attacking father for failing to protect her was achieved by her failure. Unfortunately, she simultaneously punished herself for this indirect expression of anger by suffering the effects of the failures involved. The projection of her own denied spontaneous childish and angry needs into others by her compulsive caretaking is unlikely to have originated before her mother's breakdown, when she was 5.

David

Except for his separation experience at 4, David recollected his family life as being happy until the blow, to him unexpected, of his father's leaving home when he was 17. He initially resented his mother's outrage at father's infidelity, and was upset by her insistence on father leaving home. Left at home with mother, and faced with her unhappiness and potential dependency, he felt in retrospect that he had cut off emotionally from her, and he had soon left to work in a residential job. Later, when father became severely depressed and was hospitalized, as a result of which his career collapsed, David did not go and visit him. By the time he was seeing me, however, which was a few years later, he had achieved a comfortable and mutually respecting relationship with his mother, and was seeing his father from time to time. Father had more or less re-established himself in his career and had remarried, but David saw him as a ghost of his former self, and had come to feel that, even before the breakdown, he had been something of a hollow man.

At a time in his life when he could have expected to assert his own independence from his parents, and move into the adult world with some sense of being as much a man as his father, David saw his father transformed into someone he could not admire, and had no need to compete with, and his mother as someone whose needs might block his own growth. His strategy of taking a residential job in a caring role, and of soon becoming deeply emotionally involved with his first serious girlfriend, worked satisfactorily at the time. Over the ensuing years, he slowly came to terms with what had happened, revised his simple, blaming version of the parents' difficulties, and seemed to be pursuing his own life. We are left, however, with a picture of somebody who had not yet achieved a sense of being in charge of his life, indecisive about his career choice, and still feeling the need to justify his actions and plans in terms of a relationship with a woman. I have already described (Chapter 3) how I thought that this problem represented the operation of a snag: David feeling, unconsciously and irrationally, guilty for the troubles of his father, and expiating by not claiming his own manhood. Much later in treatment, when completing ratings on his "snag", David suddenly recollected how his fear of being dangerous could have an earlier root too, in that his mother used to tell him that her illness, of which she "nearly died" was brought on by her worrying about his prior illness. David was probably vulnerable as a result of his separation from his mother and of this comment and also as the result of the separation of his parents, and his father's illness, when he was 17. That his subsequent ability to claim his life seems to have been damaged by these events is best explained if one accepts the view that his *interpretations* of these events contained assumptions based upon the understandings of early childhood. In this view, David avoided living his life fully, as if he had intended his mother's illness and his father's defeat and was therefore guilty; in particular, he interpreted his parents' separation and father's illness with the criteria of an omnipotent rivalrous child. It is not the events of childhood, but rather the conclusions we draw from them, that shape and limit our later ability to live fully.

DISCUSSION

In this chapter, I have proposed a cognitive view of the self, while incorporating important insights from psychoanalysis, especially from later object-relations theory. The self has proved a very indigestible concept in psychoanalysis, only dragged into respectability latterly as a result of work on borderline and narcissistic personality disorders. A leading figure in this late rehabilitation of the concept is

Kohut, who has struggled for a decade to integrate it into classical theoretical formulations. He wrote 10 years ago (Kohut 1970):

> It is best to confine ourselves to defining the self as an important content, a structure or configuration within the mental apparatus, i.e. self-representations which are located in the ego, the id, and the superego.

He went on to say that this would not rule out its final "acceptation" as "one of the centres of identifiable functions".

Eight years later, Kohut and Wolf (1978), writing of the narcissistic personality disorders, referred to the "*fact* that it is a weakened or defective self that lies at the centre of the disorder . . .". These authors went on to write that:

> . . . the weakness of the self was conceptualised in terms of its underlibidinisation — as a cathetic deficit, to speak in the terms of Freudian metapsychology — and the intense regressions encountered in the narcissistic personality disorders were recognised as the responses of the vulnerable self to a variety of injuries. The decisive steps forward in the understanding of these disorders, however, were made through the introduction of the concept of the *self-object* via the increasing understanding of the self in depth psychological terms. *Self-objects* are objects which we experience as part of ourself. The expected control over them is, therefore, closer to the concept of the control which a grown-up expects to have over his own body and mind, than to the concept of the control which he expects to have over others.

The extensive writings of Kohut can be pursued by those wishing to examine this view more closely; my own feeling is that the difficulties struggled with in this clotted prose are the consequences of classical psychoanalytic theory, not of any necessary obscurity in the very useful concept of the self.

In understanding the self, however, we can learn from the contribution of classical theories of defence, from the work of Erikson (1959), and from the later developments of object-relations theory. The major defence mechanisms have been extensively studied and restated as cognitive strategies by Haan (1977) who has usefully classified a wide range of functions as they appear, either as coping strategies, defensive strategies, or in fragmentation. However, she does not consider projective identification, which is a concept derived from object-relations theory, which seems to me to be of considerable importance in understanding relationships (including the transference), and which therefore I have presented in cognitive terms in this chapter.

Outside psychoanalysis, theories of the self owe much to the writings of Mead (1934) and an early cognitive formulation is to be found in Kelly (1955). The subject is reviewed clearly by Epstein (1973) who argues that individuals have implicit theories about themselves, and that therefore the self can be both the subject and object of what is known. In Epstein's view, "the recognition that an individual self theory, like any other theory, is a hierarchically organised conceptual system for solving problems" is an an important one, and explains "its total disorganisation when a basic postulate is invalidated, or when for some other reason the theory is incapable of fulfilling its function''. In a recent paper, Mancuso and Ceely (1980) address themselves to this same issue. They conclude:

> With progress in studies of the cognitive function, personality theorists will be better positioned to explicate implicit personality theories of personality, which are assumed to underlie one's theory of self . . . One can now, it is hoped, look to further studies of cognitive functioning to show us the parallels between a person's ''discovery'' of a number system . . . his discovery of persons, and his discovery of his self . . . With this kind of information we can develop a more meaningful view of how the self-as-process is implicated in the regulation of the self-as-object.

Turner (1980) has written a clear review of the child's first years, uniting perspectives from developmental psychology and psychoanalysis in a way that parallels this chapter.

It seems important that, in this study of the discovery of persons and of the self, we hold on to psychoanalytic insights into how these discoveries are characterized by confusions and conflicts, due to their acquisition with imperfect cognitive tools early in life, and important to match any attempt to describe the self against our own experience of being, and partially knowing, ourselves.

6
Teaching, Learning, and Therapy

Normal learning involves the successive revision of schemata in the face of new external situations or in the service of elaborated aims. In the neurotic patient, or other failed problem-solver, the process has gone wrong at some point. In the present chapter, we will consider in general terms the relation of theories of learning and teaching to psychotherapy, and compare the practice of teachers and therapists, before proceeding to a detailed consideration of the practice of psychotherapy in the ensuing chapters.

What patients have to do is to learn new ways of going about their lives, so that they no longer create trouble for themselves, fail to realize their aims, or suffer from symptoms. This is a learning task to do with the solution of ordinary, or sometimes unusually difficult, life problems. As such, the learning involved in therapy is learning in the precise areas where learning has been unsuccessful. Ordinary problem-solving (see the review of numerous studies by Heppner, 1976) involves a number of stages, summarized as orientation, problem-definition, the generation of alternative solutions, decision-making, and testing out. This sequence can be seen to parallel the procedural sequence described in the PSM. The particular problems of the patient, compared to those of the pupil, stem from his history of failure and from the self-perpetuating errors discussed in the last chapters, which mean that, while a pupil is in principle ready to face the task of learning, a patient is more likely to see himself as ill, unhappy, the victim of circumstance, guilty, or as a failure, rather than as a potential problem-solver.

The therapist as teacher must take account of these special circumstances, but he may still see his task as similar in many ways to that of the tutor, as described, for example, by Wood *et al.* (1976). These authors describe the tutor's role as the provision of "scaffolding", which they define as involving the following acts:

(a) Recruitment: the tutor has to enlist the problem-solver's interest in, and adherence to, the requirements of the task.

(b) Reduction in degrees of freedom: the tutor simplifies the task by reducing the number of constituent acts required to reach a solution.

(c) Direction maintenance: the tutor gives encouragement and prevents premature satisfaction with incomplete solutions.

(d) Marking critical features: the tutor notes the most relevant aspects of the problem.

(e) Frustration control: these authors note that there should perhaps be some such maxim as "problem-solving should be less dangerous or stressful with a tutor than without", a remark which could be transferred to therapy without revision. They also note the risk of creating dependency.

(f) Demonstration: the tutor may model the solution to a task by enacting an idealized version of the acts to be performed.

It is at the stage of recruitment and orientation that the therapist must exercise skills not required of the teacher; in some way or other he must transform the patient's account of distress into accurate descriptions of procedures needing revision and of problems capable of solution. How this reframing is done will depend upon the orientation of the therapist, and on the kind of intervention proposed. Thus, the behaviourist will describe the problem primarily in terms of behaviours shaped by outcomes, the analyst in terms of conflicts between drives and defences, the existentialist in terms of meanings and purposes; whatever framework is offered will have a transforming effect upon the patient's own definition of his difficulty, and will serve to recruit him to the appropriate form of treatment.

It is clear that the redefinition of problems and the orientation of patients towards their solution is a major part of the therapist's work, and one which distinguishes it from the work of teachers. In order to be able to carry out this function, the therapist must avoid premature structuring of the things the patient tells him, and must avoid responses that serve to sustain the patient's conflicts or to heighten his destructively critical self-judgements. The therapist must learn to attend to what is said and to what is not said, and to recognize from the pattern of communication the assumptions serving to shape the account given by the patient. In his non-critical, open, exploratory attitude, and in his acceptance of contradiction, he both arrives at his understandings and offers to the patient a model of a constructive form of self-scrutiny. In all these ways, the second stage of the procedural script model is being attended to, and the negative ways in which reality and possibility have been construed by the patient are being revised. Very often, this process frees the patient's capacity to proceed, and he may generate and test out new forms of action without further help, but therapists of some persuasions will offer direct guidance at this stage also.

In the approach proposed in this book, the patient's account will be considered in terms of the PSM, and insights will be shaped with the patient, emphasis being placed upon the identification of those processes which are serving to perpetuate the blocking or diverting of aims, and which are preventing learning. As this is done, and to do so is not a mechanical procedure, the patient will be helped to see how his troubles are derived from his patterns of thinking and acting, and he will learn to see his task as being a revision of these thoughts and acts, while at the same time he is being provided with concepts and methods which can make this revision possible. Many problems are manifest only indirectly, i.e. they may not have been identified by the patient and they may not be accessible to the patient's conscious introspection. However, a great deal that people do at the tactical level is patterned in a fairly obvious way by strategic or self-identity scripts which they themselves cannot articulate, but which the therapist can infer fairly easily. The early identification and naming of these higher-order scripts and the identification of the defences, traps, dilemmas, and snags that represent faults in these scripts enable patient and therapist to start work on revising patterns of thought and action. At the same time, the patient can be recruited to further diagnostic work on himself by being instructed in self-monitoring, as will be described in more detail later. The patient's work in these respects should, in my view, be sustained by by the therapist's continued support and encouragement, and by his sharing the conceptual framework being used. His assistance in pacing the rate of change, and his provision of realistic evaluations of progress are also helpful. In this, the therapist is acting in ways directly parallel to the scaffolding function of the teacher, described above.

In the course of this process, which takes place in the early stages of treatment, the support offered to the patient by the therapist's presence and by the understandings gained will often reduce anxiety and defensiveness, and access to feelings and the exploration of the personal meanings of past and present experiences becomes freer. This ability to feel and engage in looser associative thinking can be encouraged by the therapist's attention and understanding; permission or encouragement to think in this way is helpful to many people in our culture where reason and logic are seen as superior thought forms. While I have known many patients who remembered with gratitude certain schoolteachers as having encouraged this kind of thinking — usually teachers of literature or art — it is clear that most teaching does not nourish it.

There is one more important difference between teacher and therapist. The therapist must be aware of the way in which problems are not just reported by the patient, but may be enacted by him in his relationship with the therapist. For some patients, the crucial learning experience of therapy is how this enactment (the transference) is experienced rather than how it is described.

DIFFERENCES BETWEEN THERAPISTS AND TEACHERS

While the therapist's role has many parallels to that of the teacher, there are important differences which imply that certain conditions are necessary for therapy. These can be summarized as follows:

(a) The therapist avoids judgement or premature structuring of the material in order to make exploration possible, while he provides enough structure to make the patient feel safe enough to proceed with the exploration.

(b) He generalizes and reformulates as problems the difficulties of which the patient complains. This task involves making translations, investigating the meanings of symptoms, moods, and unwanted behaviours, and in most cases looking at these in terms of underlying, often conflicted, assumptions.

(c) He helps the patient recognize, explore and name his experiences.

(d) The therapist challenges assumptions and questions terms, and may suggest alternative strategies while leaving the patient free to elaborate his own alternatives as far as possible.

(e) He is aware of, and may make use of, the way in which the patient's relationship with him can be seen as a paradigm or metaphor of aspects of his difficulties.

In this brief account of therapist as teacher, I have assumed that the therapist is able to discern and name the patterns of difficulty in ways which enable him and the patient to generate alternative ways of acting. The experienced therapist can often do this quickly; he is in the position of Socrates when he was eliciting from his slave-boy the proof of the theorem by Pythagoras concerning the square on the hypoteneuse. Socrates was able to extract the correct solution of the theorem from his slave-boy because he was himself in possession of the proof and was therefore able to ask the appropriate questions. On other occasions, however, the therapist may be in the position of Socrates as imagined in a parable offered by Gilbert Ryle (1979); a Socrates who, on the following day, commenced upon a similar elicitation of proof of a different theorem from the slave-boy, only to realize that he had forgotten the proof himself. The slave-boy reminded him of the previous day's successful questioning, but Socrates was forced to acknowledge that, having forgotten his destination, he was not able to be a guide on the journey. Psychotherapy in the style of the first Socrates is often satisfactory, for "well-charted teaching can occasionally . . . dispel ignorance"; but the task may be the more difficult one of finding new solutions to unknown problems which, in Gilbert Ryle's words is "trying out promising tracks which will exist, if they ever do exist, only after one has struggled exploringly over ground where they are not." The therapist can show his support for this exploration and can offer metaphors for the journey, but he cannot provide the map. Fortunately, most patients can explore for themselves, once their self-perpetuating blocks on changing have been identified and challenged.

PERSONALITY CHANGE AND EMOTIONAL LEARNING

I have suggested that, in so far as the changes sought in therapy are conceptual, the therapist's skills in conducting therapy are an extension of those of the teacher. Therapy enlarges what the patient knows, both knowing that (i.e. his understanding of himself and his experience) and knowing how (i.e. his capacity to organize his acts and pursue his intentions). Whether such changes can be called changes of personality is a somewhat arbitrary question. Some aspects of personality are clearly pretty stable, and probably largely determined by inheritance, but much of what we call personality is the manifestation of habitual strategies employed by a person in his familiar environment. Both situational change and psychotherapy can lead to radical modifications in these latter aspects.

Neurosis is often referred to as emotional disorder, and the aim of therapy is often described as emotional learning, and hence the emphasis on thinking in this book might be seen to be missing the point. However, emotions are based directly upon the personal meanings that we accord to our experiences, and a thinking/feeling dichotomy is not a helpful one. A common aim of psychotherapy is the relief of emotional distress but the term ''emotional learning'' is too vague for this process. The various components of what is so described can be categorized as follows:

(a) A better capacity to recognize and label correctly one's emotional responses. Examples here would be the clarification of the difference between emotions and appetite disturbances in the patient with anorexia, or helping people recognize feeling states that were not named or not permitted in their childhood homes.

(b) Linked with this, difficulty in knowing or permitting emotions may be related to false predictions about what would happen if they were to be expressed. A therapist can help here by evoking and permitting the expression of such emotions, by noting their occasions in the patient's reports, and by a consideration of what forms of expression are appropriate under what circumstances. For some patients, better control over inappropriate expression of emotion may be an important aim; for others, the need may be to know and show feelings more spontaneously.

(c) Another aspect of emotional learning consists of recognizing how far unwanted emotions are the result of one's thoughts, actions, and imagination rather than changes in circumstance.

(d) Psychotherapy, by encouraging a general increase in the patient's ability to know what he wants and a greater ability to act effectively to get it, leads to more positive and fewer negative emotional experiences.

(e) Linked with this, therapy can overcome the general inertia, helplesness, and depressed mood which stem from the recognition of one's own ineffectiveness, and can relieve the anxiety that follows the recognition that one's thoughts and acts are out of control, through the development of a clearer, more positive and effective sense of self.

Taking these points together, therefore, emotional learning turns out to consist of an improved capacity to perceive and construe experience accurately and to act effectively, areas of learning which are the focus of the integrated approach proposed in this book.

DIFFERENT APPROACHES TO THERAPEUTIC LEARNING

The therapist as teacher is faced, in an extreme form, with some of the basi difficulties that face any teacher operating above the level of rote learning and drill. Learning requires the elaboration of new concepts and new skills, and these cannot be simply transferred didactically; they have to be acquired in action by the pupil. Such acquisition is only possible if the discrepancy between the experience offered and the pupil's existing capacity to cope with it is neither too small (for then there is no need to change) nor too large (for then new experience cannot be assimilated at all). The teacher has the advantage that he can control the rate of exposure to new experience, although he is also faced with the severe temptation to be to the pupil only what Socrates was to the slave-boy, denying the pupil the experience of successfully "discovering new tracks" for himself. The therapist, on the other hand, has no control over the size of the discrepancy between the patient's needs and his capacity, and is usually faced with somebody already overcome by repeated failure to solve his problems, or locked in ineffective but familiar modes of part-solution. How much support, and what form of support, the therapist should offer, in trying to help such a patient, is a difficult question. The different answers given to this question serve to differentiate very sharply between psychoanalysis on the one hand and the cognitive/behavioural approach to therapy on the other.

The psychoanalytic reluctance to offer more than reliable availability and interpretation is designed to save the patient from the slave-boy's fate. The more active therapist, on the other hand, is unashamedly Socratic, and many use even drill, while paying considerable attention, like good instructors, to the appropriate pace and order of exposure to new experience. The psychoanalytic position reflects a high ideal and would seem to offer the least threat to the autonomy of the patient, and the greatest opportunity for enlarging his sense of his own nature and capacity. For some patients, especially those who have a very diminished or undeveloped sense of their ability to order or control their lives, this very inactive holding and the permitting of this exploration is probably uniquely effective. There are, however, others — and I suspect they are the great majority of patients seeking therapy — for whom this degree of passivity and this principled refusal to guide is frustrating, and may serve to inhibit rather than to enhance the patient's capacity for self-directed exploration. The provision for patients of concepts which they can use to link and make sense of their behavioural problems, the instructing of patients in ways of thinking about their dilemmas, the planning with patients of programmes to change and control their thinking and behaviour, can all lead to a rapid restoration of morale, a loss of anxiety, and to an extension, therefore, in their sense of control and safety. It is my experience that these more active therapeutic approaches, used early in the course of psychotherapy, do not inhibit and may in fact enhance, the patient's capacity also to engage in self-directed, unstructured exploration.

DISCUSSION

To conclude this chapter, the basic assumptions of cognitive, behavioural, and psychoanalytic therapists concerning the nature of the effects which their interventions produce will be reviewed.

Cognitive models of learning

The metaphor of the "scaffolding" function of the teacher is drawn from a study of how children were helped in a block assembly task (Wood *et al.*, 1976). This work was an illustration and extension of the position described earlier in *Towards a Theory of Instruction* (Bruner, 1966). Mahoney (1974) has applied cognitive theories of problem-solving to the field of behaviour modification, arguing that the neglect of cognitive processes by behaviourists had restricted their therapeutic effectiveness; he emphasized the need to teach patients accurate self-evaluation and to encourage the generation of multiple solutions. Training in self-instruction and self-regulation characterizes the cognitive therapy described by Meichenbaum (1977) and by Goldfried (1979). The process of "systematic rational restructuring" is described by the latter as having four stages:

(a) Helping clients recognize that their self-statements mediate emotional arousal;

(b) Helping clients see the irrationality of certain beliefs.

(c) Helping clients understand that their unrealistic self-statements mediate their maladaptive emotions, and

(d) Helpfing clients to modify their unrealistic self-statements.

In terms of the PSM this approach aims to influence assumptions about one's worth and predictions about one's capacity, and about the responses of others.

Behavioural model of learning

The essential assumption in behaviourism is that behaviours are shaped by outcomes, and the manipulation of outcomes is the essential teaching device. The two best validated behavioural methods for inducing change are exposure *in vivo* for phobias, and exposure and response prevention for compulsions. The effects of these treatments can be interpreted in terms of the PSM as being ways of altering the subject's predictive evaluations, whereby an expectation of danger or failure is modified by the experience of surviving graded exposure or the non-acting of a compulsion. Rehearsal in imagination, although described in conditioning terms, is essentially a cognitive procedure, as Lang (1977) argues. This author also argues for a cognitive ("information processing") analysis of fear, and suggests that what is activated in treatment, whether by rehearsal or by exposure, are "propositional structures". He suggests that "in many practical contexts the emotional image is less usefully conceived of as an internal process, and more valuable when construed as a preparatory set to respond . . . ". In this view, rehearsal in imagination is therefore allied to cognitive restructuring as being concerned with how the subject sees the situation, understands the meaning of it, and anticipates the effects of his response to it. In terms of the PSM it represents an approach that influences both the subject's predictions and his assembly of means.

The psychoanalytic model of change

What is largely missing from these cognitive and behavioural accounts is any consideration of the effects on learning of conflicts between intentions and self-judgements. For this we have to consider the very different accounts of change given by psychoanalysis. Freud avoided the use of the word, and the concept of, "cure"; his accounts were either depressive as in "the transformation of hysterical misery into common unhappiness", or abstract as in "to strengthen the ego, to make it more independent of the superego, to widen its field of perception and enlarge its organisation, so that it can appropriate fresh portions of the id" (Freud 1933). The main agent in this process of altering the balance of power in the intra-psychic world is the transference, and the detailed discussion of it will therefore be postponed to Chapter 9.

7

Psychotherapy: Selection, Assessment, and Focus

For some of those seeking therapy, experiences that are a normal part of life, such as bereavement, pregnancy and childbirth, changing jobs, difficulties in personal relationships, marriage, or divorce, have served to reveal the limits or precariousness of their previous ways of going about their lives. Such patients are best treated while the crisis is recent or current, support being combined with therapy aimed at correcting the faulty assumptions or strategies that led to the difficulty. For others, the decision to seek therapy is based on the recognition that their physical symptoms are psychologically caused, or follows their experience of prolonged or repeated depression and anxiety, or the recognition of their inability to control aspects of their lives. Others, again, may feel more generally that life in some important way is not proceeding well, or that something is missing.

It is the responsibility of the professionals to whom such people go to be sure that the patient who asks for therapy is an appropriate case for it, and, if he is, to offer the best available kind. In suitable cases, decisions must be made whether to treat the individual on his own, in his natural group (couple or family), or in a therapeutic group. Only individual therapy is being considered in this book. Approaches to group therapy and to marital therapy are reviewed in Ryle (1976 and 1979c). If individual therapy is indicated, it is an unfortunate fact that the type of treatment offered will depend much more upon the predelictions of the professional than upon the nature of the patient's problems. In an ideal world this would not be the case, and the period of assessment would be devoted to deciding upon the method most appropriate for the particular case. In the integrated approach being described in this book, which aims to get closer to this ideal, the decision whether to offer therapy and, if so, in what form, is usually left to the end of the two-to-four sessions of the assessment period.

SELECTION FOR PSYCHOTHERAPY

The first purpose of assessment is to exclude from treatment people too well to need help, people able to get enough help from the assessment period to proceed on their own, and people suffering from conditions not amenable to therapy. This last group may include those suffering from organic illnesses producing psychological symptoms, such as thyroid disorders, as well as those too emotionally disturbed to be able to make use of therapy. The second purpose of assessment is to determine what kind of help to offer, given the available resources and the nature of the patient's difficulties.

The process of excluding unsuitable patients is, unfortunately, less easy than it might appear, because some patients with severe difficulty can make good use of therapy, while others with quite minor problems can prove very difficult to help. It is, however, certain that the risk of harming the patient (and of exhausting the therapist) is far greater where the patient has extensive difficulties, where his current relationships with others are markedly impoverished, or where there is no history of any remembered good figures from childhood or of any sustained good relationships since. In addition, patients with serious addictions or with personalities marked by much envy and destructiveness are difficult to help. The magical dependency, or the disappointed fury, provoked by psychotherapy in unsuitable cases of this sort can destroy what capacity the individual may have achieved for managing some kind of life in the world. Drug therapy, institutional care, and other forms of management may enable some of these sicker patients to use therapy later, and a few can make use of therapy that is very carefully limited, both in scope and duration. Only a few intrepid workers attempt psychotherapy with schizophrenics; in manic depression, on the other hand, psychotherapy may be helpful, although it is not possible during markedly depressed or manic phases.

STARTING THERAPY

As far as possible, patients should be seen in a reasonably comfortable room that is free from interruption, and the seating arrangement for patient and therapist should be at the same height, the most comfortable angle between the chairs being about 45°, which avoids both eyeball-to-eyeball confrontation and parallel staring into space; that is to say, it leaves eye contact possible but not compulsory. At the first meeting, the time and duration of future appointments should be spelt out clearly. If one has prior knowledge of the patient from the referring source, this should be indicated at the start of the first session. Initial meetings will be for assessment, and this too should be made clear on the understanding that discussion will take place about plans at the end of this period. The therapist working privately will spell out his expectations about fees at this point, and patients may indicate the extent of their insurance cover or other resources. If individual therapy is offered and accepted after assessment, further discussion will then take place which will outline the proposed approach, agree on a list of target issues, and will either set a termination date or arrange to consider that date at some agreed point. The therapist may also at this time tell the patient about any anticipated breaks in treatment. If patients need treatment other than individual work, then arrangements for referral will be made. Any changes in practical arrangements should be communicated in a businesslike way, in the recognition that, if an important transference relationship develops, such changes may be felt as conveying meanings that will need to be discussed.

Most patients know, or discover for themselves, the way to use the sessions but, initially, some need encouragement. If the therapist is a doctor, the patient's assumptions may be formed by his experience with doctors treating him for physical disorders and he could expect the interviews to be highly structured. If the therapist is seeing a patient who has not been assessed psychiatrically, he will need to obtain an adequately full account of the patient's history and present psychiatric status. To get this history without setting up the medical interviewing stereotype, especially when patients have been referred for therapy and are probably suitable, one can begin with unstructured interviewing, in which the patient is encouraged to give his own account of his troubles, history, and expectations for treatment with minimal prompting. This account can then be supplemented by direct questioning in those areas not covered. In the course of this unstructured interviewing, the therapist can both observe the patient's style and begin to shape the conversation towards a concern with meanings and feelings as well as facts, and towards the acknowledgement of mixed feelings, a process that will be aided by his conveying a non-critical acceptance of what is said. The general instruction to "say whatever comes into you mind" seems of little value to me, and even in intensive psychoanalytic treatment it must be honoured more in the breach than in the observance. However, by attending to hesitancies or non-sequitors, by noting connections between apparently disjointed communications, and by inviting the patient to pause and think more about the meanings and implications of particular statements, the therapist can enable the patient to realize the value of such associative thinking.

In the course of the assessment period, the therapist needs to form a preliminary hypothesis about the patient's difficulties, and to offer a problem-oriented account of them to the patient. During these first sessions, the patient is declaring his troubles and the therapist is offering a sample of his wares. At the end of the assessment period both should be in a position to agree about what might be attempted together. This discussion will, I believe, be clearer where the therapist shares his assumptions and methods explicitly with the patient. There can be no universal strategy for these meetings but, for the most part, the therapist should leave the patient to talk in his own terms, intervening only to prompt or clarify and only occasionally making his own contribution. This contribution is, however, very important; it has one aim: to make of what the patient has said something useful, that is to say, something that the patient did not know (or did not know that he knew). If the therapist can do this, and if the patient can hear what he says and see that it is of value, then therapy can usually proceed.

During these sessions, and those that may follow, the therapist will not, however, be solely dependent upon his ability to get things right. A great deal of his impact is due to the situation and is common to therapists of many different attitudes and beliefs, and doubtless also to witch-doctors, solicitors, clergymen, and many others. The experience of being carefully attended to by someone regarded as an expert produces, in the patient, a renewal of hope, an increase in self-esteem, a sense of being permitted, and often relief from loneliness and the sense of failure and shame. These effects, often called non-specific yet in reality specific but common to many approaches, are of genuine help, offering containment to the patient which relieves his disabling anxiety and enables him to think more clearly about his difficulties. They are the result of any attention that is genuine (people will soon see through ritual gestures, however) and to some extent they continue to operate throughout therapy , but they may include elements of magical hope and the hidden wish to hand over responsibility and control to the therapist, which must be countered if regressive dependency is to be avoided.

By the end of the assessment sessions, the therapist will have discerned how far his patient has realistic hopes of, and a genuine motivation for, the process which he can provide.

GOALS OF THERAPY: GENERAL AND SPECIFIC

The general goals of interpretive psychotherapy can be summarized as follows.

(a) That the patient should know the meaning of his life and his history accurately, as opposed to accepting the attributions or versions of others, as opposed to denying his own feelings and intentions or to translating them into symptoms, and as opposed to states of numbness or confusion.

(b) The patient should have satisfactory control over his acts, as opposed to feeling powerless or to repeatedly acting contrary to his intentions.

(c) The patient should have realistic and appropriate beliefs about himself and his social reality, as opposed to negative or inaccurate beliefs or assumptions.

(d) The patient should take realistic responsibility for himself, as opposed to disclaiming responsibility on the one hand, or omnipotently claiming it on the other.

(e) In his emotionally significant relationships with others, the patient should be capable of mutuality and openness, as opposed to being limited by, or feeling preoccupied with, questions of control or defensiveness.

(f) The patient should be able to live his life according to his desires and intentions rather than by evasions, restrictions, or compulsions.

The achievement of these goals involves both "destructuring" and the elaboration of new procedures. Destructuring involves the questioning and abandonment of ineffective understandings and strategies of living, and must precede the development of new and more satisfactory modes. It is accompanied by anxiety and confusion, and can only be faced if the patient can sense that the therapist, as a person and through the understandings he conveys, is with him. Restructuring demands the acquisition, in the context of this human experience, of new understandings and new ways of acting. Psychoanalytic approaches have paid most attention to the destructuring process, while behavioural and cognitive approaches have emphasized restructuring. The focused, active, integrated therapy proposed here, which may be labelled, after its origins, cognitive-analytic therapy, attempts to combine the strengths of both.

While the general goals discussed above serve to indicate the direction of change that is desirable, in formulating the detailed goals of an individual therapy one is more concerned with the identification and eradication of the *obstacles* to these general goals. We do not usually have to tell our patients how to live, although to indicate that perhaps they might live more fully is helpful; but we are always concerned to help them overcome the ways in which they are currently stopping themselves from living. The individual goals drawn up at the end of the assessment of a patient need to describe the aims of therapy in terms of these obstacles, and to define the obstacles as far as possible in ways indicating possible alternatives or necessary changes. The aims of therapy will, therefore, include overcoming blocks or distortions on perception or understanding, assisting fuller access to feelings and personal meanings, changing negative self-referrant assumptions and judgements, describing self-identity and strategic scripts of which the patient is not aware, and identifying traps, dilemmas, and snags. In discussing therapy in these terms with the patient, one is explicitly offering him access to the model of his difficulty which one is using in the conduct of the therapy; this reinforces his self-understanding and his self-control, and diminishes the likelihood that he will seek to hand over all responsibility to the therapist. It is usually helpful to discuss explicitly both the aims and the model at an appropriate level of detail, and I personally prefer to write the goals down.

Target problems described in this way provide a conceptual framework for therapy and also serve as a basis for rating progress at intervals. Formulated in this way, they point emphatically to the ways in which the patient's patterns of belief, conceptualization, and action are responsible for his difficulties, and they show him that, to lose symptoms and to alter his experiences and increase his control, he must revise his underlying procedures. Such revisions may be encouraged by many different means, including explanation, instruction, confrontation, the encouragement of different forms of behaviour, teaching forms of self-observation and self-control, and the interpretation of the transference. In addition to these methods, I believe that the act of sharing the concepts and the model with the patient is itself therapeutic. Kuhn (1962), by describing how scientific progress is held up because of the reluctance of scientists to discard old, familiar, but restrictive paradigms, offered to scientists a chance to become more aware of, and to guard against, this reluctance, which reflects the universal human need to maintain a more or less stable representation of the world, and an understandable unwillingness to discard understandings which have served in the past. By formulating the general goals of therapy in terms of changing assumptions and strategies, the psychotherapist can, in the same way, free his patients from their restrictive paradigms and help them elaborate more adequate ones.

The task of making sense in this way of the patient's account of his difficulties and of reformulating them varies in complexity. The recognition of negative assumptions or of a conditional or precarious sense of self-esteem is usually quite evident from the patient's story and also from his demeanour during the early sessions, although patients will often present themselves in these respects as if they were describing their personalities rather than their difficulties, and the therapist may need to identify these aspects of self-description as problematic and potentially changeable. Difficulties over experiencing and expressing feelings, and defensive strategies, may or may not be easy to detect; attention must be paid to what is not said and done as much as to what is, and much will depend upon the human style and sensitivity of the therapist. A full discussion of which treatment method to use, and how to combine them, is deferred to Chapter 10, by which time different therapeutic procedures will have been described.

THE INFLUENCE OF THE SETTING

The decision about what method of treatment to use cannot be taken solely in terms of the patient's problems; it must also take into account the therapist's skills and setting. In a formal psychotherapeutic situation, this will be relatively simple, but much valuable counselling and therapy takes place in other contexts with professional workers whose roles are more general. General practitioners and social workers are easily accessible to troubled people, and they are therefore frequently their first resource. Many of them accept counselling and therapy in some form as being an aspect of their work. Traditionally, the main response has been a supportive one, through the provision of a friendly ear and the offer of encouragement through difficult times. In many situations this is an appropriate and adequate response but it is not always helpful. Just as the long-term use of tranquillizers and anti-depressants to treat symptoms of emotional stress is, I believe, harmful, in that it provides a pseudo-medical label for life problems, so in some cases the provision of long-term supportive care can be equally habit-forming and equally irrelevant to the solution of the patient's problems. Most doctors and social workers will, of course, carry a few patients in their care whose lives are so troubled and whose personalities are so fragmented that long-term supportive care is appropriate; but, even for some of these, and certainly for the far more numerous ordinary troubled or moderately neurotic people, and for those struggling to adjust to everyday losses and stresses, I believe a brief, more explicit psychological intervention, aimed at extending the patient's skills and capacities, would often be preferable.

Such an approach involves the setting aside of enough time to make a proper initial assessment; but the understandings so gained allow later interviews to be brief and focused. The form of explanatory framework offered in this book, describing problems in terms of aims, procedures, assumptions, defences, traps, dilemmas, and snags, is a suitable one for work in these contexts, although the focus of the intervention will often be more restricted than would be the case in a formal psychotherapeutic situation. For example, if psychotropic drugs are being prescribed to control symptoms such as anxiety attacks or depression, the patient can also be given written instructions on self-monitoring his mood changes (see next chapter). This procedure aids diagnosis by adding information about the circumstances of the attacks, and it can also increase control of symptoms. Other symptoms or problems may respond to simple behavioural methods, and many people, given clear descriptions of their problems in terms of the concepts of traps, dilemmas, or snags, can manage their lives better without much further support being needed.

A more problematic question arises in respect of the transference, and the use of transference interpretations as a means of therapy (see Chapter 9). If strong feelings develop in the patient's or client's relationship with a doctor or social worker (and this can happen where long-term support is given) or if such transference feelings are made the main focus of treatment, then it is very difficult to provide general medical care or to carry out statutory social work responsibility, because the real and the metaphoric aspects of the relationship will become inextricably entangled. For doctors, moreover, the possibility of highly emotional and sexual feelings developing in the transference would make physical examination of the patient inappropriate. An understanding of how transference may be manifest is therefore of importance to all professionals, not least because it can occur in situations other than a psychotherapeutic one; but therapy based upon its encouragement and interpretation should only be carried out in an explicit and exclusive contract, which means that other forms of care must be carried out by somebody else.

CASE HISTORY EXAMPLES

Both David and Anne were given written instructions in the form of the ''personal therapy file'' (see Chapter 14), which consists of descriptions of how to consider and list symptoms, how to recognize unwanted beliefs and behaviours, how to monitor unhelpful thought patterns and how to recognize traps, dilemmas and snags. Anne and David had also done repertory grid tests (see Appendix); these will not be further discussed here, but the completion of them and the discussion of the analysis of their grids probably served to heighten their awareness of patterns in their relationships. At the end of this assessment period, their thoughts, as provoked by these procedures and the first sessions, and as recorded by them in their personal therapy file, and mine, as formed in the course of the sessions and from the results of the test procedures, were the basis upon which we drew up a list of treatment goals. These goals were recorded and formed the basis of rating scales, as follows. Each problem or issue, as it was at the time of the first consultation, constituted the mid-point of a vertical visual analogue rating scale. Subsequently, at points indicating the date, deterioration or improvement were recorded by making marks on a ±20 mm vertical line, labelled at the bottom ''worse'', and at the top with the treatment aim. These goals are described succinctly in terms of symptoms, beliefs or assumptions, traps, dilemmas, and snags.

David

David's list of problems read as follows:

1. Depressed mood; aim, to be normally cheerful and energetic.
2. Not feeling in control of my life; aim, to have a sense of appropriate control over my life.
3. Not able to work; aim, able to work effectively.
4. Sadness and anger over Patricia; aim, to complete the mourning process.
5. Trap (a version of the placation trap): self-uncertainty, leading to adoption of a helpful, placatory role, leading to a sense of my own needs being unmet, leading to resentment or childish reactions, leading to feeling bad about myself; aim, to assert my own needs while recognizing those of others.
6. Dilemma: *either* guilty and submissive *or* amiably controlling in relation to others; aim, more mutual terms.
7. Dilemma: *if* dependent, *then* not in control; aim, able to control by adequate autonomy and mutuality, while risking some dependence on others.
8. Dilemma: *if* submitting to others, *then* not cross; aim, able to assert own needs and defend them if necessary.
9. Snag: diminishing my own life *as if* needing to expiate for my parents' divorce and father's depression; aim, able to take control over life without guilt.

In the session at which this problem list was assembled and discussed, the last point, already raised in the second session, as reported in Chapter 4, and discussed at other times, was discussed once more, as follows.

AR: About the snag, I felt that operating very strongly when you were talking about your work. I had the feeling that you were giving away in advance any chance of a good degree, which didn't seem a realistic prediction of the effects of one term's impaired work. It seemed to me to be a way of saying, ''I'm not going to claim that'', which implies the possibility that you would feel guilty of things seemed to be going well. Now, I know it's very hard, if you don't sort of immediately feel that's right, to know whether it is.

DAVID: Well, I've actually thought along lines like those before, especially recently, but before too. I mean, trying to work out why something's gone wrong, when the capability was there to make it go completely right, and I wanted to know why.

AR: Maybe the ''why'' was because you arranged it that way?''

DAVID: Well, once these sort of pitfalls started becoming apparent time after time after time, you are bound to think like that.

Anne

Anne's list of target problems was as follows:

1. Preoccupied with the fear of nervous breakdown; aim, to be no longer scared.
2. Suffering from depression and hopelessness at times; aim, a normally hopeful mood (this description was unsatisfactory, for at the first rating she felt that she was feeling her depression *more*, while feeling *less* hopeless).
3. Inability to trust others; aim, able to trust appropriately.
4. Compulsive caretaking; aim, to be able also to be dependent in a mutual way.
5. Unhelpful thought cycles with depressive origins and depressive outcomes; aim, control over depressive thinking.
6. Social isolation trap: being self-isolating, keeping distance from others, leading to perception of others as being unfriendly, leading to further self-isolation; aim, to be able to extend friendships and social contacts.
7. Trap: self-deprivation maintained as a means of relieving inappropriate guilt; aim, proper self-care and self-permission.
8. Dilemma: *if* feeling helpful and effective, *then* imagining the future death of one or other parent, with the responsibility for the survivor, leading to guilt and depression; aim, a more realistic view of responsibility for parents.
9. Dilemma: *either* helpful and controlling (the preferred role for self) *or* dependent and potentially crazy; aim, mutuality in relationships.
10. Dilemma: *if* loved, *then* feeling trapped and guilty; aim, able to accept love and care without feeling the loss of freedom or guilt.
11. Dilemma: *if* striving for perfection, *then* stressed; *if* not striving, *then* guilty; aim, to be able to work from interest, ambition, pleasure, and for realistic ends.
12. Snag: avoiding fully achieving, enjoying, claiming, or having, a life, as if own life is at the cost of my mother's; aim, to be able to claim my life.

The role of guilt and guilt relief evident in Nos. 7, 10, and 12, was described by Anne on her therapy file as follows.

> I feel guilty and I feel I do not deserve love and affection when everything seems to be going well; when I have all, or any, or these I destroy it and feel miserable, unloved, alone, and that everything is going badly, but I feel comforted that I have got what I deserved, and feel my guilt disappearing.

These lists of aims for David and Anne represent bald summaries of the work of the first sessions, work consisting essentially of elaborating on their presenting symptoms and transforming them into descriptions that identify the underlying assumptions, patterns of action, traps, dilemmas, and snags. We can now consider how these translations are related to the basic model of the procedural script, and how they provided the basis for planning treatment.

David

In David's case, his depressed mood and work difficulty were linked together, constituting one potentially self-maintaining process, whereby negative assumptions, negative predictions, and negative retrospective evaluations of his performance had led to his giving up trying, with the development of catastrophic predictions about the future effects of this state. When he was first seen, he had already missed some weeks of work, and he had failed one assessment exercise, so there was a serious issue in reality. This was tackled from the first interview by:

(a) arranging to write to his tutors. The discussion of this revealed some aspects of David's self-deprecation; he had dismissed his past good grades as undeserved, he was reluctant to expose his weakness to them, and he felt that my certificate of impairment would constitute an unfair advantage. However, after discussion, the offer was accepted;

(b) he was encouraged to plan a work programme which was initially minimal, and to record his progress on this, increasing the requirements only when he had achieved the set tasks appropriately;

(c) he was encouraged to visit tutors and plan with them the best use of his limited current capacity;

(d) I argued with him that his estimation of the long-term effects of his present state was unrealistically gloomy.

These steps were intended to forestall and reduce any possible negative reactions from tutors, and to help him plan tasks which he could achieve, and from which therefore he could begin to rebuild some positive evaluation of his capacity, and meanwhile help him deal realistically with the implications of his current state.

The issue of being in control of his life was far-reaching in its implications. In relation to this one, he had written as follows, in his personal therapy file.

> I do not control my own life as much as some people appear to control theirs; basically, I don't care about that, though, the point here is that by my own standards I don't consider what I do enough. I don't believe in myself enough to do it. I don't often get angry with myself, though, but I usually end up by feeling sad about it. I don't mean just now, I mean always. I tend to think that I have to have a reason for doing things. If there isn't a sufficient reason, I won't do them, or find it very difficult. I won't have my heart in it. I tend to think that, unless I can benefit others by what I do, whatever I do is less valuable; I doubt, and I think I have always doubted, myself so strongly. If the only person who will benefit from an action is me, then I doubt the value of it.

From this account, it is clear that David's procedural scripts were based upon negative self-judgements, and upon eliciting validation from his relationship with others.

His sadness and anger over Patricia's loss was, in part, an appropriate response to a loss, and to the unkind way in which it had occurred. The sense of it having "happened to him" increased his depressive passivity, although he also recognized, with hindsight and self-blame, that he had contributed to the event. The depth of his response suggested that the implications were wider; it was seen as being linked with his general dependence on others for his self-definitions and this, in turn, led to a consideration of the possible implication of his separation, at the age of four, from his mother. It was as if he had assumed, from that first experience, that "if you depend on others, they will leave you". This prediction was confirmed when his first important relationship ended, but he had rapidly replaced that one with

Patricia. At the strategic level of his relationship scripts, David recognized how the options open to him in relationships were limited to those summarized in the dilemmas listed as Nos. 6, 7 and 8. As regards No. 7 in particular, he felt very unhappy at being incompetent and needy, and he had not been able to seek the support of any of his close friends, although for many of them he had, in the past, been a helpful person.

In planning David's treatment, the control of the depression in the way described above was clearly the first priority. The other issues were more extensive in their implications, but the formulations made of them served to link together the two issues which brought him into treatment: the problem of not being in control of his life, and the problem of his extreme reaction to Patricia's departure. A treatment plan was made on the basis of his early formulations, determined also by the fact that only a limited amount of time was available for him to see me. A contract was made for that period (under 4 months), during which he was offered appointments at fortnightly intervals. These intervals were determined in part by my availability but reflected also my feeling that David needed to experience coping on his own. It was hoped that this treatment plan would enable David to control his depression, to resume work, and to start some exploration of the wider issues. In view of the extent, and long-term nature, of these, I also suggested that he should subsequently join a therapeutic group. In the event, he did not do this, and I saw him individually for a few spaced-out sessions after a gap of 5 months.

Anne

Anne sought help with two problems: a fear of a nervous breakdown and depression. She used self-monitoring to understand and control her depressive thinking, with good effect. She had not realized before the extent and exaggerated nature of many of the thoughts which accompanied her lapses into anxiety or depression. The following are examples of such thoughts listed in her personal therapy file; they were collected over a period of one week.

1. I get sudden, or sometimes continuous, physical symptoms to do with anxiety, usually these are located in my right temple; as tension develops, I feel that my brain is disintegrating and splitting up, being hammered or beaten. This develops into feeling that I am having a nervous breakdown. I associate these moods with my mother's breakdown; this thought then leads to more fears and the feeling of actually having a breakdown.

2. When I haven't felt any tension for a while, I wonder if I can still remember what it's like. This produces a mood change and I get some comfort out of this, because I feel worried if I go for periods without the tension, feeling I am undergoing some other physiological change, which is also symptomatic of a nervous breakdown. That makes me depressed because it indicates how pervasive and time-consuming my fear is; then I think I'm a hopeless case, and I wonder how I'll survive life if I continue in this fashion.

3. Any thoughts about my family produce a mood change.
4. I feel a bump on my head and I imagine it's cancer and feel tense.
5. Feeling tired, I tell myself I should go to bed. The thought of sleep makes me think of mother's last breakdown, which occurred in the night.
6. I hear an ambulance and immediately think of mother being taken off to hospital.
7. I clean my teeth and look at myself in the mirror and I wonder if I look strained and old and think about myself.
8. Often, watching a film on television, I can become depressed or anxious; usually where the people are free and happy and everything is marvellous, I feel lonely and scared that I can never be like that.
9. Quite often, having thoughts like this leads me to think that to think in such a distorted way is to lead to a nervous breakdown, therefore I cannot win.

Anne's difficulty in trusting and its manifestations in therapy have already been discussed in Chapter 3, and was related also to the social isolation trap (problem 6). The description of her compulsive caretaking represents my summary of her preferred role; it describes an inferred, restrictive relationship script. The dilemmas listed as problems 9 and 10 refer to the same issue. Basically, Anne preferred giving to receiving because, in her terms, to receive implied powerlessness and guilt. In terms of the PSM, her repertoire of available means was limited to dichotomized role alternatives. Problem No. 11, her perfectionist work attitudes, describes a characteristic which she herself had regarded in the past as normal and virtuous or, at least, necessary, but which I saw as being related to the effects of an unduly harsh and critical self-judging script. The description of her snag (No. 12) and of the associated dilemma (No. 7) gave her an explicit understanding of her guilt and negative actions which she had not had previously.

As in the case of David, therefore, the work of the early sessions had converted a passive state of suffering into a preliminary understanding of the underlying issues. Anne's relatively severe distress and her clear ability to work effectively in therapy made her a suitable case for treatment, and she was offered weekly sessions for a period of about 8 months, the extent and exact duration being left for later discussion. In the event, after a 5 month gap, a second period of treatment was given.

The emphasis in this chapter, and throughout the book is on focused therapy, with goals or aims agreed between therapist and patient, after initial assessment interviews. I believe this to be a suitable model for most therapies, particularly for brief ones. It is clearly an improvement on the totally undirected approach caricatured in the comparison made between psychoanalysis and Columbus's voyage to America: namely, when he left he did not know where he was going; when he got there he did not know where he was; when he returned he did not know where he had been; but he knew he had had an experience. However, it must be said at this point that, for some people, the need is for just such an uncharted voyage, and for them the premature imposition of focal aims would be inappropriate. I am not certain whether I can describe clearly how one can recognize these patients, although in practice I usually find it obvious during the first hour or so of contact. I think there are two factors here: the patients themselves are usually people who feel incomplete in some way, out of touch with, but aware of, something valuable in themselves, perhaps as the result of a failure to mourn for the loss of an important person, perhaps from some early sense of having "gone underground" due to not being recognized for what they were. The second factor is in the way they use the early sessions, and is a transference or transference/countertransference manifestation (see Chapter 9). These patients seem to understand right away the metaphoric possibilities of the situation. All they want is to be allowed to *be*, in relation to the therapist, in ways that include the lost or submerged aspects of their natures; they want to be known so that they can know themselves. This process of getting in touch with the self is, to some degree, an aspect of most therapies, but for this group of patients it is the only one, and an emphasis upon "doing", which is implied by a problem-oriented approach, would be unsuitable.

DISCUSSION

Selection

There is no clear agreement about the criteria of suitability for brief psychotherapy. Sifneos (1972) quotes the following positive factors about the patient.

> His capacity to recognise the psychological nature of his symptoms, his ability to introspect honestly about emotional difficulties, his curiosity about himself, his willingness to change himself, his realistic expectations of therapy, and his willingness to make reasonable sacrifices of time or money for fees.

In my view, this represents a somewhat ideal list, at least for an unsophisticated patient at first presentation, although a good therapist would hope to achieve most of those criteria in his patients by the end of the assessment period. Malan (1976a) quotes the following as excluding criteria.

> A history of suicide bid, drug addiction, convinced homosexuality, long-term hospitalisation, more than one course of electroconvulsive therapy, chronic alcoholism, incapacitating phobic or obsessional states, destructive or self-destructive acting-out.

This list seems a somewhat mixed bag and unduly excluding in some respects. In my own view, treatment with the proposed integrated approach might well be offered to some people in all those groups apart from the drug-addicted or alcoholic, although additional treatment methods might be required. Suicidal behaviour and destructive acting-out are both commonplace problems in psychiatric practice, and while drug therapy may have some part to play in such cases, most could be helped by some psychotherapy; the choice will usually be between brief psychotherapy and none at all. In my experience, focused, active methods can be effective in such cases, even though subsequent long-term work, either group or individual, may be the ideal.

Some of the fifteen cases described in a recent paper (Ryle, 1980), concerning the application of focused, integrated, active therapy, would be excluded on Malan's criteria but were, in fact, helped by brief therapy. Two cases of anorexia with binge–vomit cycles (Cases 3 and 9), one case of repeated self-injury (Case 8), and one case with powerful suicidal urges (Case 11) showed definite gains from brief therapy. The exclusion of homosexuals, except where the treatment is directed at changing sex-orientation, seems quite unnecessary. Severe phobic and obsessional cases may need to be treated behaviourally in the first instance, but the majority will need, and be suitable for, brief interpretive therapy thereafter.

I remain personally unclear about the criteria distinguishing those who need a long and intensive treatment as opposed to brief psychotherapy. Some patients with major difficulties do very well with brief therapy, and some less ill patients do rather badly in long-term and intensive therapy. As the latter is, in any case, beyond the financial means of most patients or services, an initial period of brief focused therapy would seem to provide the best option; on the experience of this a proportion may well proceed to further individual or group therapy.

Therapists of the cognitive and behavioural schools pay remarkably little attention to diagnosis and selection, as a sympathetic reviewer (Kovacs, 1979) points out in discussing treatments for depressive disorders. In the case of the more extreme behaviourists, a reluctance to consider issues of self other than as a "mediating process" does not encourage attention to issues of personality structure and integration. This simple approach engenders a certain therapeutic optimism, however, and does at least lead to attention being paid to what may be capable of modification.

The focus of treatment

Behavioural therapists restrict their therapeutic endeavours to observable behaviours, and plan their therapies in terms of explicit programmes, leading to discrete goals. The definition of a focus for treatment is therefore an essential element in such therapies. For therapists of the psychoanalytic persuasion, on the other hand, the preference for time-unlimited, open-ended therapy has only slowly yielded to the idea of time-limited, focused work, even though there is by now a long tradition of heresy (see Wolberg, 1965). More recent authors (reviewed by Malan, 1976b) show some agreement about the nature of the focus, although there are still areas of dispute. Mann (1973) instituted a rigorous 12-session limit on all therapies; he put emphasis, from the beginning, on the relationship of the patient's problems to issues of independence–dependence, activity–inactivity, self-esteem and unresolved grief as provoked in the transference by the time limit. This single emphasis seems unduly restricted.* Sifneos (1972) uses a confronting anxiety-arousing technique, emphasizing the interpretation of ambivalence and resistance in the transference and its relation to past history, especially to oedipal issues His

* But Mann, J. and Goldman, R. in "A Casebook in Time-limited Psychotherapy" (McGraw-Hill, 1982) describe clearly the definition of "central theory".

approach (see Davanloo 1980) can seem confronting to the point of provocation. For Malan (1976a and 1976b) the focus represents the therapist's choice of a psychodynamic theme. Such themes may represent a nuclear conflict of deep significance, or a less central issue. The therapist maintains the patient's involvement with this theme by selectively attending to, and interpreting, only those issues related to it. Malan reports that the patient's willingness to work with this kind of interpretation, the therapist's ability to maintain a focal approach in this way, and the linking of feelings about parents with the transference in relation to these focal themes were the three factors associated with successful outcomes in the cases treated with brief psychoanalytic therapy by him and his colleagues. It should be noted, I think, that these themes are clearly the ones with which they would have been most comfortable in view of their theoretical predilections.

The process of agreeing explicit goals, described in this chapter (and in Ryle, 1979a and Ryle, 1980) is similar to the cognitive/behavioural approach in so far as goals are spelt out very clearly. However, target problems, dilemmas, traps, and snags represent a more complex description of mental and behavioural processes and assumptions than do the target symptoms and behaviours of cognitive/behavioural therapists. In the emphasis on cognitive issues — assumptions, beliefs, and processes — these goals are referring to "dynamic" issues of the sort described in different terms by psychoanalytic therapists. They represent, in effect, hypotheses about the sources of difficulty, described in terms of "current procedures" although often informed by historical material. They may include, but are not exclusively concerned with, aims and beliefs and procedures of which the patient is not, or has not been, aware. Their accuracy and relevance will be tested out in subsequent therapy and the application of the ideas in the patient's life. The explicit sharing of these concepts at this stage distinguishes the approach I propose from psychoanalytic methods, the patient being given an idea of the therapist's model and of its application to his problems. He is in this way invited to be his own problem-solver, and the use of any particular procedures will be understood by him in the context of this general picture. The inclusion in these hypotheses of descriptions of procedures that are inflexible and no longer relevant, but are not necessarily the result of dynamically repressed issues, is another point of differentiation from the focus as described by Malan. Where the limitations of time or the extent of the patient's difficulties are such that only some issues can be dealt with, a decision as to which to attend to will be made in terms of the overall understanding and of the accessibility to change of the different problems. These strategic decisions will be more fully discussed in Chapter 10, after other therapeutic methods have been considered.

8
Active Methods in Therapy

As we have seen, the diagnostic and exploratory focus of the assessment phase of therapy does not rule out the introduction of comments and procedures designed to initiate change. In the same way, the emphasis upon change during the active process of therapy does not imply that the explanatory concepts formulated in the early stages may not be modified and extended. In time-limited therapy, however, it is important to identify the main goals early and to proceed primarily along the lines determined by those goals. In every case there will be continued discussion of the central issues, namely the adequacy of the patient's grasp of the reality of his experience, his maladaptive beliefs and assumptions, the nature and possible restrictiveness of his self-identity and strategic scripts, and the blocks on his changing–described in terms of traps, dilemmas, and snags. The understandings encapsulated in these ways can be applied to the patient's history, to his current life situation, and to his relation to the therapist. For many patients, this process of grasping and using new ways of looking at their problems is all that is required, and the therapist's role is to hold him to this task, to be alert to the ways in which older patterns of thinking continue to be manifest, and to help him form realistic evaluations of his progress. Beyond this, however, patients may be helped by two rather different methods: on the one hand by various active specific procedures, and on the other through the experience of the developing relationship with the therapist. In this chapter, we shall consider the use of active techniques, leaving the question of the relationship with the therapist to be discussed fully in the next chapter.

In using active methods, the therapist is attempting to modify, by instruction, encouragement and guided experience, the self-monitoring, self-judging, and self-control exercised by the patient (PSM Stages 4 and 6) and to extend his skills (PSM Stage 3), so that he can learn to recognize and name his feelings more accurately, to understand and control his symptoms, to alter his unwanted patterns of behaviour, and to modify unhelpful ways of thinking (PSM Stages 7, 1, and 2). Behavioural and cognitive therapists operate exclusively in these ways, but in the integrated approach suggested here, these methods would always be applied in the context of a more general understanding, based upon the PSM, and would usually be combined with interpretation of the transference and the use of non-directive exploratory methods.

SELF-MONITORING

The most useful active intervention consists of instructing patients in forms of self-monitoring; a method which owes much to the work of Beck (1976). Its application in the cases of Anne and David have been reported in the last chapter. The essence of this methods, and its purpose, can be conveyed by written instructions (see Chapter 14).

The rationale for self-monitoring is that many symptoms, mood changes, or unwanted acts are provoked or accompanied by mental images or thoughts which, while accessible to awareness, are not attended to. Subjects can be taught to attend deliberately to their thoughts and to record them in writing; in doing this, they come to understand better the reasons for their altered states and are usually able to achieve some distance from their irrational, exaggerated, or catastrophic thinking. This, in turn, leads to early recognition of and, in time, control of, subsequent episodes of such thinking. In terms of the PSM, monitoring enables one to discard distortions during Stages 2 and 4. The following case provides an example of this.

Michael

Michael, a male student, aged 20, had been an obese adolescent and was now slightly underweight, with a marked preoccupation with thinness. He spent much effort in controlling his food intake, and he felt guilty after eating, at times resorting to the use of laxatives. He was also aware that he frequently became quite cut off from his feelings, something which I observed during sessions, and he smiled compulsively, especially when discussing painful events. In order to understand the feelings and meanings which, at the time, he was not able to stay in touch with, he was asked to monitor the occasions on which he became preoccupied with questions of food or thinness. After one week of monitoring his food preoccupations he reported that the associated thoughts seemed to be confined to worrying about fatness, promising himself not to eat, or feeling guilty for having eaten. During the second week, he saw more clearly that there was also a self-depriving aspect to his eating habits. At the next session, which followed a month's gap, he reported much less food preoccupation, but he had had some sharp recurrences, and he had been able to see that these had been associated with the planning or carrying out of assertive acts. Assertiveness was something which he had always found difficult and which tended to make him feel guilty. At this stage, he was able to accept a more general construction about how his attitude to food had acquired inappropriate "moral" meaning. Not eating implied being in control, not being stuffed (by his greedy self, historically by his mother); it was also a punishment for the fact that he did want to eat and, as he now saw, for assertiveness.

Charlotte

A second example of the use of self-monitoring in a patient with a more fully developed eating syndrome (bulimia) is that of Charlotte, a young woman who was much preoccupied with control of her food intake, and who went through phases of binging and vomiting. She was invited to monitor these urges and occasions to see if she could understand better the situations and feelings associated with them. She produced the following in diary form.

> *Wednesday:* Got a letter from Judith [her sister] today. It made me feel jealous, confused and a bit ashamed. Jealous because she sounded really happy and somehow it felt she had more of a genuine capacity to love than me. Confused because I kept looking for motives in my own feelings, like why did I feel unhappy for her happiness? Do I only thrive on others' misfortunes? But at the same time I really did feel happy for her and so I felt ashamed for crying and feeling sad. Anylway, the garbled confusion led to anxiety, ? hunger, stomach pains, and I sort of knew I might be going to binge. Well I ate more than usual for breakfast but did not carry on and vomit. Conversation with myself: What do you really want to do now, in this frenzy of emotions? Answer: Talk to Judith, so write her a letter. And that's what I did.
>
> *Tonight at a party:* I usually binge and vomit at parties because of the excess of food and drink available and because it is a convenient way of not talking to people, and also of feeling distinctly unattractive. I ate a lot again but I did not throw it up, and I made a conscious effort to examine my motives. Conversation with myself: why are you just standing here eating? Answer: Because it is a very pretentious party and I have had enough of trivial smalltalk. If you're not enjoying it any more why don't you go home? Because I'm scared I'll just go back and carry on binging. What do you want to do? I'd like to polish my shoes and read my book. So, do that, walk home, it'll sober you up and you'll feel better in the morning. So I walked home, polished my shoes and read my book. Very nice.
>
> *Thursday:* Rebecca (a flat-mate, also a food-obsessed woman), came in tonight and said she felt bad. I asked her what was the matter, and she said he had been compulsively stuffing this week. We explored the reasons together and shared ashamed food experiences of this past week. It was very nice because it helped to dispel the myth I have of her being such an incredible purist with whom I feel I must compete.
>
> *Friday:* Wake up feeling ill. Rebecca's over-concern. sympathy, and continuous "well you must just make sure you eat well and you'll get rid of it" made me so tense that after lying in bed until the afternoon I just went down and stuffed myself. I kept it down though. Went on feeling rather ill and tense. In the evening my best friend, Emily, came and I felt much more relaxed, Here was part of the real me that didn't care if people approved of it or didn't. She came to see me, and that's what mattered. I noticed immediately the contrast in the way. Rebecca and I related and the way I felt with Emily. Rebecca always asks, "How are you? How did the day go? What have you done? What are you going to do? Did you enjoy it?", especially when there are symptoms to ask about and concentrate on. "You must eat well dear, lots of red sage tea". Later, after Rebecca had been in and talked again, Emily said, "It's not that I'm not sympathetic about your sore throat or that I don't care, it's just that I don't feel it necessary to keep asking about it." I suppose I feel good with Emily because it's just

that I don't see her as a threat because she doesn't make me feel like it's my accomplishments that are important, rather just my personality.

I am still finding difficulty generally in listening to people and taking things in. I seem to drift off into thoughts about trivial things, food, planning times, activities, and lose track of what they're saying, so I feel guilty and stupid because I'm not capable of processing meaningful or important information, so I lose confidence and then I find it hard to express any feelings. When I realize how far I have drifted off from the conversation I feel even less able to attend to the other, and feel even more nothing myself.

Sunday: I just threw up. I knew I was going to. After Emily left I felt really lost and unhappy. I know how much more real I feel around her than among other people. I felt restless, full-up, but hungry. I started to plan times not to eat like not cooking lunch tomorrow, etc., etc., and getting anxious. I sort of knew I was going to binge and in a way I wanted to, and then to throw it all up seemed like it would be a quick and effective way of getting rid of all the chaos I was feeling inside. Before I went down to the kitchen I wanted to go and talk to the other people next door, but I felt they wouldn't want me and I would be an intruder. I knew when Rebecca came back tonight I would have to tell her all about the weekend and how my throat was, etc. etc., and I would have to ask her about her weekend and I wouldn't really be interested at all.

Later on in the day: One binge and vomit has just started a whole succession. When I have emptied from the vomit I feel scared and anxious so I eat, vomit again, eat, vomit again, and so on.

Monday: I woke up this morning and felt slightly disgusted with myself, depressed and anxious. I couldn't tell whether I was hungry but I thought this could be, since I emptied myself out yesterday. It looked cold outside, snowing, and I still didn't feel very well, although I know I was getting behind on work and should go to the library. These thoughts made me feel more anxious and I started to get a nervous tension stomach-ache. This kind of stomach-ache always makes me panic and I think maybe if I eat something it will go away, but since I am never actually hungry, just tense and anxious, food never does any good. I just eat more and more, and then say, "What the hell" and throw it up. That's what I did this morning."

Charlotte is described further in the next chapter.

Another form of self-monitoring, also described by Beck, can be used by patients to help correct their blanket judgements about how they are living their lives. One self-perpetuating aspect of depression is the negative retrospective evaluation of achievement. Sometimes the patient's evaluations of activity are borne out by monitoring, but even then it serves to provide a realistic basis for therapy by making self-judgements more accurate and discriminating.

Cora

Cora was a young woman who spent a great deal of time "arranging" not to do the things she needed and wanted to do. She was helped to recognize this by keeping an hour-by-hour chart of activity, which she then coded as either "coping" (which meant working or getting on with the ordinary businesses of life) or "enjoying", and also a third category that we called "limbo", which was a suspended state exemplifed, for example, by lying in bed, drinking endless cups of coffee, or making needless forays to the shops. She was able to learn from the use of this diary both how often she had under-reported those things that she had done effectively, but also how much of each day she did in fact make null and void. (This tendency was linked in her case to an extensive underlying snag, and with the common dilemma summarized as "if I feel I must, then I can't or won't").

Some workers add to these forms of self-monitoring, which serve to make patients aware of how their self-evaluations are unrealistic and negative, an explicit training in more adaptive and realistic self-instructions. In my experience, most patients develop their own self-instructions on the basis of their own more adequate introspection, and from the discussions of the results of monitoring which take place with the therapist.

BEHAVIOURAL METHODS

Monitoring techniques play an important part in the planning of behavioural forms of treatment.

Sally

Sally suffered from panic attacks in many situations. Monitoring these situations for a week enabled her to list the hierarchy of difficulties, from the most to the least, as follows:

(a) Public situations when seated away from the exit.
(b) In company in any kind of formal situation where she felt observed and could not get away.
(c) Out of doors, in crowds.
(d) Alone in her room for long periods.
(e) Being with a close friend.

Under this last condition she very seldom felt any anxiety. Her symptom was an expression of a pervasive over-dependency upon the judgements and validations offered by other people of her existence. Related to this, she was controllingly dependent upon her boyfriend, and acted in ways which neither he nor she liked, Sally was advised, on the basis of this, to try two different ways of controlling her panic. The first was the behavioural approach of rehearsal in imagination, and graded exposure. She was told to enter the easier situations first, and to rehearse before going there. To do this she was told to get herself as relaxed as possible, and then to imagine in as much detail as possible how she would feel in the situation, while maintaining her relaxation. However, when she tried to do this, she suffered unacceptable levels of anxiety. Supervised sessions of relaxation and rehearsal might have been effective, but in fact she obtained rapid control of her panics by the technique of paradoxical intention.

In paradoxical intention, the patient is instructed to try to produce the symptoms. The rationale in the case of panic attacks would seem to be that the essence of the symptom is one of loss of control, and that by attempting to produce it deliberately one is inevitably asserting control. More generally, paradoxical intention may help to control any symptom which is maintained by performance anxiety. By instructing the patient not to attempt to control the symptom, the anxiety about not being able to stay in control is dissipated. Sally obtained rapid relief of her panics by this means and treatment was discontinued after five sessions. Most of the treatment time had been devoted to discussing her controlling dependency on her boyfriend, that is to say with the hypothesized underlying self-identity and strategic scripts. At follow-up, 5 months later, she reported no further panic symptoms, and said that her tendency to be controlling, both of her boyfriend and of her other friends, was much diminished. At a casual encounter 2 years later she reported that she was "fine".

For patients with variable, situation-dependent symptoms, paradoxical intention can be tried out in combination with instructions in self-monitoring. The patient is told to enter the situations where symptoms occur and to try to experience the symptoms as fully as possible, with the aim of recording an accurate account of what has happened. There are three possible responses to this instruction: the patient may discover that he cannot produce the symptoms, and he can then be told to use the instructions as a means of control in the future; he may carry out the instruction but still suffer the symptoms, in which case the monitoring aim is still being fulfilled; finally, he may fail or refuse to carry out the instructions, in which case one is left with the need to explore further the reasons for his refusal or failure, a situation which occurs not uncommonly when behavioural methods are used.

Behavioural techniques depend essentially upon the careful analysis of symptoms or difficulties as behavioural sequences in relation to situations. In terms of the PSM, the emphasis is on Stages 4–6 of low-level, tactical scripts. When strategic issues are being treated, such as marital difficulties or problems like shyness, behaviourists will focus upon the sequence of small-scale acts and situations through which the larger problems are manifest, seeking to generate a change in detail, and then to generalize from this. The specific and commonsense nature of this approach is appealing and offers the possibility of accurately evaluating the changes produced. One can accept the effectiveness of the methods used, without accepting the adequacy of the underlying theory. In terms of the PSM, it is clear that extending control at tactical levels can lead to a revision of negative self-efficacy assumptions, but not clear that this is always the full extent of change needed. To this neglect of the wider meanings which are commonly, although not always, attached to symptoms must be added the tedium involved for patient and therapist in carrying out behavioural treatments. Moreover, though it is commonly believed that behavioural techniques are quicker than interpretive ones, this is not necessarily so, as the following case illustrates.

Bridget

Bridget consulted at the age of 22 because of depression and a phobia. Her phobia had started when she was it school, and had been present, with variable intensity, for 10 years. It consisted of a panicky dread of being sick or seeing someone else be sick, and it had led to avoidance of situations where there were many people present. If such situations were entered, she had to sit by the exit. Bridget chose to combine interpretative therapy with a behavioural approach to this phobic symptom. She prepared a hierarchy of difficult situations and enlisted a friend's co-operation with the aim of getting the friend to talk about, and later to mimic, vomiting. However, before she embarked upon this programme, she realized, as a result of her reflections following her first three assessment sessions, that the phobia of throwing up was linked with a forbidden *wish* to "throw it all up". The symptom expressed symbolically a major problem in her relationship to others. In terms of the PSM, self-acceptance was conditional upon her evaluation of herself as being clever, good, under control, and not angry. She could give herself no permission to do other than work hard and compliantly, and her symptom had served as a means of evading this strict requirement but also of punishing her. Once that was understood, symptom relief was rapid, and the extensive and personally important issues were dealt with in the course of, and after, her subsequent therapy.

Simple cognitive and behavioural approaches can often be incorporated in treatment with minimal supervision, and written instructions can cut down the time needed to apply them (see Chapter 14). Self-monitoring is easily learned and patients are quick to see its the value. Most people can understand the concepts of rehearsal, graded exposure, step-by-step change, reinforcement and extinction, and if control of symptoms can be achieved by these means, confidence is restored, and time and energy are left to attend to other matters. Long-established and severe phobias, and elaborate and pervasive obsessive–compulsive disorders, are best treated by specialist behaviour therapists in the first instance: the former by graded exposure to the feared situation, under the control of the patient; the latter by exposure combined with some form of response prevention. However, it is my firm opinion that active methods should always be applied in the context of a treatment approach which gives consideration to the full range of meanings of the patient's difficulties, and to the implications of his change.

DISCUSSION

Recent years have witnessed the evolution of a spectrum of behavioural and cognitive/behavioural therapies. The purest, or most extreme, form, is based upon the principles of operant conditioning and specifically excludes or forbids attention to cognitive processes which are seen to have no initiating or causal role in the determination of behaviour. The main therapeutic methods used by this school are the application of reinforcement or punishment to influence carefully analysed small units of behaviour. The main application is to subjects under the control of others, that is to say adults or children in institutions, or children in families and schools.

Many behaviourists applying classical stimulus–response (S–R) ideas to the treatment of neurotic problems allow complex mediational processes to perch upon the hyphen between the "S" and the "R", but even though rehearsal in imagination is one of the common techniques employed, the use of the word "cognition" is not encouraged, and the attempt is always made to refer treatment to principles based upon laboratory experiments with animals, a position quixotically identified by the protagonists as being scientific.

Social learning methods of therapy, as described by Bandura (1977a), incorporate the full range of behavioural techniques, and edge into the consideration of cognition. Behaviour, including symptomatic behaviour, is seen to result either from a response to an environmental stimulus or as an instrumental act shaped by the consequences of the act, or as being determined by central "mediational processes" where such learning is stored as hypotheses, rules, strategies, etc. The self is frequently referred to, but is defined rather seldom; in particular, much attention has been paid recently to the question of self-efficacy and its relation to performance (Bandura, 1977b). In this model, therapy is made up of a number of discrete, highly-specified acts. *Modelling*, which is the most specifically social aspect of the theory, represents the modification of the existing response patterns through the observation of another's performance of the act, in which the other performs differently, with different consequences. Modifications of behaviour based upon modelling need to be reinforced for the individual by direct positive outcomes provided either by self or other. Such modelling is seen to occur in any interpersonal and social relationship, not always helpfully. Bandura argues that therapists should take care to provide the patient with a model of self-exposure and personal accountability. Unwanted behaviours are altered by controlling reinforcement so that desired behaviours are rewarded (*conditioning*) and undesired behaviours are either not rewarded (*extinction*) or are met by *aversive conditioning* in which punishing outcomes are provided. In *counter-conditioning*, anxiety or other unwanted effects are replaced by incompatible responses during a process of controlled graded exposure, either to the actual feared situation or symbols of it. In some cases, this must be supplemented with training in appropriate coping skills. In aversive counter-conditioning, used especially in the treatment of alcoholism and sexual deviation, control over deviant acts is developed by associating the acts, or the stimuli leading to the acts, with punishing outcomes.

In this model, consciousness, or awareness, is seen to enhance, but not to be essential to, the process of learning, although "individuals eventually infer, from observation of their behaviour and its differential outcome, the correct reinforcement rules which partly control subsequent responding". The main feature of Bandura's model can be incorporated in the PSM but the emphasis on cognition in the PSM is not accepted by social learning theorists. The strength of social learning theory lies in its specificity and its basis in reasonably well-controlled and observed experiment. Its main deficiency is in its neglect of self-evaluation and self-judgment; these issues receive only one out of more than 600 pages in Bandura's book (1977a). One can only agree with the following observation, while wondering why it has not been given more consideration in practice:

> Since the person's own self-demands and self-respect serve as his main guides and determinants, behaviour that is under the latter form of self-control is apt to be less affected by variations in specific situational contingencies.

As Bower (1978) argues, the distinction between social learning theory and a basically cognitive psychology seems difficult to maintain. This convergence is also exemplified in Mischel's (1973) social learning theory of personality, which emphasizes person/situation interaction, and sees the relevant variables in the individual as being his competence in constructing schema, his mode of categorizing, his outcome expectancies, the subjective values he attaches to possible outcomes, and his self-regulatory systems.

In terms of the PSM, operant and S–R based treatments aim to intervene at the tactical level: they influence the individual's retrospective evaluation of his acts by manipulating the consequences in ways that serve to alter subsequent predictive evaluations, so that different acts can be selected. It is inevitable, however, that higher level self-identity and self-efficacy assumptions should be influenced by the non-specific factors operating in any treatment situation and by observation of the changes produced.

Accounts of paradoxical intention are to be found in Haley (1963) and Cade (1979). These authors emphasize the use of the technique to outwit the patient who is using his symptom controllingly, an approach I feel to be somewhat manipulative, although Cade defends himself against the charge. Ascher and Turner (1980) report that a straightforward account of the rationale behind the procedure is as satisfactory a method as one in which the description is adjusted to match the patient's beliefs. Paradoxical intention operates at the stage of predictive evaluation of performance, by circumventing the cycle of negative prediction followed by confirmation by failure: once control is established, self-efficacy assumptions will also be revised.

Treatment based on cognitive or social learning approaches is consistent with the PSM, as we have discussed already. Different approaches under these headings show variations in the particular focus of concern. The rational-emotive therapy of Ellis (1962) seems to consist largely of bullying the patient into agreeing that many of his beliefs and assumptions are silly. In Beck (1976), self-monitoring and self-evaluation of thoughts not normally attended to serve to illustrate the irrationality and emotional significance of underlying thoughts and beliefs. Other writers (Meichenbaum, 1974; Mahoney, 1974; and Goldfried and Goldfried, 1975) pay more attention to teaching problem-solving strategies and, in particular, to the explicit teaching of more effective modes of self-instruction.

The best evidence for the efficacy of behavioural and cognitive treatments is found in methods involving direct exposure, notably to feared objects or situations in phobias or obsessions (Gelder, 1979; Emmelkamp and Wessels, 1975). The evaluation of narrowly focused treatments in terms of observable behaviours is, of course, much easier than the evaluation of treatment with more complex aims, and it remains uncertain how often such treatments are adequate on their own. The behaviourist literature reports only rare examples of "symptom-substitution" following successful behavioural treatment, but the concept of symptom-substitution is a very narrow one, and ignores the many possible effects of behaviourally-induced change on other aspects of life. The narrow definition of neurotic difficulty employed by behaviourists inevitably determines the range of phenomena to which they attend and, hence, changes in patterns of relationship or in subjective experience are neglected or conceived of as unrelated to the "symptomatic behaviour". When a wider focus is employed, wider effects are noted. Hafner (1977 and 1979), for example, showed how the cure of agoraphobia in housebound housewives produced jealousy or morbidity in a proportion of their husbands. A more serious indication of the narrowed attention of some workers in this field is given by Bayer (1972), reporting the successful behavioural treatment of compulsive hair-pulling (trichotillomania) in a depressed young woman. To therapists interested in the self, this symptom is expressive of an angry attitude towards the self, and the comment that "treatment was interrupted by the patient's unfortunate death in an automobile accident" would have been less baldly presented. In terms of the PSM, it seems quite possible that the removal of the patient's self-attacking symptom might have led to an increase in guilt and, hence, to increased risk-taking or risk-seeking, so that the accidental nature of the death was not entirely beyond question. This is not to suggest that behavioural methods are not apropriate for symptoms of this sort; they are clearly effective, but their relation to more serious and extensive difficulties must be attended to. An example of "symptom substitution" is given in Chapter 12.

Wilson (1978) takes the evidence for the superiority of direct exposure over rehearsal in imagination and other cognitive approaches, as providing evidence for the redundancy of any cognitive concepts in therapy. However, the efficacy of direct exposure is as consistent with the PSM or other cognitive models as it is with the behavioural one, for clearly one most effective revision of negative predictive evaluations of performance is to observe the self performing satisfactorily. Wilson concludes his discussion of this issue as follows:

> Another advantage of social learning theory is that the concern with cognitive mediating processes is deliberately tied to overt action. This interdependency between cognitions and behaviour underscores the fact that, whereas cognitive mechanisms may underlie behaviour change, they are not the treatment targets per se.

This represents a statement of faith or, more critically, the self-imposition of tunnel vision. Changes in cognitions seem to me to be important and appropriate aims of therapy, and I have reported how one can define desirable cognitive changes at the start of therapy and demonstrate that they have been achieved at the end, using repertory grid techniques (Ryle, 1979a; 1980).

Even in the hands of humanly open and generous-minded therapists, the various behavioural and cognitive approaches described in this chapter fail to attend to a number of issues which are comonplace and important in the work of any therapist who is less confined in his attention, notably those concerned with personality structure, and with the question of intrapsychic conflict and the pervasive importance of guilt and guilt-avoidance in maintaining neurotic difficulties. In the PSM, the crucial role of self-defining and self-judging scripts is acknowledged, and the defensive strategies (psychoanalytic defence mechanisms restated cognitively) are accommodated. Moreover, while the PSM explains the effects of therapeutic methods that act upon only part of the system, it also points to wider issues and to the implications of change achieved by such local interventions.

9

Transference: the Metaphoric Relationship between Patient and Therapist

In the last chapter we considered various active psychotherapeutic methods. We will now consider an additional major source of understanding and of change: the relationship that develops between patient and therapist. In getting to know any other person we are guided by our previous experience of people and, as each of us has had a different experience, each develops a personal set of assumptions and expectations. We differ, for example, in how far we tend to see others as weak, friendly, trusting, humorous, patient, strong, controlling, threatening, or destructive. We also differ in how we see these and other traits to be connected to each other. For one person, strong others may be seen as threatening; for another, they may be perceived of as reliable; for one person, friendly people may be seen as weak or stupid; for another as trustworthy. These differences are expressions of what one could call different implicit theories of relationships linking our perceptions of individuals to our repertoire of relationship scripts. On meeting a new person, we perceive their qualities, more or less accurately, and attribute other qualities to them on the basis of our particular scripts, and then act as seems appropriate in terms of our particular aims and available means. Much of the suffering of neurotic people can be attributed to the particular implicit theories of personality which guide them in their relationships.

It is in our emotionally significant and less structured relationships, such as those with friends and lovers, rather than in relationships with, say, shop-assistants or policemen, that our individual expectations and our personal repertoire of perceptions and responses play a powerful role. Moreover, in such relationships we tend to have chosen people, although not always consciously, who seem familiar and ready to play through the drama of relationship according to the plot for which we are already rehearsed; this process of selection serves to confirm the "rightness" of our beliefs.

There are, however, surprises; surprises of two sorts. The first arises from the fact that our consciously recognized version of ourselves and of what we seek in others is seldom the whole story; much is left out, and there is often a counter-plot implying quite other needs and expectations. The sources of these limitations and divisions in the self have been discussed earlier, in Chapter 5. The second sort of surprise is based upon the fact that what we perceive in the other person, and the pattern of relationship which we expect, may not correspond with their identity and their intentions. In this mismatch between the template of our expectations and assumptions, and their surprisingly different assertions and realities, we are presented with the opportunity to modify our system of understanding. Because such learning is difficult, we will often prefer to lose the relationship or try to bully the other into fitting the prescription we offer; but sufficiently strong and sure others who can stand their ground and refuse to be so reduced offer us a real possibility of change. The failure of our mental schemes to assimilate their reality, and the failure of our habitual relationship scripts to evoke the expected reciprocation, force us to enlarge our ideas about the limits of our being, and about what we want and can expect from others, and give us the opportunity to develop more complex and less inflexible scripts.

This understanding is crucial to therapy, for the psychotherapist can be a person who offers these two sorts of surprise. By giving the patient the opportunity to manifest and recognize his own contradictions, and by not accepting his invitations to confirm his assumptions, he can offer a unique opportunity for change.

The process of engendering a relationship that can expose these contradictory wishes, while gratifying none of them, is a central method of psychoanalysis and the main source of psychoanalytic understanding. In the orthodox analytic setting, the patient lies on the analyst's couch, usually for several hours a week, and the analyst is both literally invisible and personally opaque. This method tends to maximize the patient's sense of helplessness and dependency, and serves to make manifest the less respectable and more infantile aspects of his nature. In psychoanalytic terms, this situation is designed to create a regressive, dependent transference. The resolution of this by interpretation and working through is the central therapeutic method of psychoanalysis. Transference is defined as the patient's partly or wholly unconscious tendency to view the psychotherapist in illusory ways determined by his own expectations and wishes, rather than on the basis of the actual behaviour and characteristics of the analyst. Forms of transference, however, occur in settings other than that prescribed by orthodox analysis, including many situations where it is not recognized. The transference which occurs in less rigidly defined treatment situations where, for example, patient and therapist sit in view of each other and where the therapist's interventions may not be exclusively interpretive, may also be utilized therapeutically. I have argued earlier (in Chapter 6) that the psychoanalytic assumption that the orthodox psychoanalytic role is a neutral one seems doubtful; for many patients, the inaccessibility and remoteness feels hostile and may mirror their own inability to stay in touch with others. Such patients may struggle through to the recognition that the analyst is offering care but, in my view, the way to this recognition need not in most cases be made so hard.

The idea of transference is now fairly generally understood, but often in the somewhat crude version that "patients look for parent substitutes in their therapist". The description "metaphoric relationship", proposed in the title for this chapter, is suggested to avoid such simplification. The world "metaphor", from the Greek, is equivalent to the Latin-derived word "transference", but the different sense conveyed by the two words in English points to a distinction which I would want to make. To say that a patient has "transferred" an attribute or expectation from a parent to his therapist seems to describe a relatively crude and simple act, whereas to say that a patient uses the therapeutic situation, consciously or unconsciously, to experience and enact metaphorically various "as if" versions of his sense of himself and of his wishes, needs and expectations, implies, I think correctly in most cases, a more creative and delicate use by the patient of the opportunity provided by the therapist.

Metaphor is meaningful because the structures of meaning expressed metaphorically correspond to the structures of meaning being explored. One skill of a therapist, therefore, is to allow his patients to use the relationship as a stage on which to play out versions of his scripts, especially those felt as unacceptable or not fully known. Another therapist's skill is to recognize and use fully those small-scale interactions that take place on the therapeutic stage to illustrate the higher-order scripts which are responsible for the patient's life difficulties.

At this point it should be noted that not all that takes place between the patient and the therapist is at the potentially more obscure level of metaphor. The meeting of patient and therapist is a real event, recognized by both as serving a particular purpose, and each inevitably presents the other with a sample of himself. What particular sample of himself the patient offers will, in part, be rooted in the obvious and real nature of the therapist; for example, as older person to younger patient, as white therapist to black patient, or as male therapist to female patient, or the reverses of these; and these realities must be fully acknowledged in understanding what transpires, and may set a limit on what can happen. Within such limits, however – and the limits will be wider to the extent that the therapist can convey his openness to possibility – the individual patient's self-presentation will reveal his particular formations and his particular limitations that stem from his history. As therapy proceeds, such samples may be selected, consciously or unconsciously, as being related to the larger themes, and patient and therapist may develop together a mutually understood symbolic process.

There is one other aspect of the situation that determines which samples of himself a patient brings; namely, the fact that the patient is in need and the therapist is offering help. This inequality, and the anxiety, shame, or anger so easily generated in our culture in adults by the recognition of their dependency, means that some of the experience of the patient in therapy is always difficult to acknowledge. The manifestation of these less acceptible aspects is usually, initially at least, partial and indirect, and is often apparent to the therapist before it can be consciously named or acknowledged by the patient. The process of unfolding the more difficult aspects of the truth about himself is helped by the therapist's basic acceptance of the patient, and by the sense of sdafety engendered by his feeling understood. The patient's statements, silences, dreams, or demeanour, will usually acceptance of the patient, and by the sense of safety engendered by his feeling understood. The patient's statements, silences, dreams, or demeanour, will usually combine some concealment with some expression; the therapist needs to clarify and make explicit what is being hinted at, and to imply permission for the expression of the difficult thoughts and feelings that he suspects to be present.

In many treatments, the transference serves to illuminate particular issues, or provides further experience of problems which have already been faced in other relationships; but in some this metaphor becomes the dominant factor and the relationship with the therapist carries the weight of the central issues of the patient's life. In some way, unconsciously chosen but allowed by the therapist's conveying his understanding of it, the basic issues of the self are raised: who am I; am I allowed and, if so, on what terms; can I give or receive love; is my anger too dangerous to admit? Along with this, concealed or forgotten aspects of the self and the blocks that prevent change become focused upon that encounter, and may be lived through there to a different conclusion for the first time.

In these more total metaphoric relationships, the therapist needs to be deeply sensitive if the patient is to be spared humiliation, and if he is to learn from the process. This involves the total acceptance of the reality of the patient's feelings, coupled with a clarity and delicacy in exploring their origins and meanings. The patient feels "as if" the therapist is someone other than, in reality, he is, but there is nothing "as if" about the feelings. Provided the therapist has established his genuine human commitment to the patient, the patient can accept the therapist's non-reciprocation of the extremes of love and hate that may be experienced and can, in time, come to value the real care offered (which is therapy) above the more dramatic feelings experienced and the more dramatic responses sought. This process, whereby needs and desires are recognized only to be abandoned, is both painful and strangely liberating. In the remainder of this chapter, we will look at examples of how meetings between patient and therapist can be used in this way. We will start by considering the manifestations of transference in the treatment of Anne and David.

David

David was seen on seven occasions before a gap of some months; because of this and the plan for later group therapy I did not emphasize the transference relationship. It was discussed around two themes: firstly, through my early recognition of his difficulty in accepting the patient role, which was linked with his more general tendency to adopt the care-giving role in his relationships. The second issue was in anticipation of the end of treatment. The experience of being alone after Patricia had left had been a painful one, which he had needed to go through. When, in the sixth session, it became apparent that he had forgotten the date of our next meeting, I felt that this was probably the result of him not wanting to think about yet another defection, although when I said this he did not accept that is was true. At the seventh session he was given a further appointment 5 weeks later for which he arrived a day late, and it may well be that his failure to meet, which could not be remedied at that time, was an expression of anger or the need to avoid the feelings around the termination of treatment.

Anne

In the case of Anne, as we have seen, transference issues came up at the very start of therapy over the issue of trust. As she developed more trust, the basic pattern of the relationship was characterized by her feeling safe with, and working hard for, me as a good parent. While my "good parent" role was helpful in encouraging Anne towards more self-care, the recognition of mixed feelings was important and, as therapy proceeded, she became more able to be both present in the session and to experience her negative feelings more directly; she was able to shed tears for the first time. As the long break in treatment approached and as she recalled many painful memories, Anne experienced much sadness and some anxiety, but she developed a confidence that she was managing, and she contrasted this sense of "work in progress" with her previous need for everything to be perfect and totally under control.

FOUR EXAMPLES OF TRANSFERENCE UTILIZATION IN TREATMENT

We will now look at some other examples of transference which illustrate the various ways in which it may play a part in treatment.

Peter

Peter was referred for treatment by his tutors because of his failure to complete written assignments. After he had been in treatment for some time he agreed to record, anonymously, an account of the understandings he was gaining of his work difficulty, for my use in a conference for teachers on learning difficulties. The following excerpts are from this recording. It illustrates a recapitulation in treatment of the work difficulty and his growing understanding of the relationship of this recapitulation to his work difficulty and to crucial events in his childhood.

> I made an appointment to record this material yesterday but, due to reasons that are not of great significance, like lying in bed in the morning, I failed to turn up and I am recording it a day late. This may not, at the outset, seem very relevant, but you will see the significance of it. My problem first occurred during the Christmas vacation; I had been working fairly well during my first term and had produced one or two pieces of work of good quality. During that first vacation, when we had a normal amount of reading and writing to do, I experienced a total work breakdown. I knew that some students who showed a certain amount of superficial early promise "blew their fuses"

when they came to do real work at University, and I assumed that my relatively good grades had exhausted what little intellectual ability I possessed. With this theory in mind, I went to the Dean, not to apply for treatment, but tell him that it would probably be better for the University and for myself if I were to leave. The Dean evidently realized that, although I may have had problems, they didn't lie in the field of intellectual exhaustion, and he recommended that I should discuss the problem further with somebody else . . .

In my early therapy sessions, I described what happened when I worked: how I would spend a great deal of time sitting with my books and trying to read, to such an extent that where I was living I acquired a reputation for being something of a swot; but for myself, I think I spent most of my time dreaming and going round and round in my mind why I wasn't working, what was going to happen if I didn't work, and how it would be if I did, and how greatly I would achieve, if I did; and I lived altogether in a sort of fantasy world in which I was the conquering hero or was sinking slowly lower and lower to the gutter. I felt I was being unfairly insulated against the coldness and hardness of the world, but that sooner or later it would all catch up with me and I would get my desserts and be seen for what I really was – a rather miserable failure.

Well, what we discovered in the interviews was that all these work difficulties, which had been present since I was at school, were in part reactions to significant male figures. At this stage, perhaps, the thing will fall into perspective when I say that from childhood I have not had a father; he committed suicide when I was seven, and now, in treatment I have found what I had in a vague way suspected: that I hadn't known at all what that had meant . . .

It seems that one of the major things I have been seeking has been some kind of retribution, as if I had been responsible for, and actually was being punished for, my father's death. At school, I had attempted to achieve that first by being very aggressive, bringing down the retributory wrath of the authorities, but the need was evidently not assuaged; so I had switched to being compliant to an extreme degree but then, instead of bringing down the direct wrath of the authorities by deviant actions, what I did was to fail 'O' levels, to fail one of my 'A' levels, to fail my Oxford and Cambridge Entrance, and almost to fail to get a University place . . .

It was the year after I was born that my father became chronically ill. I think I had a real problem with him as, in becoming ill, he seems to have returned to the infantile situation, so that both he and I were like male infants demanding our mother's love. My mother's great need for love to be given in return was turned on her children, especially on me, her only son, and I think I felt the pressure of that over-demand for love from her. In my therapy there was a process of becoming consciously aware of what was going on and of what the situation had been in the past with regard to my father and mother. Underneath that, my subconscious seemed to lag behind so, although I was aware of what sort of syndrome was operating, it continued and still continues, to some extent, to operate.

I also react, but not so much now, to the doctor as a mother, a sort of symbolic mother whom I need and love, but who is demanding things from me. I react to him also as a father figure, and I want to express aggression to him, and I react to him in the same way as I had wanted to react to my father but, as a child, I had learnt that anger to fathers made them die. While, on the one hand, I wanted him to drop dead, on the other hand to express aggression was to have him do so. So, this aggression had to be expressed non-verbally, in lateness for appointments, by not turning up for the recording session yesterday, it had to be expressed in forgetting to bring the dreams I had remembered and written down to talk about, just as it had been expressed in not writing essays for tutors. I also reacted to my doctor as an invader because, although distorted, the structure I had built up was, while frightening, yet in a sense safe and secure, and the doctor was someone who was going to come into my squalid but known mental situation and change it. So, while I wanted it changed, to do so meant a painful experience, it meant exposing myself to new feelings which I also saw as painful, and for this reason, too, I resisted the doctor and wanted to express my aggression to him.

So, this is how the process of recovery seems to be operating. Although the mean line of the graph of progress is constantly upwards, the actual line is one of advance and regression, although in general the regressions are never so far back as the previous ones; so, although I wanted to assert myself, wanted to express my personality and my individuality, and my aggression against the doctor by refusing to come to the appointment yesterday, nevertheless I have recorded this today.

Charlotte

Charlotte, already described in Chapter 8, was a young woman incompletely recovered from anorexia nervosa, still suffering from marked food preoccupation, with phases of binge-eating and vomiting, and suffering from depression and difficulties in close relationships. The treatment included the use of active techniques, notably self-monitoring, but transference interpretations played an important part on some occasions. The first occasion was at the end of the first assessment session, when I suggested that she was scared of her wish for total care, and was hence having great difficulty in accepting any care at all. This same fear was important in understanding her relationship dilemmas. In the ninth session, I suggested that her indirectly expressed anger with me was linked with the way in which she seemed to perceive me as demanding that she should behave well as a patient, in which she saw me as being like her mother. In the twelfth session, following a break in treatment, she arrived announcing that she was arranging to consult a nutritional expert, a move which I saw as representing a denial of the understanding she had achieved of the meaning of her symptoms and, hence, as representing an indirect, unacknowledged act of hostility towards me; it was also an attempt to escape from the dependency which she had allowed herself. From the fifteenth session to termination at the twenty-first I repeatedly returned to the theme of the approaching termination and of her apparent incomplete ability to acknowledge the fact of it or the feelings about it. These difficulties were seen as linked with her frequently repeated pattern of relationship, a cycle of denied need, fear of closeness, cutting-off, symbolized and magically controlled by her anorexia, gorging, and self-induced vomiting.

In the cases of Peter and Charlotte, there were many similarities between the patients' behaviour in the transference and their behaviour in some relationships in the world outside. In the next case we will consider, the expression of the issues was less direct, representing a metaphoric recapitulation (unfortunately without resolution of the difficulties experienced in life) rather than a repetition.

Nora

Nora was a young woman who consulted for the second time at the age of 25. Four years' previously she had consulted with depression and a sense of not being in control of her life, related to the recent experience of a frighteningly intense emotional involvement with a girlfriend. Two assessment interviews at that time suggested that these problems reflected a harsh, denigrating attitude towards herself, and an inability to allow herself full expression or achievement, due to guilt at having rejected her family's strong religious beliefs. She had accepted referral for group therapy at that time, but had only attended two group meetings. When she returned, at 25, she reported feeling better about herself in general, seeing herself as more in control of her life, and her main complaint was one of persistent sexual difficulty. She had never had an orgasm despite the recent experience of a profound and prolonged relationship with a man who was currently abroad. This relationship had not been ended but she was now involved in a second relationship which was also intense, but was similarly incomplete sexually. She had consulted at a time when she was only available for treatment for 3 months, and I had been uncertain about whether to offer treatment, or not. When I said, at the third session, that we would see what we could do in the time available, she countered by saying that she now felt she would not proceed. I interpreted this response as representing her need to control by withdrawal, and linked this with her previous leaving of therapy, with the fearful experience of over-involvement with the girlfriend, with her current ambiguous commitment to two men, and with her sexual problem which represented, I felt, a defensive absenting of herself at the point of sexual commitment. This defensive control seemed characteristic of many of her relationships, although it alternated in some instances with placatory behaviour followed by resentment. These themes were explored over five further sessions, two sessions having been postponed by her. She dealt with her two-man problem by arranging to go abroad away from both for a further year, and postponed her last session; she failed to contact me for an alternative time.

Win

Win had 30 therapy sessions over the last 18 months of her University career, the reason for seeking help being a morbid obsession with death, panic attacks, many psychosomatic symptoms, and depression. In the course of her treatment, her self-attacks, her symptoms, her fears, and her self-diminution reduced in intensity, and her tendency to see destructive attacks from others, which were based on projection, was much lessened. Termination was accompanied by sadness and by the feeling that she was not ready to leave. Follow-up contact was arranged but, for geographical reasons, this was infrequent. Over the ensuing 15 months, however, she wrote a number of letters in which she expressed very fluently her sense of "unfinished business", and described eloquently the painful experience of living through the resolution of a powerful transference which had clearly not been adequately dealt with at the time of termination. In Win's early letters she was preoccupied with her sense of loss and with her awkwardly conveyed shame at having sexual feelings for me.

> Sometimes lately I've wanted to feel that you were hurt like me, but I expect it's some odd wishful thinking. I am not clear why I want to produce pain in you when you took so much of it away from me. So now I'll come on to the other reason for my feeling that you would be ashamed of, or angry with, me. What a pity that I can't think of any other way to put it down that doesn't sound absurd, especially since it's simply that I want you physically as well as the other ways . . . Nothing I can think of consoles me. It makes me very angry with you for making me feel it, and with me for feeling it . . .

Later (4 months after ending) she went through a period of great desolation, described as follows.

> Some nights ago . . . I suddenly, for no reason I could see, began to feel worse than ever before. I can't explain exactly what it was but the end result was quite different to anything experienced at other times. (I no longer seem to have the death fears.) I became quite convinced that I was the only living thing left on earth. I went frantically calling the cat to be able to hold on to a breathing, living creature. I couldn't find it, and ended up watching the cars go by to reassure myself. Since then, I came to hate everyone for not wanting me. By the time I wrote to you I had worked up 100% hate. I hardly knew where it all came from. Then, for some completely unknown reason, everything lifted like a fog. No delirious happiness, nothing excessive, just a nice, calm, reasonable peace. My boyfriend says that he won't leave me and he wants to stay. I think I was relieved most of all to know how much I wanted him to, rather than whether he wanted me . . .

Two months later she was able to write as follows.

> It is hard for me to write, for although I know where to end I hardly know where to begin, so I'll start by saying what I intended to leave to the end, which is a very simple and, to you at least, obvious statement that I know I must become alright without you. I am afraid of becoming whole since, paradoxically, unity also means apartness . . .

In her next letter she explained how difficult it was to name her feelings for me without risk of distortion or of my being reductive.

> I consider that I have loved a few people before, although my boyfriend is the only person of whom I have said it. None of these feelings encompass the kind of thing I feel towards you, nor even in their own way were they so strong. I swear that if these people went from my life I would grieve, but that I would see an end to it. Perhaps I am doing myself a rather twisted injustice, but what I mean is that I cannot see an end to grieving now, and the pain does not seem justified by the cause . . .

Two months later she described how the pain of ending had initially felt like the appropriate punishment by her "gaoler" (her name for her self-destructive and self-restrictive parts):

> Now, when I should feel peace, when I can grow away instead of being pushed away as I felt it was, I wait to be punished . . .

These issues were referred to over the ensuing months, with increasing self-assertion, and finally, 15 months after the formal termination, she was able to write her last letter.

> I wasn't intending to write to you but as I put down in my diary my version of what I was thinking and feeling, I found I was posing a question to which I didn't have the

answer. Since it is a question about you, I am turning it into a letter. Something happened which in itself isn't very important, but which made me very depressed. After a week of being down, I found myself crying and not able to stop. This went on for about 3 hours, during which time all the feeling I had had for you and all the sadness that went with it returned. I thought it had disappeared but it was only buried. And yet, it wasn't the same depression or the same pain, and this time I could see through that state into the time beyond it. The next day I felt rather better and in a week quite strong and recovered. I began to dismantle the particular problem and to reason it out in the light of what I had learnt from you. Reasoning is always a good sign for me because I can only do it when I'm not afraid. The reasoning itself wasn't very wonderful or profound but the meaning it holds for me is. I tried to think of the pattern of the things you've said, and put them in order, not to regiment them but to make them stand still and be looked at. It made sense. I found myself trying to see you away from what I wanted, in the past, to force you to be, so I will try to tell you what you mean to me now. First, I can't, and probably never will, understand why I had to go away that first time before I was ready. I felt like a ghost going from your room, as though I had ceased to exist. I hope there is no worse feeling to be experienced. Sometimes I think you might have been surprised at how really bad I felt, but of course I couldn't ask you if you knew. I hope you didn't because it would have made you very cruel. I couldn't believe that. Well, I came back and I wrote, and if I was persistent, unreasonable, and a nuisance, it was at least partly your fault. Nevertheless, you were good to me. You were always there and comforted me, and later you let me be angry with you which I badly needed to be. I could really have smashed you sometimes. You were still there, and answered my letters despite my idiocies and spite and the difficulties. When I reflect on my foolishness now, it doesn't please me, but it doesn't upset me as before. It's just a part of what I was, and am now, in different forms. It doesn't govern me. Then I went through a phase of wanting to be without you, being afraid to try it. This took the form of me managing and being independent and you being hurt and upset without me. As I wrote, I realized that it was this question I was posing, and this fear was still hanging about. So this letter is just a way of discovering if my independence, which seems to me to have become a bit loud and aggressive in my last letter or two, was hurting you or not. I have been so happy lately, and still am, and it took some misery to bring the question to my attention. I don't think there are any more questions. Puzzles perhaps. With love from Win''

A DISCUSSION OF THE FOUR EXAMPLES

We will now consider the last four examples in terms of the PSM. In the case of Peter, the transference relationship was a repetition of a pattern recognizable in his relationship to tutors and teachers for many years, and bearing traces from his earlier relationship with both parents. He consciously sought high achievement and worked appropriately until nearing success or completion, at which point he stopped. These self-engendered failures were both acts of defiance (historically having the meaning of not doing what mummy wanted) and invitations to punishment (historically a kind of baring of the throat to the fathers who, in the fantasy generated by his own father's death, would not survive or permit his direct anger and maybe not even his success). He was trapped into the dilemma ''either compliant or defiant'' and success was prohibited by a snag; in psychoanalytic terms, these were manifestations of anal and oedipal issues. In treatment, he alternated between compliance and defiance and he finally chose to end therapy himself, a decision which probably included both elements of defiance and some proper assertion of autonomy. Symbolically, being able to go off on his own terms, feeling that he had made progress and yet had left me neither punishing nor punished, was a challenge to the snag. His problems were not completely resolved, however; throughout his undergraduate and postgraduate career, which was ultimately a successful one, he repeatedly failed to obey the letter of the law, and in particular was often late in submitting work.

In the case of Charlotte, the basic dilemma she showed in her relationships, and repeated in the transference, was one of being either controllingly withholding, or involved and out of control. This was parallelled in her attitude to food, in which she was either meticulously self-depriving and self-controlling, or greedy, binging, and out of control. Clearly this dilemma, in psychoanalytic terms, relates to the early oral issues of trust and dependency. The transference interpretations I gave her were fully accepted intellectually, and she became much less food-obsessed and much more able to express her feelings, but she remained a waxing and waning presence and, as with Peter, treatment had mitigated rather than fully resolved the basic dilemma.

When Nora missed her last appointment, I felt that she had been untouched by treatment, having simply re-enacted her controlling, withholding script with me. Her sexual problem was an expression of an existential one in which basic trust in others was lacking and the integrity of the self was felt as in jeopardy. While these issues point to a developmentally early origin for her difficulties, it could be that the very competent strategies she had evolved for remaining safe constituted the main reason for the persistence of this pattern. Some weeks later she wrote that the sessions had been "an introduction to a series of valuable explorations which I hope somehow to continue . . . they have without doubt unravelled a little of the internal confusion and I can sense an allayment of some of those suicidal fears." So, while the therapy remained as incompletely consummated as her sexual relationships, some shift may have been initiated.

For Win, the living through of the transference relationship was the whole point of therapy, and most of the crucial work was done after the end of regular sessions, by letter. The continuing source of Win's troubles was her harshly self-critical and self-punishing "gaoler", which was slowly mitigated by my becoming both the object of her love and desire, and an alternative and kinder judge. (In psychoanalytic terms, as described by Strachey (1934) and discussed below, I was the object of her id drive and a quasi replacement for her superego.) The sexualization of the transference can reflect an inability to hold onto the metaphoric quality of the relationship (a sign of severe pathology) or it may represent a resistance to the work of therapy. In Win's case, however, it seemed to be no more than the intense manifestation of what was primarily a powerful maternal transference, in which the basic issues of trust, and separation without damage to either, were eventually lived through. It was a painful experience, but by the end she had clearly achieved a much less conflicted and kinder attitude towards herself.

DISCUSSION

In terms of the PSM, the metaphoric relationship of patient and therapist offers an opportunity for the patient to engage in a relationship in a situation with special possibilities which can allow the expression of aspects of the self normally concealed or unrecognized. Patients can be expected to relate to the therapist in terms:

(a) of their general relationship scripts;
(b) in terms of scripts selected on the basis of their initial construction of the therapist, for example as authoritarian or maternal, and;
(c) in terms determined by the actual evolution of the therapeutic relationship.

Whatever is manifest in these ways may be usefully commented upon by the therapist. As regards (a) and (b), the patient's perceptions and actions may reflect narrow, inflexible scripts which have served satisfactorily in the past, with or without the addition of the defensive strategies such as repression and denial, or the distortion of projection. The patients' usual procedures may be manifest in a range of tactical level acts and experiences, both in everyday life and in the transference, which can be seen by the therapist to reflect the terms of higher-order scripts of which the patient is not aware. These higher-order scripts can be described by the therapist, and such descriptions are accepted and found useful by patients. As regards (c), the evolution of the transference will be shaped in part by the realities of differences in status (self-exposing, help-seeking patient, more or less un-self-revealing, help-giving therapist), in part by the particular style of the patient and therapist, and in part by whatever it is that the patient's needs determine. The therapist's offer to the patient, of non-critical listening and the absence of conventions of logic or politeness, communicate the particular privileges of treatment, which allow the patient to experience and enact aspects of himself that are normally concealed. In particular, childhood-based feelings, and meanings normally hidden or guarded against, may find expression even if regression is not actively fostered, because of the safety that can be established in the therapy situation, and as this safety and the therapist's acceptance are understood, riskier and more anxiety- or guilt-arousing issues can be presented. Not everything that develops in the transference relationship is regressive or shameful, however; often the patient's real wish is for the therapist's recognition of his capacity to be effective and to love.

Transference, a psychoanalytic concept ignored by other schools, is the subject of an enormous and often confusing literature within psychoanalysis. Sandler *et al.* (1973), in discussing the evolution of the concept, propose that it should be distinguished both from the treatment alliance and from those traits that are equally manifest in other relationships. In this view, transference is a unique process evoked by the treatment situation and characterized by the development of specific illusions about the analyst and by attempts to provoke particular responses from the analyst, in ways representing the repetition of aspects of past relationships. However, Sandler *et al*, also concede that such distortions and manipulations may occur, though without being recognized, in non-treatment situations, so that this proposed, exclusive classification is not entirely satisfactory.

In the evolution of psychoanalytic practice, the interpretations of the transference has become the central, for some virtually the exclusive, intervention. For a specific and highly influential paper on this subject, we can turn to Strachey (1934) who approaches his issue with considerable detail and clarity. Strachey retraces the evolution of Freud's thinking from an early concern with the recognition of unconscious desires and drives to his recognition that "as analysts, our main task is not so much to investigate the objectionable unconscious trends, as to get rid of the patient's resistance to it." The energy for this task of overcoming resistance was seen to come from the transference:

> Instead of having to deal as best we may with conflicts of the remote past, which are concerned with dead circumstances and mummified personalities, and whose outcome is already determined, we find ourselves involved in an actual and immediate situation in which we and the patient are the principal characters, and the development of which is to some extent at least under our control; but if we bring it about that, in this revivified transference conflict, the patient chooses a new solution instead of the old one, a solution in which the primitive and unadaptable method of repression is replaced by behaviour more in contact with reality, then even after his detachment from the analysis, he will never be able to fall back into his former neurosis.

Transference analysis has as its main aim the modification of the superego. Strachey, influenced by Klein, sees the superego in the infant as built up out of a vicious circle of re-introjecting projected oral aggression. This circular process (anything but a merry-go-round) begins with the child's destructive feelings for the frustrating mother; these are projected into, and then experienced as coming from, the mother, and by this means a mutually sustaining savage id and savage superego are built up. In the normal child, the balance of positive feeling emerging around the genital stage is supposed to relieve this vicious circle, but in the neurotic it persists and will be manifest, evidently or latently, in the transference relationship with the analyst. The "mutative interpretation" which, in Strachey's view, is the essential instrument of change in psychoanalysis, recognizes and names both the violent, forbidden impulse, and the violent defence against it, and relates this polarization to the confusion seen to exist between the analyst as he really is and the "archaic phantasy object" projected onto him in the negative transference, Such interpretations are effective because the analyst has become the object of the patient's id drives and the quasi replacement of his superego; the repetition of interpretations of this process leads to the permanent modification of the patient's superego.

On the basis of this account, Strachey, and psychoanalysts in general, insist upon the need for "neutrality" on the part of the analyst because "it is a paradoxical fact that the best way of ensuring that his ego shall be able to distinguish between phantasy and reality is to withhold reality from him as much as possible.'' It is argued that any act of the therapist will be experienced by the patient, unconsciously, as representing either an invitation and hence heightening id pressure and provoking increased superego repression, or as a punishment and hence heightening superego pressure. It will thus inevitably feed into the savage id–superego vicious circle. If this point is taken as true, the proposal to combine transference analysis with active methods, which is a central proposition of this book, is clearly absurd.

I think one has to accept that any act of the therapist may have a powerful meaning to the patient, and if a strong transference relationship has developed this will include meanings articulated at a primitive level. What I am not so clear about, however, is whether there is any way of being with an analyst for 5 hours weekly, at considerable expense, that does *not* accord to him a powerful reality. The analytical argument is really for the provision of a particular kind of presence; that of a literally and personally invisible, largely silent and withholding, deliberately opaque, occasionally speaking, and implicitly helpful presence. Such a presence may be appropriate for some patients, but I cannot see that it is necessarily so for all; it will have very different meanings according to the patient's history. For some, and especially for those previously exposed to, or themselves operating in, similar controlling and withholding ways, it can represent sterile mirroring, or can be sensed as persecutory. (Perhaps the preoccupation of Kleinian theory with schizoid–paranoid phenomena and the predilection of Kleinians for violent language stems from their patients' reactions to this opaque stance?). Moreover, the personally inaccessible analyst, when he does speak, offers a form of interpretation which throws into question at a very fundamental level the patient's self-understandings. I cannot believe that these somewhat Olympian pronouncements, even if accurate, are not at times experienced as powerful challenges to the patient's reality sense, even though Strachey says that ''the patient's ego is so weak, so much at the mercy of his hidden superego that it can only cope with reality if it is administered in minimal doses and these doses are in fact what the analyst gives him in the form of interpretations.'' I find myself doubting both the description of the interpretation and of the patient implied in this passage. Those neurotics with clearly weak egos (the borderline cases and narcissistic personality disorders) seem to do rather poorly in classical analysis. Those who do well are the healthier ones, most of whom have shown an ability to cope with some areas of their lives, and many of whom have demonstrated considerable strength and courage in surviving past bad experiences, and in managing the conflicts and pressures they impose upon themselves. Some of the ego weakness apparent on the couch may be a weakness induced by the couch.

Further questions about this model of change are raised by a more recent brief paper addressed to the same general issue. Khan (1970) argued that the major problem that faces the analyst, especially with the more sick patient, is not his "authentic illness" (by which he means, I think, the condition capable of description in classical psychoanalytic terms) but rather the patient's "practice of self-cure". This practice of self-cure, Khan argues "is rigidly established by the time he reaches us. To treat this practice of self-cure merely as resistance is to fail to acknowledge its true value for the person of the patient". I would personally extend this somewhat backhanded recognition of the patient's capacities by suggesting that, if we look at how most neurotic patients live their lives, we will often find their problems are not primarily those of a beleaguered ego crushed in the vicious circle of savage id–superego conflict, but are rather those of people operating with a set of strategies somwhat less adaptive than those of their neighbours. Most of these strategies will, however, have served well enough in the past; the inadequacy of them at this point in time has been exposed by their failure to cope with new situations or by the recognition that they are restricting growth. Although to some extent the neurotic person's strategies will differ from those of his neighbour in that they are more concerned with ego-defence (that is to say, they will involve more restrictions on awareness or action), many of his difficulties are the result of ways of thinking and acting which were once, but have now ceased to be, effective. These ineffective ways are often easily visible to the therapist, and, once named, are recognized without resistance by the patient. If the therapist names these strategies clearly, and perhaps uses some of the active methods discussed in Chapter 8, he will often find that the patient's weak and beleaguered ego turns out to be remarkably resourceful. Given a conceptual tool, "it" will get on with the job. Moreover, as "it" becomes more effective, "it" becomes stronger and less in need of defence or, as I prefer to say, as the patient gains a sense of greater control, capacity, and value, his need for strategies which distort reality and limit action is reduced. The classical analytic technique has left analysts and their patients ignorant of the effectiveness of all the more direct means of help because analytical theory rules them out, and imposes on the patient a passive and regressed role.

In my experience, the early sharing of accurate descriptions of faulty procedures and of active methods does not prevent the development of transference or the possibility of working with it, although the transference itself will have fewer regressed and paranoid features.

This is not to say that active methods should always be applied; there are patients for whom the right to shape and explore what can be done with the therapist, is very important, and to whom active methods can seem intrusive or irrelevant. A less active approach is often appropriate for the patient who has been unable fully to mourn a past loss; the therapist, by becoming the metaphor for the lost person, allows the process of loss, repeated with the termination of therapy, to be gone through to completion. In this way, those scripts designed to deny the reality of the loss, or diminishing the value of the lost person, and hence of the self in relation to the lost person, can be revised.

Gallwey (1978) has contributed a useful consideration of the transference with special reference to the problems of aim-restricted psychotherapy, by which he means therapy conducted once weekly or for a limited period. In his discussion he notes that quite primitive pathology may be present in the transference without any general regression taking place. He relates this possibility to the mechanism of splitting, contrasting this with the previous analytic ideas in which such primitive pathology would always seem to be the result of regression to earlier modes. In terms of the procedural sequence model, these primitive transference involvements represent unintegrated relationship scripts, the avoidance of which may have dominated the actual form of relationship experienced by the individual. In Gallwey's view the issues of deprivation, limitation, and loss are particularly central in the management of aim-restricted therapies of this sort, and not all patients are able to cope with those problems on once-a-week treatment. He stresses the importance of early recognition of the problems and early involvement between patient and therapist, saying:

> Patients in weekly psychotherapy with whom one does manage to make good early contact can get into the stride of the work in such a way as the times in their weekly sessions take on a regularity characteristic for themselves . . . so that their internal "clock" seems to regulate the experience appropriate to its meaning with extraordinary facility.

The difficulties of time-restricted therapy may be more those affecting the confidence of the therapist than those of the patient because:

> . . . it is much easier to lose track of the reality of the importance of oneself and the work for the patient's unconscious, and become slipshod, particularly if the patient is improving . . . or is effectively concealing his feelings. It is a very pronounced thing about transference work that however much evidence one gets that, when correctly carried out, it militates against regression and makes patients less dependent upon oneself in a clingy, infantile way, the impingement of disturbed dependency within the transfence . . . inevitably leads one to the feeling that one should not attempt to contact it for fear that it will be exacerbated. The very reverse is in fact the case . . .

This paper, which includes sensitive clinical examples, also includes an appropriate warning against bad transference work.

> There is one common shortcoming, however, and that is for therapists not only to shy away from examining and endeavouring to interpret the transference, but to believe they are making transference interpretations, when they are forcing the material into a mother/father/sibling constellation, and relating it ad hoc to themselves. Such facile constructions are sometimes combined with implications that the therapist represents an ideal authority. The combination of banality and pseudo-superiority is at its best ineffectual and exasperating . . .

The closing words from this paper will serve to close this discussion also, as they summarize the situation very clearly:

> . . . I think we intuitively know that the responsibility of involvement in the transference is unique, and once one has made contact at an intimate level of understanding, then the therapeutic effectiveness that it enhances cannot be easily set aside. However, if there is fair contact with one's own weaknesses, support from

colleagues, and involvement with other people's work, then there is immense interest and satisfaction to be had from the utilisation of the most sensitive and informative of all psychological instruments.

10

Instructions, Constructions, Interpretations, and Strategies

In the last three chapters, the selection of patients, the setting up of therapy, the establishment of its goals, the place of active methods, and the use of the transference have been considered. It has been argued that therapists must know how to create a situation in which patients can reveal their troubles and know how to make sense of, and reframe, these troubles. Beyond this, they need to have certain practical skills at their disposal which they can teach patients to use in the pursuit of self-knowledge and self-control, and they should be familiar with and, in some contexts, able to use, the transference. In the present chapter, further attention will be paid to what therapists say and do, and to the question of planning the strategy of the treatment.

It should be emphasized at this point that, in my view, psychotherapy involves more than techniques: it is the skilful use of the human encounter. The development of closely specified treatment methods and the production of standard treatment manuals have served to introduce some rigour into the field of training and outcome research, but such treatment packages, fortunately, are still delivered by human therapists of all shapes and sizes, in very different contexts. In my own practice, while drawing upon some of the specific techniques of cognitive and behavioural workers, I never conduct therapy on lines restricted to any one such approach, and the foundation of treatment is always a sharing with the patient of my overall understanding.

The aim of a therapeutic programme is to obtain maximum impact with minimum means. One of the main contentions of this book is that this is best achieved by the early elaboration of treatment goals in the form of high-level explanations or hypotheses about the patient's self-perpetuating faulty procedures. In this, the approach differs from both psychoanalysis and behavioural therapies, where the emphasis is more upon detail: in psychoanalysis, through attention to the minutiae of recollection, fantasy and the transference; in behaviourism by the careful microanalysis of small units of behaviour. In both these approaches, recovery is seen as taking place through a process of generalization. While such detailed attention has its place, especially during the diagnostic phase, the relabelling or reconceptualizing of a problem-maintaining procedure, especially one expressing (although often in many detailed manifestations) a high-level self-identity or strategic script, can free the patient and enable him to alter his behaviour and experience over a wide range, in ways less immediately dependent upon the therapist. I believe that the power of such explanations has been underemphasized. Any act and any understanding that demonstrates or enlarges the patient's capacity to control his life will be therapeutic; but the impact of such gains will be greater to the extent that their relation to central procedures is clear. When the utilization of a concept, or the trying-out of a new way of acting in a small-scale context, is understood to be an application of a general understanding about procedures, the successful small-scale evidence serves to modify the whole class of procedures of which it is a member. Mathematics teachers impart principles, and then set their pupils problems which are to be solved using the terms set out, thus enabling their pupils to make the necessary strategies their own, but they do not set problems and expect the pupils to generate the principles themselves. Patients who are demoralized by making consistent errors in solving their problems surely deserve the same kind of help.

Once a set of overall hypotheses and goals has been developed with the patient, identifying his procedural faults, the therapeutic method can be similarly jointly considered. A few patients will need to work primarily in the transference; but for the majority, the agreed goals and hypotheses will form the basis for continued exploration, in which both active methods and interpretation may play a part.

The cognitive/behavioural techniques appropriate for most neurotic patients are not complicated and do not usually demand a highly detailed behavioural analysis or programme. Self-monitoring, instruction in relaxation and rehearsal in imagination, programmes for graded exposure to overcome avoidance behaviours, and the use of paradoxical intention, can all be described briefly and, with the help of written instructions, patients can be taught to be come their own behaviour therapists. In so doing, they may also gain a more concrete sense of the relationship between acts and outcomes. Patients with highly elaborated behavioural problems or those with suitable types of difficulty who fail to respond to a combination of simple approaches and the general understanding being offered, should be referred for specialist behaviour therapy, but they are a small minority of most neurotic populations.

The active technique of most general use is self-monitoring. Any individual whose symptoms or unwanted behaviours are intermittent, or variable in intensity, can carry out self-monitoring during the assessment phase, with advantage. The minimum gain will be the collection of details of diagnostic importance; often patients report their depressed and self-attacking feelings more explicitly in these writings than they do verbally. Many patients find that monitoring brings to their attention the unrealistic nature of their thoughts, and this commonly enables them to distance themselves from them, recognize their recurrence more quickly and, in time, gain more control over them.

Im terms of the PSM, active methods are effective by altering maladaptive assumptions and evaluations, and by correcting associated trap behaviours. The focused work done on the basis of the dilemma, trap, and snag formulations – identifying blocks to relearning – is effective by increasing the accuracy and sophistication of the patient's self-evaluation, so that his hitherto accepted maladaptive assumptions and strategies become identified by him, relabelled as problems, and opened to modification. While most patients can recognize the truth and relevance of these reformulations (at least provided they are well-rooted in the information provided by the patient and are not a product of the therapist's theory or of his fantasy) many need time to explore and grasp fully their implications and some will, in this process, elaborate or revise aspects of them. This further exploration and elaboration may be assisted by various forms of imaginative exploration and by the more traditional forms of interpretive work which draw upon psychoanalytic theory and involve, in particular, attention to the transference and to dreams.

Even when active methods are used, most of the time spent with the patient can be devoted to discussions of current life situations, of memory, fantasy, and of the transference, and the form of sessions can be left largely unstructured, and determined by the patient.

The sense of control gained by the early provision of a general explanatory framework, and by the early experience of increasing control over symptoms and behaviour, assists the patient in the task of abandoning restricted defensive strategies of thought or action, and serves to support, rather than interfere with, the work of dynamic therapy. Such an assertion does not essentially contradict the psychoanalytic view that the aim of therapy is to extend the power of the ego, but it would nonetheless be regarded as inappropriate by most workers in the psychoanalytic tradition, even by those working in time-limited therapy, where the need for therapist activity and goal specificity are acknowledged. The conventional wisdom rests upon the polarization of regressive–reconstructive and repressive–constructive treatments. Conventional psychoanalytic treatment, in this view, offers regressive reconstruction and is hence virtuous in that it does not impose solutions on the patient; whereas active methods are repressive–constructive and, even if effective, are not virtuous. The assumption that the only way to strengthen the ego is to induce its temporary (i.e. for up to 5 or 7 years) regression in the relationship with a powerful analyst, is paradoxical and requires more evidence in its favour than has been provided so far. Active methods, and the interpretation of the transference in non-regressed patients, do not impose values or solutions on patients, and it is wrong to describe such methods as repressive. The provision of concepts and cognitive skills to patients allows them to pursue their own solution and frees them to explore and re-assess their strategies and to pursue their own aims on their own terms. If the large explanatory theories developed at the start of treatment turn out to be wrong, or wrong in detail, their revision by the therapist and patient together is a useful enterprise and a good learning experience; if they are more or less right they offer a powerful means to the patient of revising ineffective procedures.

By the time assessment and the joint consideration of method has been concluded, therapeutic change will usually have commenced and a therapeutic mode satisfactory to patient and therapist will have been established. The patient has said, in effect, "These are my troubles and this is who I am." The therapist has answered, "This is how I understand what you say. This is how I see how things go wrong. These are the ways I think I can help you. These are the things you can begin to do." In terms of the PSM, the possibilities of the therapeutic situation have been clarified, the nature of therapist and patient roles have been established, the therapist's belief in his own and in the patient's efficacy has been conveyed, and there has been some discussion and some trying out of alternative means, usually with some positive evaluation of the effects.

SHARING UNDERSTANDINGS WITH THE PATIENT: CONSTRUCTIONS

In psychoanalytic terminology, constructions – or reconstructions – represent the more or less elaborate linking up of hypothesized events in infancy and childhood with current difficulties. This reconstruction is genetic, that is to say it seeks to make sense of what is now experienced in terms of the meaning system derived from the earlier stage. The status of such construction is, of course, hypothetical: "Only the further course of the analysis enables us to decide whether our constructions are correct or unserviceable" wrote Freud (1937), but the "assured conviction of the truth of the construction ... achieves the same therapeutic result as a recaptured memory."

Memories, in the cognitive view, can be reconstructed but never recaptured; moreover, as memory is a store of schemata organizing perceptions, understandings, and actions, the revision of this store, whether by rewriting the past by way of a recaptured memory, or by the use of a serviceable (but perhaps not necessarily "correct") construction will affect the current system of scripts.

One of the major differences between time-limited psychoanalytically based therapy and the time-limited cognitive analytic therapy that I am proposing, revolves around these constructions. The emphasis of most psychoanalytic workers is on the interpretation of the transference around specific events. While such interpretations may sometimes be the main form of treatment, most patients, in my experience, gain considerable early relief and control from the early presentation of more general constructions of their self-perpetuating ineffective scripts. These formulations do not set out to be genetic reconstructions, although they may draw upon historical data; the emphasis is upon identifying current, self-perpetuating, negative procedures.

It is not the patient's history, *per se*, that interests the therapist; it is the conclusions that the patient has drawn from it.

INTERPRETATIONS

Interpretations are understandings of specific incidents or experiences. Sandler *et al.* (1973) write as follows:

> . . . it would appear that therapeutic change as a consequence of analysis depends, to a large degree, on the provision of a structured and organised conceptual and affective framework within which the patient can effectively place himself and his subjective experience of himself and others.

Interpretations are ways of making explicit sense of a patient's particular experiences, including those aspects which are incompletely known and recognized by him. The subject matter of interpretation is any reported situation, memory, fantasy or dream, and the patient's behaviour towards the therapist. Interpretation can involve translating hints, disguised statements, or symbols offered by the patient; it may include noting contradictory or conflicting elements in what is being presented, and will often involve noting what is *not* said and *not* done as much as what *is* said and done.

It is usually implied by psychoanalytic writers that the patient's inability to understand fully the meanings of his own acts and communications is necessarily due to the operation of defences. I have argued earlier that patients' failures to name their higher-order scripts, which are serving to pattern individual acts, may be based on no more than the easily remediable lack of appropriate concepts with which to name them. It is for this reason that the early provision of broad, accessible constructions is of such value. However, transference interpretations become of crucial importance when the transference relationship illustrates the enactment without resolution of the issues named in the basic dilemma, trap, and snag formulations, and it is particularly clarifying where the more primitive and disorienting processes of projection and splitting are manifest.

The conventional form of giving an interpretation is somewhat tentative, the aim being to avoid suggestion. There are, however, many occasions, particularly in brief therapy, when it is quite appropriate to argue, confront, and suggest. For example, a patient crippled by harsh, self-judgemental scripts, who can accept and understand the need to mitigate unjustified attacks on the self, may learn more, and faster, if one is prepared not just to interpret the evidence for a "harsh superego", but to provide detailed suggestions on how to improve self-care. In doing this, one must be prepared to justify proposed acts in terms of equity and justice; one must be prepared to argue forcibly with the assumption formed by the patient's history, and one should be prepared to define the values on which the suggestions rest, in order that the patient can choose whether to accept or resist them. In terms of the PSM, one is attending in this way, not only to the patient's biased reading of the situation and to his destructive self-identity judgemental scripts, one is also helping with the generation of alternative methods of proceeding and modifying negative self-efficacy assumptions by enhancing his capacity for self-care.

Such active interventions are usually ways of challenging undermining, negative self-judgements. Sometimes, however, the naming and challenging of self-prohibiting scripts is not adequate, and in that case additional help may be required in the interpretation of what, in psychoanalysis, would be called "id drives", i.e. suppressed aims to do with sex or aggression. Difficulties in the expression of feeling that stem from self-punishing inhibitions are often experienced in ways that can be described as dilemmas (e.g. feelings are *either* totally controlled *or* chaotic). In such cases, the elaboration of effective forms of alternative action can be a great help. The transference may provide the patient with his first experience of a feeling that is both acknowledged and contained, but he may also be helped with detailed consideration of his procedures in other relationships. The ability to act on the basis of feeling demands both that feelings be acknowledged and permitted and that their expression is under control.

DREAMS

One particular focus of interpretation that played an important part in the evolution of psychoanalysis is that applied to dreams. The following example illustrates the use and interest of dreams in therapy.

Rachel

At the end of the first assessment session with Rachel—a young woman who had incompletely recovered from anorexia nervosa, who seemed over-controlled and out of touch with her feelings—I asked if she dreamt and suggested that one could sometimes find out about oneself by considering one's dreams. During the night before her second session, she dreamt for the first time for two months; in this dream, she was forced to work all day at a boring job in order to pay for her studies which she was obliged to pursue at night. This illustrates many of the reasons that make dreams of interest to the psychotherapist: the fact that she remembered the dream and the timing of it expressed co-operation or compliance, while the content of the dream with its heavy burden of nightwork told of a more complaining response. Rachel is further described in Chapter 12.

The interesting thing about dreams is that they are made up by the dreamer. The remembered dream is inevitably an edited one, for most dream images are muddled and vague, and it is in our "effort after meaning" (Bartlett 1954) that we put structure upon them. In that process of putting structure, we will select certain meanings and suppress others, a process that becomes more marked still when we communicate the dream to another. The recounted dream, therefore, is a conflation of the original images and the meanings applied to them; but the fact remains that both the images and the editing are the product of the dreamer and can convey news about him. Thinking about a dream and trying to explore what other possible meanings the images might have often reveals ambiguities and can illuminate the underlying conflicted meanings in the person's mind.

In the context of psychotherapy, the dream becomes a communication to the therapist. What is dreamt, and how it is told, will be related to the stage of therapy and to the transference relationship with the therapist. The value of dreams lies precisely in their basic vagueness and in their apparently unbidden quality, which allows the patient, in some degree, to disclaim responsibility for them, and therefore to present aspects of himself that are not fully or easily acknowledged. Moreover, especially for some creative dreamers, the way in which thoughts or ideas are expressed can often be in a highly condensed and symbolic form. Discussion of a dream with a patient, therefore, is an opportunity for the therapist to extend and to share subtle understandings, while simultaneously showing his acceptance of the contradictory and "forbidden" aspects of the patient's thoughts and wishes. Many dreams, of course, cannot be understood, and indeed some seem to be transference challenges defying understanding, but the establishment of the use of dreams in therapy, in which the transference implications are explored in relation to the patient's problems, can be a considerable aid to progress. In order to demonstrate some aspects of dreaming, we will return to the two patients, whom we have followed through the book, Anne and David.

Anne

Anne discussed dreams on four occasions during the first phase of her therapy. The ninth session followed the first interruption in therapy, during which she had in general managed rather well, and had felt much more in control. Half-way through the period she had a dream in which she was in a mental hospital under my care: I had been taking her pulse and arranging an electrocardiogram, and she thought to herself, "It can't be a mental hospital, it must be an ordinary one". Then she thought, "Oh, on, he's just doing the cardiogram in order to placate me. It really is a mental hospital all the time." This dream illustrates, but does not extend particularly, our understanding of Anne's fear of mental illness and her mixed feelings and mistrust of me during my absence. That session ended with the discussion of mealtimes at home, terrible occasions of immense tension, at which she had been required to get meals ready as a sign that she loved her mother, eat them quickly, not talk to daddy, and when she had finished eating, get up immediately and wash the dishes. At the next (tenth) session, she came with a dream continuing these "oral" preoccupations. She and her siblings had been kept for years in a garage, and they were thin, like the photographs of starving children used to obtain support for Oxfam. In the dream, she and her siblings had escaped, but the others had been too weak to keep up with her. Father had chased them but had been unable to reach the roof that she was on, and she finally escaped to a neighbour's house. There, she found her father, but now she had a pistol in her hand; she fired at him but it was only a toy pistol, at which point she just patted him on the face. Anne was able to see how the early part of this dream represented a fuller recognition than she had been able to give before to the deprivation of her early years. As a result of the dream she had been able to talk much more openly with her husband and had discussed how, before her acute symptoms had come on, she had felt a number of strains in herself, and between them, which they had not been able to discuss at that time. The dream also conveyed a deep ambivalence towards her father (and probably to me). The siblings who failed to escape could represent her actual siblings who were still living at home, or could represent that part of her which was not yet free. The conventional, and probably appropriate, interpretation of the pistol as a penis symbol was not discussed.

At her fourteenth session Anne told of a dream in which she was in a building somewhere between a supermarket and a prison, with her mother, and by an enormous effort she had managed to squeeze herself out through a crack in a locked door. She had then taken shelter in a bar (with a barman in the background), where she gathered strength in order to go to the bookshop where she was to meet her husband. The first part of this dream seemed to express her sense of excape and struggle; the second part, the bar and the barman, stood for the shelter and refreshment of therapy, and the bookshop rendezvous was, perhaps, a reference to the tendency towards intellectualization she shared with her husband. When I commented on the last point she said that the day before they had had one of the most effective and freeing rows that she could remember.

The seventeenth session of therapy had been marked by initial blankness, and then by a surprising and painful experience of direct sadness during which she cried, although she had very quickly dried the tears away again. She had been in and out of a depressed state following that session. Shortly before the eighteenth, she had a dream, located in one of the houses the family had lived in when she was a child. There was woman there, not recognizable, who was dying of a heart attack, who later in the dream transformed clearly into her mother. Her mother was screaming at her; she had been trying to get the ambulance but could not get the address right. The scene shifted to another of the family homes, and her mother was shouting at her father in a way that reminded Anne of the jealous scenes which had recurred during her adolescence. Anne called out three times to her father, "Why don't you leave her and come and live with me". This dream was followed by a lot of painful recollection of family scenes. The end of the dream gives expression to a feeling which had never been consciously acknowledged; it seemed to support my feeling that her anger with, and mistrust of, me, early in therapy (see Chapter 4) had, as I had suggested, a basis in denied wishes for closeness to her father and older men.

David

David was aware that he dreamt quite a lot, but he had a more or less deliberate policy of not attending to dreams because he was worried that to do so would contribute to his bad sleep. In the course of his brief therapy he reported a dream on one occasion, in the third session. He was driving an open car with Patricia, and in front of him saw a similar car which spun round and drove back against the traffic; he saw that this car was driven also by himself and was being chased by another car, and the car he was in joined the chase also. There was a crazy ride across uneven country, and then the second car crashed and the car he was in ground to a halt at the foot of a rubbish dump; rubbish began falling down all round them, and Patricia complained that he was failing to protect her from it. This dream seemed to contain many of the aspects of David's emotional response to his situation (see Chapter 5) but I was unable to make very much sense of it beyond that; perhaps for that reason he did not bring any more dreams.

DISCUSSION

Evidence of the helpful effects of combining behavioural techniques with psychodynamic psychotherapy is provided by a number of authors in Marmor and Woods (1980). Of particular interest to the argument I am putting forward is a paper by Segraves and Smith in this volume, describing simultaneous treatment of patients by a behaviour therapist and a dynamic therapist. Three case histories are given. The two therapists confined their interventions to the terms of their respective theoretical positions. It is evident from the case histories that the emergence of transference issues and the recovery of important memories and understandings, occurred specifically in relation to the progress of the behavioural therapy and in the context of the patient's relationship with the behaviour therapist. The working through of such issues was left to the dynamic therapist. Other authors in Marmor and Woods report the use of combined methods by single therapists, which is clearly more economical and perhaps less confusing for the patient. Olds (1981) reports the effectiveness of introducing active techniques (rehearsal in fantasy, record-keeping, paradoxical intention) in accelerating psychoanalytic therapy. Planning of such treatments would obviously be easier if the dynamic and behavioural methods, currently based upon quite different theoretical models, could be related in the single cognitive model which I am proposing in the PSM.

For many people, the distinction between active and interpretive methods in therapy is equated with that between superficiality and depth. The concept of depth is psychoanalytically derived, referring to the infantile stage at which the patient's trauma or developmental failure occurred ("early" implying "deep"). As regards therapies, Cawley (quoted in Brown and Pedder, 1979) suggests a three-level classification from:

(a) the most *superficial*, consisting of the patient's unburdening of his problems, ventilation of feelings within a supportive relationship and discussion of current difficulties with a non-judgmental helper;

(b) *intermediate* (overlapping the above and the deeper level), consisting of clarification of problems within a developing therapeutic relationship, confrontation of defences, interpretation of unconscious motives, and transference phenomena; and

(c) *deep,* consisting of exploration and analysis through repetition and remembering and reconstruction of the past, regression through less adult levels, and resolution of conflicts by re-experiencing and working through.

This classification is based upon an implicit equation of the depth of the difficulty and the depth of the treatment, and reflects the belief that really fundamental change demands analytical treatment. This view, in turn, conflates the belief that adult difficulties are historically-determined, especially through the persistence of unintegrated conflictual issues dating back to infancy (which is clearly often the case), with the assumption that regression and resolution through re-experiencing (the psychoanalytic three Rs) is the only route to recovery. It is here that the cognitive-analytic approach I propose parts company with the traditional psychoanalytic one. The reports that active methods are slightly better than interpretive ones for patients with more serious disorders (Sloane *et al.*, 1975), that profound dynamic changes can follow minimal therapy or life events (Malan *et al.*, 1975), and that in practice at least one analyst (Balint) was both active and didactic when treating an ill patient with focal therapy (Strupp, 1975), argue against the orthodox position and there is no really satisfactory support for the belief that full-scale analysis produces more profound changes than shorter methods (see also Appelbaum, 1977). This does not mean that it may not offer some people a valuable and desired experience.

The fact that our present understandings are built upon our historical experience is true; thought and memory are, in an important sense, indistinguishable. But we continue to elaborate and refine our understandings and strategies without having to dismantle the whole structure and start again (not that we can, anyway, start again in any real sense) and in my view it is the obstacles to such elaborations and refinements that are the proper targets of psychotherapy.

The tactical implications of this view are important. Instead of consigning patients to the superficial approaches of ventilation and non-judgemental chat, we can offer all patients a reframing of their troubles by identifying the obstacles to change and, at least in some areas and aspects of their difficulties, we can try out the effects of teaching relevant skills. For some, this approach can profoundly influence their lives; for others, the correction of old assumptions and strategies may require to be dealt with through some form of transference work, although this can usually be relatively brief and need not involve regression.

One must assume that there are some patients for whom the experience of full-scale analysis for 4 or 5 hours weekly for several years, with the development of a regressed transference, is necessary; but the analytic literature provides little guidance towards the recognition of such patients, the basic conviction seeming to be that it is the ideal treatment for all able to pay for it. The refusal to countenance active methods is in no way a necessary corollary of the model of mental processes proposed by psychoanalysis; it is based rather upon tradition and faith, and upon a system of training whose primary aim is the preservation of this tradition. Perhaps therapeutic methods, as well as training, have as one main function the defence of the purity of theory and tradition?

Schafer (1978) proposes that the distinctive features of psychoanalytic treatment are as follows:

> First, psychoanalysis is the consistent attempt to understand the analysand's reports of private and public psychological events, especially in the transference and resistance, as actions that are susceptible to interpretation and re-interpretation . . . These reports are considered . . . as actions, some of which underemphasize agency and others of which overemphasize it. Second, the psychoanalyst develops a focus on the archaic, more or less bodily and unconsciously maintained, meanings of these actions, and third, the analyst states these meanings in terms of conflictual, sexual, and aggressive wishings and imaginings, and in terms of those relevant infantile zones, substances and situations, which seem to threaten or enhance the self and others in relationships.

The first of Schafter's points defines for me the essential nature of interpretive psychotherapy; the second and the third refer to psychoanalytic theories of infantile development which may serve to inform the analyst and will help enlarge his understanding, for example of metaphor or of symptoms, but how often, how far, or in what sense the psychotherapist needs to *focus* upon these archaic meanings and state them in terms of "relevant infantile zones" etc., seems very uncertain. I suspect that for most patients full recovery is possible without this, and that in many cases the induction and interpretation of the regressed transference is unnecessary and possibly disabling. At least one has to accept that evidence to contradict this belief is largely lacking.

11
Difficult Patients

The secret of success for a psychotherapist is to treat patients who are not too seriously troubled. This is not a cynical remark for, in terms of human happiness, brief therapy with a basically healthy person with a definable problem is extremely worthwhile. However, attention needs to be given to more troubled patients for a number of reasons, including the fact that, in the ordinary professional work of psychiatrists, general practitioners, psychologists, and social workers, such patients are unavoidably present and often demanding, and in the experience of the trainee psychiatrist will tend to form a large proportion of his non-psychotic population. Moreover, psychotherapy with some sicker patients can be extremely effective and not necessarily lengthy; but it can also do harm.

The difficult patient is not necessarily the very sick one. Sometimes the difficulty may reflect an inappropriate selection for psychotherapy—something which careful assessment and an explicit discussion with the patient, of the aims and methods, can make less likely. At other times it can represent a difficulty in the therapist in the form of faulty technique or an awkward counter-transference. However, patients who threaten suicide, who overdose, or cut themselves, and patients who lose sight of the "as if" quality of the transference relationship are usually sicker than average. They also provoke, and may be responding to, more difficult counter-transference reactions. Because some covert and unacknowledged aspects of the therapist's response may be contributing to the difficulty, the therapist looking after such patients will always be helped by supervision. In most cases, if the therapist can calmly hold the line and make sense of the transference by relating it to the focal issues of the therapy, the situation will be contained, and this containment is a helpful experience and gives the patient more control over his own feelings. The reverse situation, in which the patient perceives or is given a collusive response, is experienced as alarming. Patients in whom such difficult transference—counter-transference reactions emerge are likely to be labelled as "schizoid", "borderline" or as having "narcissistic personality disorders". These labels are used in the psychoanalytic literature, but unfortunately there is no agreement as to the precise diagnostic criteria. In the medical psychiatric diagnostic scheme, patients in this category may appear variously, and not always helpfully, labelled according to their predominant symptoms; for example, as "personality disorder", "psychopathy", or "addiction". The basis of the psychoanalytic classification is a developmental one, and the terms used draw attention to developmentally early failures. Such patients are different from less ill ones in that their problems in life and in their relationships are expressions of a poorly and incompletely developed self-structure. For the psychotherapist, it is crucial to recognize these cases because of the much greater risk of evoking damaging regression in them. The impaired ability of these patients to maintain a sense of self and a satisfactory relationship with others is manifest in many different ways, often in more than one way in a given patient. These ways include hysterical behaviours, such as uncontrollable bursts of disordered feeling, histrionics, clinging dependency on others, sexually perverse behaviours, frightening experiences of personal disintegration, feelings of unreality, paralysing obsessive states, massive use of the defence of projection with areas or episodes of paranoid thinking, and attacks on, or serious deprivation of, the self. While the "ordinary neurotic" may be gravely restricted by the various devices he relies upon to feel safe, such as denying feeling, bodily symptoms, symbolic or magical thinking and acting, and the placing of restrictions on his personality and forms of relationship, these sicker patients have lost control; they act out what the less sick patient contains or structures into some kind of a life.

In terms of the PSM they have a more precarious and contradictory self theory, a more arbitrary and inconsistent basis for self-judgement, greater confusion of contradictory intentional scripts, a more distorted, poorly integrated and simpler schematic representation of the world, and a confusion of self–self and self–other scripts, manifest in projection and projective identification. As is evident from this summary we are dealing with questions of degree rather than category, and hence the selection of patients for therapy remains problematic. While multiple symptomatology may draw attention to severe problems, recognition of the degree of disorder held in check by obsessional devices or by schizoid (i.e. cold, uninvolved, intellectualized) modes of relating to others may be more difficult. If there is evidence of areas of sustained competence in the history of a patient being considered for psychotherapy, or if there has been, or is, a good positive relationship with some human being, the therapist may derive some reassurance and be less alarmed by other areas of extreme disturbance. Most people would agree that frank schizophrenia or severe endogenous depression make a patient inaccessible to psychotherapy and indicate the need for pharmacological treatments, but there are many patients who have had psychotic episodes, or who experience some psychotic symptoms, who may be accessible to therapy. The judgement that this is the case would be based upon the "mitigating circumstances" named above, and also on the evolution of the patient–therapist relationship over the assessment sessions. If there is early evidence of contempt or destructive envy, or if there is idealization probably covering over such feelings, the therapeutic path is likely to be a stormy one, whereas the expression of some realistic understanding of the therapeutic process, and the contacting of some depression or concern at this stage are positive signs.

The decision about what form of treatment to offer and how extensively to aim to change the patient is a difficult one, about which little agreement exists. Orthodox psychoanalytic treatment is probably unsuitable, even for those few for whom it is available, for these patients can easily become locked in battling and erosive treatment relationships. Variations in analytical technique are a current topic of hot but unresolved debate. Winnicott (1965) has argued that the need of these patients is for the provision of a symbolic ''holding'' and ''unclever ego-support'' which ''like the task of the mother in infant care, acknowledges tacitly the tendency of the patient to disintegrate, to cease to exist, to fall forever''. Treatment of intensity and long duration may be the only way to provide a good enough basis for re-integration. This type of work is outside the scope of this book, but some of the literature referring to it will be mentioned in the discussion section of this chapter. The approach may involve accepting a degree of regression in the patient which is only justified if circumstances can permit a long-term contract. Other approaches, however, seem to be satisfactory for many patients. Group therapy, which carries fewer risks of severe dependency and regression, can often be very helpful to these patients and less sick group members may be helped by their presence in the group (Pines 1981). Working in the group does require, however, some capacity to share, and that is not always available.

Two other approaches will be discussed in this chapter. The first is the deliberate provision of a very limited amount of therapy time, designed to minimize the chance of regression and to maximize the patient's awareness of ambivalence while, at the same time, energetically and supportively offering explanatory concepts and using direct methods that can enlarge the patient's control. This approach is based upon the belief that in these, as in less sick patients, the addition of active methods enlarges the patient's sense of his own capacity, while the limited care offered implicitly conveys the expectation that the patient can find new resources, and in this way serves to alter his assumptions and predictions about his value and performance. The experience of an intensely ambivalent transference is less frightening when it is not linked with the heightened sense of helplessness that can accompany the regressed transference in treatment carried out in purely interpretive ways. The second approach involves the brief provision of carefully planned institutional care.

STRICTLY LIMITED THERAPY: TWO CASE HISTORIES

Kate

Kate was under psychiatric care between the ages of 16 and 20, during which time she spent a year as an inpatient with a diagnosis of schizophrenia. She was treated at that time with electroconvulsive therapy and with prolonged drug treatment. She was referred for a psychiatric opinion once more at the age of 30, at which time she was complaining of depression and of phases of extreme lack of confidence. At her first interview she talked about hearing voices instructing her or debating her behaviour, but she said she always felt able to act independently of them. Her main complaint was that "I don't know who I am". Kate had left school (illegally) at the age of 12, and, although she had obtained some further education and training later, she had been unable to find work for the past 2 years. Despite this unpromising history, Kate, once given the chance to talk about herself and her life, used therapy very constructively. She was seen for 25 half-hour sessions over a 15-month period. During this time her previous pattern of relating, which was marked by idealizing attachments to (lesbian) partners which had always been followed by disappointment and rejection, was given up. She became much more accepting of herself and more able to be at ease with other people, and she reported no further hallucinatory experiences. At the end of treatment she found suitable and interesting work. Quite early on in her therapy she brought the following poem, which had been written some 2 years previously; the last line of the poem seems to indicate unextinguished hope which, in some sense, was realized metaphorically in her brief therapy.

MOTHER MOTHER

Mother I fear you reard me wrong cause I pick up my head, can't tell where I belong, Mother something's hurting me bad, Something's hurting me real bad, Life has begunning for something that I never had, Sometimes I feel my life has come and gone, I have in this world, But I'm only looking on, I can't understand, Its too far over my head, I'm living in the life, But I'm really dying instead, Yes mother, I'm really dying–dying–dying, but you'll never understand (you-fucking-stupid-bitch), You reard me wrong cause I lift up my head and I can't tell where on this earth I belong, Mother something's terribly wrong
Mother here I am.

This case is an example of the value of "unclever ego-support". From disturbances of her childhood and adolescence, and from an experience of hospitalization, recalled as incomprehensible and unhelpful, Kate had derived a view of the world as hard to predict and of herself as unacceptable. Her attempts to find total acceptance had led to further rejections, and her unemployment was a further contribution to depression. Therapy was an opportunity for her to tell, and make better sense of, the story of her life, and to understand her needs, while giving up the hope of ideal solutions to them.

Ronald

Ronald, a young man of 23, consulted after having been hospitalized briefly for a "heart attack" which, in fact, had been the worst of a series of panic attacks accompanied by palpitation. This last attack had occurred when travelling by train back from a visit to his girlfriend, Mary. The symptom seemed associated with anxiety and the need for the reassurance of the presence and admiration of others.

He described quite unrealistic ambitions professionally and revealed a "superman" view of himself which divided the world into superpeople like his girlfriend and himself, and the second-class majority. He was initially given a general interpretation of his other-dependence, accompanied by some behavioural advice (rehearsal in imagination and graded exposure) which gave him control over the symptoms. Over the next two sessions, which were at monthly intervals, a picture was gained of his background. His mother was both adoring and critically demanding of the patient. She denigrated his father, who was seen as amiable but effaced and ineffective–a view epitomized by mother's account of Ronald's birth: it was a home confinement, the sun, of course, was shining, but it was also very cold, and father had become so distracted by reading the paper with which he was supposed to light the fire, that the room was too cold for Ronald's arrival. Another memory of importance was at the age of 11, at which time he remembered being very depressed, which he related to his final exclusion at that age from the parental bed.

Ronald traced the evolution of his superman self to the sense of feeling unwanted at the age of 11; he saw himself then as bravely facing the pain of that situation and as adopting a nihilistic view of human activity, in both respects seeing himself as superior to his fellows. At the same time, he saw his persistent need for approval as leading to conflict with his more self-accepting peers, which set him apart as different – more serious and misunderstood – but once more as superior. A third strain was linked with his identification with Nietschze, who was seen as both superman and as going off the rails; to reassure himself that he need not go off the rails, he had to dismiss as inferior anybody who seemed hostile to, or who disagreed with, him; while the approval of those who were sympathetic, and preferably older, was crucial if his doubt and fear were to be contained. These threats had combined to present him with two dilemmas: "*either* superior *or* mad", and "*if* not admired by admirable people, *then* contemptible".

After the third session, his girlfriend gave him up and shortly after that he became much more anxious and depressed. From this time on, he began to dismantle his self-idealization and became able to tell his friends something of his troubles and to mix with the common herd to the extent, for example, of watching football matches which previously he had always avoided doing. A date was fixed for the end of therapy, and the sessions were increased to become fortnightly rather than monthly. Therapy aimed at supporting him during the process of losing his idealized girlfriend and losing his self-idealization, while simultaneously dealing with the involvement and anticipated loss of his therapist. He developed some homosexual anxiety in the company of friends during this time, which was relieved following the interpretation of some unacknowledged passive homosexual feelings in his transference relationship.

In Ronald's case, his narcissistic problems represented a continuation of mother's critical idealization. While her care included affection, it had been at the cost of denying any strength to the father, and had left him with either idealization or denigration as being the only modes of relating to himself or to others. In losing his idealized girlfriend, and in having to accept that he was not my only, or most favoured, patient, he went through a lot of emotional pain, being partly sustained in this process by some residual idealization of himself as a good patient, which I probably colluded with to some extent. It was also true that he showed courage and worked hard at this task. At a follow-up interview about 8 months after termination, we looked back on the therapy; the following are excerpts from a tape-recording of this interview:

> To some degree, since I started the therapy and broke up with my girlfriend, I have had no close friends. The way I treated my close friends, I didn't want to do that any more, so basically I decided to go it alone. The need is still there to have people tell you how great you are; I just avoid it to some degree . . . As I see it, one by one I've withdrawn from those special people. I started off having my mother, in childhood, with me; then I had Mary, so I had two; then possibly with you I had three. But I think you were, from the beginning, saying "I'm going to go", which was very constructive, it sort of hooks you exactly where you want to be hooked and makes you very powerful. It also means you've got to manage without . . . It didn't impinge on me rationally, but looking back on it, the deprivation was a far more important aspect of it than I had recognized . . . If I had seen you once a week or more than that I'd have been in real trouble. I was always in danger of having my own personality submerged by yours or in giving out everything to you . . . I would have loved to have been you twice a week and if I had there are all sorts of problems that I wouldn't have faced. Between those fortnightly meetings there was always a drawing up of charts and thinking about it and that was all part of doing it on your own. Since I last saw you, it has been the same thing. It has been to some extent recognizing that I have seen things, and if I had seen you during that week it might have gone further and faster. But the fact that I have done them on my own, that I haven't got you, was useful . . . When the final deprivation comes, you have been through it ten, fifteen times before and it is just a bigger one of those and you can just start to mesh reality in with your picture of it . . . From quite an early stage, I was starting to say, you know, 3 or 4 months, how many more weeks have we got, and at the end it came like a sort of fear of death; the end became very significant, but towards the end it seemed to me in a sense I was wanting just to get free of you . . . I was expecting it to be a relief, I was expecting to get part of myself which I had given away back but I didn't feel like that, I was very depressed and confused but I think but it was a sort of confusing out of which something comes . . . The most important change is to be in touch with feelings. I mean, you said, "You're not very much in touch with your feelings" sometimes, and that basically is what it comes down to – to be in touch with your feelings. What I learnt from therapy was that your expectation immediately is that you're going to be put in touch with nice feelings, you know, things will become rosy and marvellous, and that was the first disappointment and disillusion . . . But if you have completely lost relationship with your feelings, nothing good has any satisfaction for you. If something good happened to me I couldn't value it because it was never good enough. It doesn't make you the superman you want to be, it just means, it makes you feel, well, I'm 6 feet tall, I'm not 100 feet, you know it's no good, everything good is more or less lost to you and when things that are bad hapen to you you can't face them head on, or come to terms with them, or even cry about them. I mean, grief is a sort of therapeutic process, but instead of feeling sad it's all converted into hostility towards yourself, mocking yourself, anger towards yourself. . . . Initially what happened to me was that being in touch with my feelings meant being in touch with a certain amount of grief and guilt and anxiety; now, if someone says, "Are you anxious?", I say, "Yes" because I recognize I am, although far less anxious than I was.

> The thing is that being slightly anxious and recognizing you're anxious, or even being very anxious and recognizing it, is much easier to bear than being terribly anxious and not recognizing it at all. Also, it's only very recently that I've grasped that by not being a superman I'm not being a failure. Before, if someone said, "Look, you're not a superman" I would think I'm a failure. It's only very recently that I started to recognize I'm not a superman, that I am human, therefore I'm not a failure.

In a follow-up letter two years later, Ronald reported that his realistic career plans were proceeding well. He was still busy thinking about himself, he felt he could do that quite successfully, concluding with the words:

> My relationship with my new girlfriend is fraught with problems but seems to work somehow; I make all the same mistakes I made with Mary but I try to resolve them differently in the light of experience ...
>
> It can scarcely be said – and here I am close to tears – that I have made a swift recovery ... while mourning the loss of Mary, I have taken time to do a thorough job and mourn my childhood too ...

The letter ended with a discussion about whether to seek psychoanalysis.

Nearly 4 years after the end of treatment, 18 months later, he reported progress in his profession, a continuing and closer relationship with his girlfriend, and better terms with his parents. He wrote:

> How do I feel? Melancholy, despairing, anxious, still cursed by a pervasive optimism, nervous, ill-at-ease, frightened, ashamed, depressed, and lacking a secure sense of self-esteem. I still feel very often that meeting people is a performance in which I must attempt to impress them. What is different is the degree. All of these feelings are weakened. My self-knowledge has grown. And in recent months – for the first time – these unpleasant feelings have become tolerable ... most gratifying is a noticeable increase in the clarity of my thoughts, which has always been dogged by confusions, forbidden areas, paradoxes, rationalizations ... I am happier and sometimes plain "happy" ...

The symptoms which brought Ronald into treatment were the physical effects (and secondary anxiety about these) of a mismatch between self as perceived and the idealized self he required himself to be and required idealized others to see him as. Therapy had first had to control and translate the symptoms, and thereafter had initiated a slow process of self-acceptance on more ordinary terms.

SYMBOLIC REGRESSION DURING BRIEF INPATIENT CARE

Despite the general emphasis in this book on preventing regression, there are occasions when permitting a limited, controlled regression is profoundly healing. Our culture frowns on helplessness and offers few opportunities for it, yet, for some people, being allowed to go back into permitted helplessness enables them to revise the terms of their relationships and their independence towards a much healthier state. I have seen two patients in whom severe injuries from road traffic accidents necessitated prolonged hospitalization. In one, the accident was the result of a suicidal attempt, made after 5 years of drug therapy for schizophrenia. The surgeon stopped all medication and she used her "licenced" dependency in the surgical ward to begin a process of recovery that 5 years later was still progressing. The other patient was an unhappy, withdrawn young woman, whom I had treated psychotherapeutically without much success. In this case, she was not responsible for her accident. She too was deeply moved by the care she received and, despite chronic pain, was relieved of much of her inner bleakness by the extensive care she received following the accident. These stories serve to reinforce my belief that therapists should not turn their faces inexorably against the possibility that regression can be a benign experience.

I believe there are some adult patients similar to the unintegrated children in residential care described by Dockar-Drysdale (1968) who, before they can grow, need the experience of a permitted, controlled, time-limited period of symbolic regression, as inpatients or, sometimes, as daypatients.

My experience in this form of management is based upon work in the University Health Service at Sussex, which has a small inpatient unit. (In describing this work I would like to acknowledge the collective contribution of my colleagues there, and especially the work, in developing the approach, of three senior nursing sisters, Nancy MacKenzie – who, partly as a result of this work, is now a psychotherapist, Cecily Manser, and Ginette Dight.) Because of the high level of staff communication involved, and the inevitability of staff tensions evoked by these patients, the approach I am going to describe would not be manageable in a large unit caring for patients with a wide range of problems. However, the provision of a small "intensive care unit" within the context of a general admission ward would not be impossible, and would, I believe, make the containment of such patients less disruptive and more therapeutic.

Selection of patients for this kind of care is a difficult matter, demanding that one distinguishes in advance benign from malignant regression, and my own experience has included wrong choices in which the experience was not helpful and was, in some cases, probably harmful. These patients, in some sense "negotiate" the right to regress, and the nature of this negotiation is predictive of the likely outcome. In the cases which went badly it was marked early on by threats, blackmail, and destructiveness and by the failure of myself and the staff to satisfactorily block acting-out and establish adequately strict limits. This led to recurrent bitter struggles and the generation of extreme staff dissension. With more experience in handling the therapy, the management, and the staff reactions, however, such faulty decisions became avoidable.

Where this intervention was successful, the therapist and patient had already established a good working relationship, in the course of which the patient had become centrally preoccupied with certain historically early issues. The patient evoked in the staff the kind of concern similar to the maternal preoccupation described by Winnicott. They saw themselves as revisiting aspects of the past, or as going through some kind of necessary journey. One such patient, for example, drew the curtains of her cubicle on admission, saying that for the time being she only wanted to concern herself with the weather inside and, during the 6 weeks of her admission, she slowly parted these curtains as she prepared herself to return to the world.

Many of these patients were preoccupied with the stories of, or enacted deeply ambivalent fantasies about, their births, which they saw as having been dangerous for both themselves and their mothers. One, for example, whose admission was prompted by a hypomanic episode, summed this up by saying, "When I was born, my mother nearly died and I was slow to breathe". During their admissions, most of the patients listened to music a great deal, painted, and wrote, often using these products as communications with the therapist. In all cases, they asked for the return of this material at a later stage in therapy, as if they now felt strong enough to take charge again of their chaos or did not want to leave it in the control of somebody else. The drawings and paintings were usually initially unformed, violent in mood, most often in black, red, or brown. Later, they often included images of birth or of body parts, breasts, penises and body cavities predominating, even in patients quite innocent of any knowledge of Freud or of Melanie Klein.

The process was usually clearly related to some kind of metaphoric rebirth in which the transference was initially positive or idealizing, as representing the missed or forgotten experience of good mothering, followed by the emergence of destructive anger and sadness as separation was faced; but the power of these destructive feelings was now made tolerable by the fact that they had experienced the ability of the therapist and of the nurses to be strong as well as caring. During these admissions, which were usually about 3 weeks in duration, therapy sessions were continued and briefer contact might be offered three or four times a week, with the therapist and nurses in constant communication, in order that the transference meanings of all that went on could be shared. Patients, during their admission, were required to dress, make their beds, and take meals in the common room with other patients, but in other respects could choose between staying in their rooms, listening to music, or painting in the common room. Many expressed a need for solitude, and restricted or refused visits from friends. The timing of their discharge had to be determined by the therapist, always over some resistance. As in therapy in general, emphasizing the time-limited nature of the admission serves as an ever-present reminder of the fact that it represents a metaphoric revisiting, not an attempt to make good past hurts and deprivation. After discharge, many of these patients sustained some connection with the staff, usually by visiting as daypatients, and in time our experience of this led us to design a special room furnished with cushions, a record-player, and paints, called "the time-out room", representing essentially a privileged space where the right to be unhappy, or silent, or anxious was granted. Once that room was established many patients in therapy made some use of it, and it served as an even more safely restricted but, for some, adequate experience of care, and reduced the need for admission

Close and detailed communication between all staff members involved with the patient is essential. Without it, the patient will continue to use his usual self-defeating strategies to extract from staff those responses which have been so pain-producing and persistent in the world outside, seeking care by means of incapacity, provoking rejection by provocation, and maintaining his fragmentation by locating different and often warring aspects of himself in relationships with different people. Staff tensions in units caring for such disturbed patients can sometimes be the source of a patient's deterioration; sometimes they are the indirect reverberations to a patient's state. Either way, staff must share their experiences of the patient to prevent harmful effects on both themselves and the patients.

In terms of the PSM, the effect of controlled regression is upon the self-identity criteria. Inability to care for the self, punitive attitudes towards the self, unclear definitions of the boundaries of the self, and the confusions of relationships with others due to projective identification have characterized such patients. What is offered is a combination of a safe, holding environment, with interpretation and explanation. The safety is both in the care and in the understanding, and in the explicit definition of boundaries that is achieved through careful defining of staff and patient roles. In this respect the geographical line between patient accommodation and the kitchen or staff quarters served frequently as important physical representation of separateness and differentiation.

The intense enactment of these issues seems to achieve a critical shift in the intrapsychic "balance of power", so that destructiveness, previously acted out upon the self or projected on to others, or guarded against by massive self-restrictions, becomes less frightening, and trust and hope become stronger. To complete this chapter, I will give a patient's retrospective account of her admission.

Beth

Beth sought therapy at the age of 28, for depression. She had felt unhappy at the age of 19 and had received some therapy at that time. Her present, more severe, depression dated from the birth of her child 3 years before, and from the breaking up of her marriage soon after that time. She had failed to engage herself satisfactorily in a career and she was currently in an emotionally confused tangle with two men. Beth was the only adopted child of relatively elderly parents. Her adoptive father, whom she remembered as warm but ineffective had died some years before, and she and her adoptive mother had a difficult, rather distant, relationship. Beth's admission to sickbay was precipitated by the end of her relationship with one of the two men. The following is Beth's recollection of her "breakdown" and admission to sickbay, which occurred some months after starting therapy; the account was written 2 years later.

> This is truly like remembering labour pains. Almost now I remember my descriptions of the time, as they were told to others, as much as I remember the experience . . . I sank into the mental cushion of the sickbay; that in itself was felt as a great death, out of socially-mediated life and living to dependency: letting-go, asking for help, recognizing pain. To begin with, for a couple of days, just ache and conscious withdrawal, getting through the day with polite interactions with others, hugging the ache. Then a more

profound withdrawal from the social world, a real journey inwards with its accompanying passage through time, back. This was being in "my" room, noise an agony, people exhausting to interact with because they had to be engaged with completely as the defences went down. But at the same time as they were related to completely in the present, they were also slotted into the internal world, they became actors in past events and feelings simultaneously. This must make such an experience truly becoming a child. The world exists as an extension of "I" and only in that way does it make sense. It felt like living consciously and unconsciously simultaneously; the latter a world where time didn't pass out of sight but was somehow incorporated in the present sensation. I seemed to go back and back, or rather wider and wider in my emotional map, so that all things had great significance. It was like unrolling the map of meaning and perception from how one recognizes that a knitting pattern is a message to your moral code. Things jumbled out, all elements of synthesized presentations to the world; for example, finding the fairy-tale ancestors of the poems I had written . . . I was trying to reconstruct, attached to my therapist, held by my therapist, who as guardian of the ego allowed me to redraw its shape. I remember waves of mental pain as this process went on, coming and going. My therapist seemed in absolute communication with me. I remember a moment of panic when I felt shut in and struggling to get out, as if I had reached my birth again. With that sensation came a knowledge inside me that I believed I had destroyed my parents by existing. I struggled through the mental birth canal using my therapist's presence and hope and will-power. It began to be *my* life, *my* entrance in the world. I had made a claim on existence. It seemed if I looked and kept looking at the feelings, if I swam through them, then I would get out the other side. I wouldn't sleep because the man who had recently left me could enter my mind's window. I wouldn't leave my room because people, like emotional giants, would absorb my energies, and even in my room, noises hurt my skinless mind. I stayed physically still and felt something run the tape of my history through me. But once I believed I existed I began to head out towards some undefined state of the future. I committed myself to a future, and to being different, and headed for that."

DISCUSSION

The first two cases discussed in this chapter are examples of patients with quite major problems, treated satisfactorily with brief therapy. Psychotherapy limited in intensity and duration may not be adequate for all such patients, but provided no unrealistic hopes are raised, which means that the point of the "principle of deprivation" in such treatment is fully explained to the patient, it is not likely to do harm, and may be surprisingly helpful for some. For any patient well enough to pursue some kind of life in the world, it seems logical to try such an approach before exposing the patient to the risks either of intensive therapy or of hospital admission. Therapists in training, working in this way under supervision, will learn much from the experience of the treatment of these difficult but very educational patients.

Sicker patients may be so cut off that any kind of therapeutic contact is hard to make; or so disturbed that it is hard to sustain. This group of borderline patients is very difficult to define, and the extensive literature reviewed by Perry and Klerman (1978) revealed a degree of vagueness and diversity in the diagnostic criteria startling even for psychiatry. Holzman (1978) argues that the central feature of the heterogeneous group gathered under the title of "borderline" is that of unstable psychological organization, manifest in what Menninger had called *dys*function. In the psychoanalytic view, these poorly integrated states are rooted in early developmental failure. Pine (1979), discussing psychopathology in relation to the developmental studies of infants (Mahler *et al.*, 1975), suggests that a key factor determining this kind of pathology may be how far issues in the relationship with the mother were unresolved prior to the development of a sense of separateness, or are rooted in problems around the separating experience. Steiner (1979), writing most eloquently from a Kleinian view point, suggests that "a full account of the borderline patient ... requires a description both of the depressive anxieties he is not able to tolerate and of the schizoid mechanisms which he is obliged to make use of". This view is part of a three-way understanding of the term borderline. He sees these patients to be diagnostically between neurosis and psychosis; he sees their experience as being represented metaphorically by their feeling always on the edge of, or between, conflicting identities and social realities, and he sees their theoretical position in Kleinian terms as being between the paranoid–schizoid and depressive positions. In Steiner's view, the difficulties of therapy are based upon the pervasiveness of the primitive defences of splitting and projection, and upon the angry and dispiritingly negative transference, which must be endured if depression and reparation are to be contacted. However, he suggests that therapy should not be put off and notes that very significant change can be achieved "even if once-a-week treatment is all that can be offered".

Other analytical accounts are to be found in the writings of Winnicott (1958; 1965) and Guntrip (1968) and in the remarkable account of a very prolonged therapy by Milner (1969). Blake (1968) provides a straightforward account of the very taxing therapy of borderline patients, whom she defined as:

> ... people who have not developed a capacity for concern or for whom concern is such a limited or painful experience that, in their efforts to cope with their environment, they still feel so persecuted and anxious that they need to operate as if concern is either a luxury ... or a handicap ...

She describes how such patients often have "special" needs to modify, usually in minor, possible ways, aspects of the conventional therapeutic arrangements, and suggests that premature interpretation of these may be experienced as punitive and may deprive the patient of the experience of being symbolically held, in Winnicott's sense. Other analytical accounts are to be found in Kernberg (1967, 1974) and in the voluminous writings of Kohut and his followers, summarized in Kohut and Wolf (1978). These professional accounts may be supplemented by the autobiographical novel by Green (1964) which remains one of the most moving accounts of severe mental illness in the literature. Finally, anyone attempting to combine psychotherapy with inpatient care will need to read Main (1957) with his clarification of how patients can exploit or engender staff conflict in tune with, and to the exacerbation of, their psychopathology; and also the more systematic study by Stanton and Schwartz (1954).

12
Marking Progress and Ending Treatment

The explicit listing of the focal issues of therapy at the end of the assessment period, in the ways discussed earlier, represents an explanation of the patient's difficulties and an indication of the current obstacles to change. When therapy is set up formally as a structured and time-limited contract, the ending is anticipated from the beginning, and will be referred to as an issue throughout. While this already serves to focus the work, it is also helpful to review how far each issue has been resolved by considering progress at intervals throughout the course of therapy.

MARKING PROGRESS

To rate progress, each target issue is made the basis of a simple rating scale, set out as a vertical line on which the initial state represents the mid-point of the line. The horizontal dimension marks the passage of time. At each review of progress, change is recorded in relation to the vertical scale, marks below the mid-point representing deterioration, marks above, improvement; the top of the scale being labelled with the agreed objective. The patient carries out these ratings every few sessions, taking account of what has happened in his life and in the therapy since the last rating occasion. The therapist can comment and, in particular, needs to look out for signs of inaccurate, compliant rating, or for other transference manifestations, but the patient decides where to put the final mark. These reviews record progress and often enhance the patient's realistic self-monitoring; they also frequently serve to remind him of progress and restore a sense of being in control. The ratings may also identify neglected or unsatisfactorily resolved issues and will lead to examination of the reasons for failure to progress, and may suggest a need for the use of other methods of treatment. The relation of these ratings to the time elapsed and the time remaining in therapy also serves to frame the work and to prevent the kind of comfortable stalemate or infinite postponement which can develop in work done without time limit.

An example of the use of these ratings through the 26-session, 18-month therapy of Rachel (described briefly in Chapter 10) is given in Fig. 12.1.

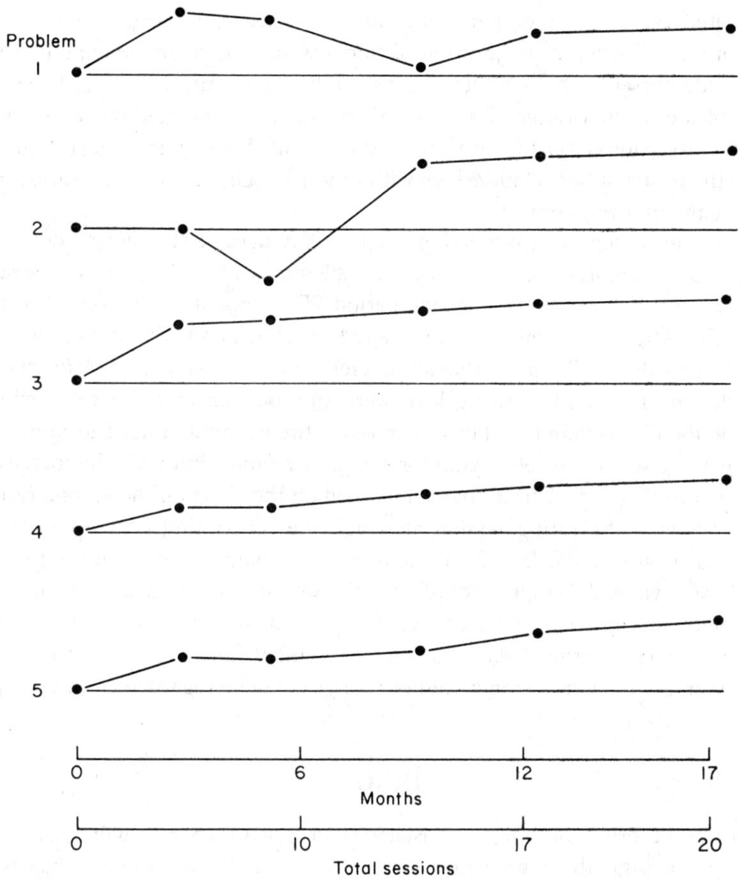

1. Prone to panic attacks (aim: to be symptom-free).
2. Marked preoccupation with thinness, self-induced vomiting at times (aim: ordinary concern with food and weight).
3. Tendency to be remote from, and in control of, others (aim: to be able to be more exposed and less controlling.
4. Dilemma: if depending and submitting then not cross (aim: to be able to assert and defend own needs).
5. Dilemma: either in control or in chaos (aim: to feel safe in self and able to let go).

Fig. 12.1 Example rating scale.

Rachel

Rachel was a young woman of twenty-two, with a past history of anorexia nervosa at the age of fifteen, and of a referral to Child Guidance at the age of nine. She had now consulted on account of panic attacks and a travel phobia. She was still markedly preoccupied with the question of thinness and she often ate compulsively and then made herself sick, by which means she had maintained her weight at the lower end of the normal range. The aims of treatment, formulated on the basis of the assessment sessions, were focused upon the loss of these symptoms and on the revision of the terms of her relationships with others which, in my view, constituted a more fundamental problem.

Looking at the ratings of progress (Fig. 12.1) it is noticeable that her tendency to remain remote from others (3) and the two dilemmas (4 and 5) showed steady improvement throughout the treatment period. The appetite symptoms became worse initially. After 3 or 4 months in therapy Rachel had embarked upon her first happy and sexually fulfilling relationship. Her feelings about the relationships between allowing food and allowing love were summarized in a dream in which there was no food in her kitchen, but a very warm fire burning in her bedroom; she observed that she seemed to be paying for this new relationship with the increased self-induced vomiting (Problem 2) that is recorded on the chart on the second rating occasion. Following the rating session at which the contrasting changes in these problems had been discussed, and the nature of her binging and vomiting again considered, she virtually stopped binging although she suffered a setback with regard to her panic attacks (Problem 1). She remained free of any major food preoccupation when treatment ended a year later and at follow-up, 8 months later. The short-term contrary movements of her ratings could be regarded as an example of "symptom substitution".

ENDING

In most cases of brief therapy, a satisfactory degree of change will have been achieved by the time the termination date is reached. Where therapy has been confined to the more didactic active methods, in which the patient has been taught ways of increasing his capacity to monitor or control his actions, progress will have been clearly marked by an extension of autonomy for the patient, and in such cases the therapist will not have invited a transference relationship. In so far as the transference is manifest, it will usually be in the form of a direct response to the therapists's role as parent or teacher, and will take the form either of compliance or of resistance. Such responses need to be dealt with but if the essential relationship has been a satisfactory teacher–pupil one, then it can usually be relinquished relatively easily. Active methods are therefore particularly suitable for short-term work, or work in contexts where the development and interpretation of transference can conflict with other aspects of the professional role as, for example, in the case of general practitioners or probation officers.

However, active approaches are not adequate in many cases. To the extent that the patient's problems have become defined and dealt with through the metaphoric relationship built up between patient and therapist, the patient's autonomy may well be impaired and will need to be restored before therapy can be considered complete. The issue of termination is, therefore, a central one in such therapies. Only in relinquishing the support of the therapist are the lessons finally learnt, and the personal growth of the patient finally achieved. To the extent that the metaphoric nature of the experience is partly lost sight of by most patients, so that the therapist is seen to provide a replacement of the early significant others, or is seen only as providing a repetition of the frustrations and angers previously experienced, the process of termination will be a painful one, but one which is potentially therapeutic. The therapist must ensure that the disillusion and mixed feelings are both experienced and survived for, if impossible hopes can be given up or if the patient can be freed from his need to continually seek their satisfaction, or from the need to avoid expressing any needs because of their depth and inappropriate nature, then the patient's capacity to pursue attainable and appropriate aims can be enhanced.

In all cases therefore the meaning of the approaching termination must be fully considered by patient and therapist. Some patients will have difficulty in acknowledging its significance and will try to avoid sadness or anger associated with the loss of the therapist. Where an incompletely mourned previous loss has played an important part in the patient's difficulties, living through the end of treatment and fully experiencing what it means is a crucial aspect of the therapy. Even where past losses are not the main issue, most patients will experience some reliving of past disappointments and disillusions, and some facing of the need to give up fantasy and magical expectations. In the course of doing this they will experience, often for the first time, uncomfortable mixed feelings. Such experience is helpful in healing previous splitting mechanisms, whereby others were seen either as idealized or as disappointing and frustrating figures, and leads to a more satisfactory pattern of relationships and of self-care. In patients treated with the therapeutic methods described in this book, the intensity of transference feelings is often eased by the fact that the patient has already acquired many skills and capacities through the use of the explicit framework and active methods. His experience of the therapist and of leaving the therapist will still be an illustration of important themes, but it will be an illustration in the context of a relationship which has included sharing of concepts and understandings, and the dependent transference will not bear the whole weight of the therapy.

We will now consider the use of these ratings and the issues around termination as they presented in the case of David and Anne.

David

In David's case the shortness of the initial therapy was such that only one rating was carried out, at his last (seventh) appearance. The rating scales used allow for a change of plus or minus 20 mm. David recorded no deterioration on his ratings, and the following improvements: depressed mood – +8; not feeling in control of his life – +7; not able to work – +5; sadness and anger over Patricia – +15; the placation trap — +4; the dilemma, *if* submitting, *then* not cross – +3; on the remaining dilemmas and the snag (see Chapter 7) he rated no change. At the rating session, he reported that his friends had commented on his greater capacity to make claims for himself, and he also described a clear and realistic decision about his future career plans, based upon following a long-standing interest in a field not related to his previous work. Whether David's confusion about the time of his eighth appointment represented a denied aggressive act is uncertain, but the likelihood of there being some disappointment at losing my support, given his previous disappointment in his father and his recent loss of Patricia, seemed high. I suggested this at the sixth session, but he denied strong feelings. Had he come to the eighth session I would certainly have returned to this theme, in case he had failed to acknowledge fully the meaning of the event to him.

David has seen for further individual sessions after a 5-month gap. By that time he was involved in taking his final examinations, which he had prepared for doggedly and methodically. He was seen with long intervals (3–5 weeks) between sessions.

Anne

Anne's initial therapy (22 sessions over 8 months) ended with an agreement to review the situation after 5 months; at that time a further period of treatment was offered. Progress was rated on two occasions during the first phase and once after 8 further sessions. At the time of the first rating occasion, Anne had begun to experience sad and angry feelings about her past life, although she felt these only intermittently. She was anxious about doing the ratings, but in the course of filling them out, came to realize that she had made real progress on many of them. Discussing this perceived improvement with her husband, she was pleased to find that he was in no doubt about it being the case. Her second rating was carried out 6 weeks before the gap in treatment; once more, in doing these ratings, she realized that, regarding the patterns of her relationships with others, she had made further progress. The last sessions of this phase were concerned with her being emotionally present rather than working hard at being a good patient, and with acknowledging her feelings as she became more deeply aware of the meaning of remembered episodes from her past. I did not repeat the ratings at the end of this phase of therapy as I felt this could have been an inappropriately task-oriented approach at that time and as, in any case, it was clear that she had held on to the gains that she had reported at the second rating occasion. During the 5-month gap in therapy, Anne wrote the following letter:

> This is a very difficult letter to write because I had been waiting for a crisis to come to write to you about but, for some reason, it hasn't happened; nor have I actually felt ready to regain contact with you until now. These two things have surprised me, partly

> because I had fears of not coping while you were away, and also because I had expectations of having to write you frequent letters to calm myself during your absence. Not only that, my destructive impulse has not even sought to disturb this relative mental calm that I have enjoyed over the past 2 or 3 months. Although part of this, I am sure, is symptomatic of my distancing myself out of self-protection, I also feel that the period, as you predicted, has been useful because it has enabled the slow, gradual absorption of everything we talked about. Although I have had periods of tenseness, they have not been characterized by my old friend, the fear of losing control. Generally they have expressed themselves as phases of depressiveness, irritatedness, or complaining; although it is difficult to tell, I think they are sparked off by both/either guilt from not working and/or an abstract need for a session of psychotherapy with you; I say ''abstract'' because during the whole period of your absence I have felt no need to go and see anybody else because of any problems, yet I have missed talking with you. Although problems like fears of nervous breakdowns are no longer prominent — either resolved (I hope) or put out of mind — my fear of cancer still plagues me occasionally. . . On the whole my relationship with my husband is much healthier, and I am much more confident about showing my feelings, and that includes anger very occasionally. I have been to my parents' a couple of times and have managed OK. One change was that I felt real depression about my mother's sorry state, after a long talk with her one evening, rather than anxiety or fear. It seems to me to be the more appropriate feeling.

Anne's last phase of treatment was concerned with experiencing more deeply what she had learned earlier, and with preparing for termination. Her ratings on the third occasion, after a total of 34 sessions over 15 months, were as follows: pre-occupied with the fear of a nervous breakdown – +17; inability to trust others – +12; compulsive care-taking – +18; depressive thinking – +18; social isolation trap – +17; guilt relief by self-deprivation – +19: *if* hopeful or effective, *then* imagining death of parent – +13; *either* helpful and controlling *or* dependent and potentially crazy – +17; *if* loved, *then* feeling trapped – +19; *if* striving for perfection, *then* stressed; *if* not striving, *then* guilty – +12; snag-avoiding fully achieving, enjoying, claiming or having a life, *as if* own life is at the cost of mother's – +15.

To conclude this chapter. I would like to consider further the way in which termination is defined and carried out. For most patients it is quite simple: the job is done and one says ''goodbye'' forever. For others, the work has indicated that some further therapy of a different kind may be indicated; for example group, family, or marital therapy. In other cases, it may be appropriate to offer follow-up appointments, and in some cases these may continue for a long time. Such follow-up appointments do not mean that the patient is denied the experience of termination; it is rather that they represent a sign that the work is expected to continue, and that there will be a witness for it. The therapist is often the only other person who can really understand the way in which the issues discussed in therapy are still of active concern. This process of continuing work can be difficult, and it cannot easily be shared with others, for friends, especially those who are emotionally close, often find the importance attached to therapy and the therapist incomprehensible or absurd.

Ultimately, the revision of strategies and assumptions, and the more integrated and effective sense of self which successful therapy achieves will be sustained by the patient, and the necessary separating and mourning process will be completed. The therapist, who was a new "other" to the patient's self has offered forms of understanding and of relationship which have allowed a modification of the terms on which the patient's life is lived; and, as these terms are claimed by the patient as his own, the living therapist can be forgotten. In terms of the PSM, the sense of competence has been enhanced, the identity of the self is more fully known and integrated, self-knowledge and self-monitoring are more accurate, and the criteria of self-judgment are less critical and are based on a clearer understanding of the limits of responsiblity.

The resolution of splitting and projective identification, whereby the perception of others is distorted and the division of the self is perpetuated, will be achieved most securely by the experience of relating to the therapist, who elicits and accepts aspects of the patient on both sides of the split. The therapist, in ending therapy and in all the other ways in which he fails to meet the patient's more regressive and often unconscious wishes, will evoke disappointment, sadness, or anger. If he allows and acknowledges this as well as being, and being seen as, a good and caring figure, then the patient's tendency to see others as polarized between idealization and denigration, and himself as either perfectly cared for or utterly rejected, will be mitigated. Many relationship dilemmas, as described in terms of the PSM, are maintained by such polarized role perception, as was discussed in Chapter 5. However, the interpretation of the projective elements in the transference may not be the only way to resolve these problems. The revision of the terms of current significant relationships, on the basis of understandings achieved and the encouragement given in brief therapy based on sharing understandings, in the terms described in previous chapters, may be achieved without depending exclusively on the transference.

DISCUSSION

The detailed specification of goals of treatment, and the recording of progress towards these goals, often by way of successive sub-goals, was evolved largely by behaviourists. Where it has been adopted by therapists of other persuasions, the purpose has been to assess change rather than to organize the course of treatment (e.g. Battle *et al.*, 1966). The approach proposed here, and first described in Ryle (1979), aims to extend this behavioural approach, which is restricted to the modification of observable behaviours and symptoms, by specifying in addition the conceptual and procedural problems that require revision. The rating of progress on target problems, traps, dilemmas, and snags serves, as in behavioural treatment, both to focus the work of therapy and to provide a basis for the assessment of progress at different stages. Improvements recorded by a series of fifteen patients on rating scales of this type were accompanied by appropriate changes in repertory grid measures relating to dilemmas, indicating cognitive revision, and on scores on a symptom inventory (Ryle 1980).

As regards the issue of termination, only psychoanalysts have considered in depth the meaning of the therapeutic relationship and of its ending, and the importance of dealing with these meanings explicitly in brief interpretive psychotherapy has been stressed by many authors, notably by Malan (1976a) and Mann (1973). "Transference cures" achieved by the patient's need to please the therapist, or by their "internalizing" the therapist as a "good object" may be satisfactory for some problems, especially where positive transference has been utilized to guide the patient towards more effective forms of self-control and self-care; but in some cases changes achieved in this way will be unstable or insufficient.

13
On Becoming and Being a Therapist

To become a therapist is a strange choice. How could one choose to spend one's time with people whose defining characteristics include unhappiness and getting along badly with others? There is no single or obvious answer to this question but common antecedents (some of which played a part in my own choice) include one's personal difficulties (being a therapist as self-cure), a history of being caretaker to one's own family (needing to be helpful to feel good), a difficulty in getting in touch with one's own deeper feelings (seeking vicarious knowledge), and finding a safe form of intimacy (therapy as being in control). Such observations are likely to provoke dismay in would-be patients, for how can the blind lead the blind? The dismay is fed in part by the idealizing opposite wish (that therapists would be perfect human beings) but it cannot be dismissed as entirely unreasonable for, while it is true that even a fairly neurotic and imperfectly resolved person can be a therapist, the task being a professional one of providing certain conditions and understandings rather than one of showing the way, it is also true that a therapist will be better to the extent that he has achieved insight into, and resolution of, his own personality. The fact that his original motivation was in part "neurotic" or partly unconscious does not mean that a therapist should withdraw from the field, for most life choices of any value are similarly charged. In most jobs, however, these irrational and often unconscious motives can go unexamined, but for the therapist awareness is essential: in the course of his training, in addition to seeking intellectual understanding of his work, he needs to examine himself and come to know the meaning of his choices as fully as possible. Without this, a therapist dominated by the need for self-cure may use his patients to fulfil his own needs or a therapist needing to feel helpful may resent his patient's independence, or may transfer to his patients the mixed feelings stemming from his helpful, but perhaps unconsciously resented, family role. The vicariously exploring therapist may be a poor judge and guide to the person inhabiting the psychic desert he is interested in, while a therapist needing to control or to remain inviolate and detached can seem unhelpful or persecutory to his patients. Self-knowledge and a critical examination of his therapeutic work are therefore essential, and must be sought through therapy and supervision.

This view is one derived from psychoanalysis and finds its fullest expression in formal psychoanalytic training, which has come to be characterized by many years of personal analysis. This training requirement is enormously expensive in both time and money, and the decision to pursue it, and in doing so to commit oneself to a particular ideological position, should not be taken lightly, or before a period of wider based experience and training. It is to this more general basic training, which may lead in various directions, that I shall now address myself.

BASIC TRAINING

There are three interrelated skills required of the therapist. The first is to arrange his meetings with his patient in ways that enable him to find out what he needs to know about the patient, and which enable the patient to hear what he has to say. The establishment of this situation is partly a technical matter of times and places but depends eventually on the therapist's human qualities; in particular on his ability to anticipate and recognize the patient's anxieties and to communicate his own general concern and interest. The second skill is to be able to make sense of the information he gathers from the patient's account and from his relationship with the patient. The third skill is to know how to use all that he learns in the service of the patient's care. The second and third tasks, while still requiring the human ability to sustain a relationship, in addition require concepts and skills. As in so many of the issues discussed in this book, which aspect receives emphasis in training depends upon the theoretical orientation of the training programme, although recently broader-based programmes have become more available.

SUPERVISION

Early in his basic training, the trainee therapist using basically interpretive methods should start giving therapy to a well-selected case under close supervision. Such supervision has two elements: technical and personal. The technical part consists of discussion of what is said and done, and of the reasons for what is said and done in terms of the therapeutic method and of the theory being applied. The personal part involves the careful consideration of all those attributes of the trainee which are manifest in his therapeutic work, both those that are helpful and need encouragement, and those that are unhelpful and need examination. To make this possible, the supervisor needs to establish a stance that has something in common with the accepting and non-judgemental attitudes of the therapist, and in doing so he also acts as a model. But he has to do this while, at the same time, making it clear that it is the trainee's responsibility to tell all he can about what goes on between him and his patient, accepting that his own part in that will be scrutinized and is open to criticism. In so far as a trainee's personality is expressed in his work, it is a professional, not a private matter, and open to comment. The same rule or expectation can apply to group supervision, whether by a senior or jointly with colleagues. It is from the experience of such constructive, but often painful, sharing of his work, that the would-be therapist may begin to change and may also come to face wider issues for which he may seek personal therapy.

Supervision, combining technical and personal elements, is the foundation of traditional training in interpretive methods. Two additional approaches offer valuable, different opportunities for learning. Video-tapes of actual sessions, either exemplary interviews by experienced workers or, probably most effective, of the trainee himself, offer the chance to recognize useful and revise unhelpful forms of intervention. An even more flexible and economical method, allowing fuller exploration, is role-playing. The trainer can play the role of a patient he has treated himself in a group training situation, in which group members in turn conduct the interview (including ''replays'' using different interventions). The interview is broken off at intervals,

(a) to consider how effectively it has enabled the patient to reveal himself, which provides training in interviewing skills,

(b) so that the group reflects on the material and begins to make sense of it in terms of the theoretical concepts being taught,

(c) to enable the group to consider on that basis what interventions and treatment strategies are appropriate.

While reasonably experienced trainees can present their own cases in this way, (and this is an interesting variant on conventional supervision and gives a powerful sense of being the patient), inexperienced therapists, or those presenting cases only seen for a short time, cannot play sufficiently coherent roles. If the trainer plays the patient, however, he can select cases and manipulate interactions in ways that highlight the particular issues he wishes the group to consider. This very flexible method involves the participation of the whole group and is surprisingly subtle, often evoking, for example, transference and counter-transference feelings that can also be considered.

Assuming that the trainee's first experience has been in individual work on a basically interpretive model, he will need to get some training and experience in cognitive/behavioural approaches, some experience of group work, and some experience of family and marital work. These different experiences will be accompanied by instruction in the appropriate theoretical backgrounds of behavioural psychology, the cognitive therapies, and the different theories of group and family functioning. Group work and family work may further expose the trainee to a consideration of his own characteristics through forms of self-exploration such as group membership and sculpting, experiences which may facilitate important personal changes, sometimes more effectively than individual therapy pursued out of routine obligation.

COUNTER-TRANSFERENCE

A therapist's response to his patients combines rational judgements, perceptions, and styles of address reflecting his particular background, and also factors deriving from his particular history of which he is not aware. The need is to understand both general assumptions and strategies, and to recognize problems that are due to factors that are inaccessible because of defence mechanisms. The quickest way to self-understanding is to be exposed to the reflections of others who do not see possibility circumscribed by what we see as self-evident. The patterning of our individual responses by our higher-order schemas can be pointed out to us, and often accepted without difficulty, and this can enable us to extend, modify, or make allowances for, our particular assumptions. We may also be confronted with ways in which our defences interfere with accurate understanding. Some of these may yield to the effects of good supervision and the confidence that follows upon developing competence, just as patients become less defended as they gain control and understanding, but therapists in training will benefit from individual and/or group therapy.

As well as learning to see more clearly and respond more accurately, we can learn to recognize and use our idiosyncratic responses as diagnostic tools, translating our personal irrational responses to patients into news about the patient. One example often cited is that of the clenched fist in the pocket, said to be diagnostic of hysteria, but in fact all such responses are quite idiosyncratic and our job is to learn what our own particular responses mean in terms of what the patient is doing, or seeking to do. If we can manage this, we can often, without having consciously to articulate the connection, respond in a way that seems intuitive to what the patient is doing, or trying to do, and does not yet know about.

THE TRAINEE PSYCHOTHERAPIST

The therapist who manages to obtain a training of the kind of breadth and depth suggested above should have a reasonable degree of self-knowledge and a flexible therapeutic approach. From this he might choose to continue to work on a broad front, or to pursue a chosen special method. The advantages of a general initial training over a narrow approach based upon one theoretical model or confined exclusively to group, individual, or natural group settings is, I hope obvious. The disadvantages are those to do with identity and support in that there is at present no one theoretical system and no all-embracing institution able to unite those seeking to work in eclectic or integrated ways. However, by the end of a few years of training and experience, a therapist is likely to have acquired an extensive system of understanding and to have undergone a fair amount of personal change, on the basis of which he will have chosen forms of work that match his personal style. The field is wide enough to house happily a wide range of temperaments and ideologies and there is obviously no single model of the good therapist. We may all aspire to become like the mature, ideal parents, supervisors, or therapists we had, or wish we had had, combining the wisdom of age with the energy of youth, uniting "masculine force" with "feminine understanding", knowing when to open a new question and when to point to a solution, capable of always giving enough and never too much; but meanwhile, we can begin to have some confidence in our offer, and some awareness of our limits. The incorporation into our therapeutic work of some form of evaluation of progress, such as a periodic review of progress with patients in relation to predetermined aims, provides the best basis for making an accurate assessment of our effectiveness, and is a protection against complacency.

MAINTAINING THE CONDITIONS FOR THERAPY

Having considered the process of becoming a therapist, I will move on to some questions of practice, by discussing what conditions are required by therapists for their work, and what conditions they should provide for their patients.

The first requirement for the therapist is that the nature of the act be sufficiently understood by his colleagues. Junior staff in training, in particular, have to learn to insist upon space and time free from interruption to see their patients, and the right to seek supervision and perhaps personal therapy. Later on, pressures upon services being considerable in most circumstances, the disposition of time between long-term and short-term work, between treating cases, or teaching or supervising others, between consultation and therapeutic work, can be problematic. Psychotherapists, with their particular concern for the private and individual, often handle their social, professional, and political relationships badly, and become isolated and vulnerable as a result. Moreover, their isolation and narrowing of attention to the detail of clinical work does not serve the interests of the population of potential patients well, as is evident from the heavy concentration of psychotherapy resources upon middle-class patients. Other pressures are self-generated, perhaps as a result of unresolved omnipotence. Doing therapy is inevitably tiring, but how tiring depends upon the kind of work being done and on the ease one has with oneself in doing it. The therapist should try to adjust his workload within the limits of his resource, giving time and energy to thinking and reading and to living his own life. The worst solution is to limit the extent of one's availability during actual patient contact; I believe we could often do better to spend less time with patients and more time thinking about them. The dangers of settling down to a routine, with the therapist a passive sponge or uninvolved chess-player in relation to the patient, is greatest in open-ended, unfocused, interpretive therapy and reduced in the integrated approach I advocate, with its greater variety and openness.

The control and definition of the therapeutic process itself is a more complicated issue. Where the therapy is confined to the use of active and didactic methods the principles are not too difficult to enunciate, being determined largely by pedagogic considerations. The therapist needs to explain clearly what he offers and should provide it reliably and skilfully. The use of a broader approach, involving the consideration of assumptions and strategies and working to overcome dilemmas, traps, and snags, may similarly demand no more from the therapist than the type of scaffolding function referred to in Chapter 6 but, as transference may occur and may either interfere with treatment or add a new dimension to it, it is my view that the conditions offered and sustained by the therapist must be seen in the light of this metaphoric transaction.

Once that is accepted, then the guiding principle behind the therapist's control of the therapeutic situation is clear. He must recognize that, whatever goes on will have, as well as its obvious and surface connotation, a possible meaning in terms of the patient's self-identity and strategic scripts, especially with respect to those of which the patient is only incompletely or uncomfortably aware. It is the therapist's responsibility to recognize and clarify these meanings with the patient; rather than allowing the patient to evoke a confirmatory response, he uses the transference as a learning experience.

Those who accept that transference is a central issue in therapy may still apply this recognition very differently. Disagreements about the therapist's role may be described in various ways; one distinction is between those who stress the personal encounter between therapist and patient, and those who stress the professional nature of the contract. Laing has written extensively on the crucial importance of the human connection between patient and therapist, but in terms of practice it is not always clear what the implications of this are. Lomas (1973) makes it clearer but, in doing so, appears to disclaim any professionalism at all. The more establishment figures, on the other hand, would be closer to the position of Strachey, discussed earlier, and would regard any departure from the opaque, interpretive stance, as offering more reality than the patient could bear, and as being likely to feed into unconscious conflict and delay the progress of analysis. As, despite this view, many psychoanalysts occupy themselves with brief psychotherapy and recognize that the implications of this include a much greater activity and visibility on their part, this issue is clearly far from being resolved. My own view can be summarized as follows:

(a) The human relation between patient and therapist is an unequal one.
(b) It is directed towards the patient's needs.
(c) Because of the vulnerability of the distressed patient and because of the power of the transference, the therapist must accept responsibility for the control of the relationship.
(d) Knowing how to control and how to utilize this relationship is a professional skill.

In establishing the terms of therapy, the therapist exercises and sets up the conditions of his control. How this is done will be a matter of personal style: it may be done stiffly or informally, implicitly or explicitly, but it needs to be done clearly and not foggily. The control, which is the frame within which therapy proceeds, has two main purposes: the defence of the therapist and the defence of the patient.

Therapists must defend themselves against the pressures of their patients, some of whom at least are likely to feel desperate, to be manipulative, and to have difficulty in acknowledging the needs of others. The therapist's patience and his ability to turn these pressures into understanding is possible only because his degree of exposure to his patients is limited. This control is exercised in the first place by making the terms of the contract clear; the psychotherapist makes the offer of a regular meeting of a certain duration in his office for the purpose of talking about the patient's problems, and he undertakes to be present as an attentive and skilled helper. Moreover, although his is a human presence, the agenda does not include *his* life, *his* personality, or *his* problems. The therapist must be prepared to give the reasons for the terms he sets, but cannot basically offer to compromise with them. This confined, well-bounded offer is a relief to most patients, and frees them for the work of therapy. It is an annoyance to others, but this feeling, as much as any other, can be accepted and openly discussed and it is probable that it will throw some light on the patient's life problems.

How opaque as a person the therapist is, or chooses to try to be, is a matter of theory and of style. Most therapists working in brief and more active therapies will not deny their patients all gestures of concern or all evidence of their own personalities, but limits on personal exposure and involvement are still necessary. The dangers of being a charismatic presence are obvious enough: cure by persuasion or inspiration is likely to be unstable. The possibility of sexual exploitation of patients whose transference involvement may include powerful, and often partly sexualized dependency, is also obvious. The inequality of roles, the unequal vulnerability, and the fact that such transference feelings reflect poorly assimilated, unresolved childhood feelings for parents would make any sexual response on the part of the therapist exploitive in general, and specifically antitherapeutic. The dangers of a calculated degree of human availability as opposed to invisibility are less obvious. Provided the therapist is cautious in the pace at which he becomes visible, making this judgement on the basis of the early meetings with the patient and the patient's history, I believe that the advantages of a reasonably human presence outweigh the possible costs, and such a therapist will still attract the range of transference reactions available and necessary for the patient's progress. Neurotic people are plagued by the tendency to repeat the same errors over and over again, and they will do so with a visible and present therapist, given half a chance. It is also clear, as I have argued earlier, that the personally invisible, withholding therapist is not a neutral presence, he is a very powerful and controlling one.

However the therapist resolves the question of how present to be, he must remain in control of the agenda of the meeting and must always turn it back to the issues on which the therapy is being conducted. Patients will sometimes ask about the therapist's private life, although they do not always really want answers. Such direct enquiries can sometimes be answered or an answer can be refused on the grounds of one's right to privacy, or partial answers can be given; whichever is done, the reason for the question's being asked can also be explored. A rigid stance on this question can lead to silly power struggles and guessing games, which should be avoided. As therapy proceeds and the patient comes to differentiate between the metaphoric transference relationship and the working relationship more clearly, and to see the therapist in a less clouded way, there is a shift in the direction of greater equality and openness but, up to the time of termination, the agenda must always remain the patient and his problems.

The therapist who does not solve the problem of his visibility by adhering to the conventional analytic prescriptions of minimal exposure, and who does not strictly limit all communication to occasional interpretations in a 50-minute session, will still need, as much as will the rule-follower, to take note of everything that happens between him and his patient, and to look for evidence of transference and counter-transference. I have argued earlier that the inclusion of active methods in the therapy does not prevent the emergence of transference, and I have expressed my belief that a patient's capacity to use transference interpretations to abandon restrictive and defensive strategies is often enhanced rather than reduced by such activity.

SOME DIFFICULT TECHNICAL ISSUES

Any therapist working on weekly or less frequent sessions needs to consider ways of easing, and ways of speeding up, the process of therapy. I would like to consider three specific questions at this point. Should the therapist allow telephone or letter access to patients? Should therapists ever touch their patients? Should therapists ever reveal their counter-transference? Each of these is essentially a professional question, but none is simply resolved.

The question of giving patients telephone or writing access is largely one of the therapist's own needs. It is particularly likely to arise in therapy with long intervals between sessions, or at times of interruption in therapy. Telephoning represents a major intrusion on the therapist's life and should be kept to a minimum, but there are times of crisis or of angry transference when it is only humane to give patients access, in order that they may confirm that the therapist is still with them and alive. Writing letters is less intrusive, and for some patients represents a way of saying things which cannot be said so clearly during the session. I personally, therefore, do not put restrictions on this (as is clear from the letters quoted in this book), believing that such communications are often valuable. What is communicated in such letters should be discussed at the next meeting with the patient. As with any other act, the patient's use or abuse of telephoning or writing may itself need to be understood in terms of the problem being treated, and the transference.

The issue of physical contact with a patient is seldom discussed, and needs discussing. To suggest that any contact at all might take place arouses fears of sexual exploitation or of inducing dependency, and challenges the more general taboos on physicality which dominate western culture. The simple answer is never to permit it but that is not, in my view, always the correct one. There are occasions in therapy, for example, when patients first fully feel the extent of their despair or loss, when not to take a hand or put a hand on a shoulder is inhumane. Even if such gestures are misjudged, and many patients have extremely awkward feelings about their bodies, their response may be more illuminating than their non-response or unexpressed response to a non-gesture would have been. Anne's anger, reported earlier, is a case in point.

Jane

Jane, a woman of forty, had sought treatment for phobic symptoms. These were related to a long–term unacknowledged depression. Jane became flustered when, after a very painful session, I took her hand as she was leaving, and at her next visit she talked about how important that gesture had been in helping her understand the extent of the prohibitions of her childhood. She wept as she recalled an occasion when her younger brother, of whom she was very fond, had returned from a long stay in hospital. She had sat by him, just wanting to be near, and sometimes touch him, but her father had said, "Leave the lad alone, won't you", and had made her sit on the far side of the room. At later sessions she referred back to the occasion of my taking her hand as having been a critical moment in her understanding of one source of her depression.

One further issue needs to be discussed. Knowing and clarifying the transference is a central task of many therapies, and learning about the counter-transference an important part of training, but how far should the counter-transference itself be reserved as a mine of private information at the therapist's disposal and how far, if at all, should it be shared with the patient? Clearly, if the therapist is aware of a response that is simply a function of his own private history, current mood, or unresolved neurosis, his main job is to ensure that this awareness is used to defend the patient against distortions of his understanding or response. Often, however, the responses which patients evoke in therapists are similar to those they evoke in others in the world outside and here an explicit description of the response can be useful. A patient who is being passively unco-operative and withholding, and who is irritating his therapist might be given the interpretation: "I feel you are putting your anger into me." I would prefer something more direct such as: " I find you impossible to get through to today; it makes me feel pretty irritated. I wonder if other people get to feel the same way when you are like this. Can we try to understand what you are feeling?" One may at times share one's own idiosyncratic counter-transference usefully; for example, I know and do not respect in myself a certain vulnerability to the appeal of helpless and hopeless waifs. By recognizing and naming the impulse to give care and protection while, at the same time, withholding it and making it clear that I know such a response to be inappropriate and collusive with a self-diminishing strategy on their part, I offer both an interpretation and a model of controlling an inappropriate impulse, and I convey trust in the possibility of the patient acting differently.

We need always, in judging our acts and non-acts, to try to anticipate and make sense of how the patient understands what we are doing or not doing. If a particular patient becomes the subject of more than the usual variations in our practice or the subject of unusual preoccupations, that is to say, if a particular patient evokes a powerful or confusing counter-transference, we should seek supervision or share the issue with a colleague. Many would argue that strict rule-following by the therapist is the safest path, in that mistakes will be avoided, but that view leaves out the fact that the omissions, the silences, and the inexpressiveness of the therapist are also acts and may also be mistaken.

DISCUSSION

Different school of psychotherapy use very different training methods, but most share one feature: a failure to evaluate the effectiveness of their training programmes by research. Matarazzo (1971), reviewing research in this field, awards the Rogerians highest marks for training evaluation research, in particular noting their widely quoted (and incompletely replicated) demonstration of the relevance of therapist attributes to outcome in therapy (the attributes being accurate empathy, positive regard, and genuineness) and noting the extension of this finding to a similar characterization of successful supervisors. Behaviourists' research in training, also reviewed by Matarazzo, concentrates on the training of new practitioners in problem identification and in the selection of appropriate techniques. Demonstration (role-modelling), supervised treatment, role-playing, and didactic instructions are all used in the training of behavioural therapists. Predictably, psychoanalytic training is the least rigorously evaluated. Traditionally, this training combines formal instruction in theory, personal analysis, and the conduct of training cases under close supervision. The role of the supervisor is seen as a matter for some dispute: some see it as primarily interpretive, in which the trainee–supervisor relationship is as much a focus for attention as is the trainee–patient one; whereas others place the main emphasis in supervision on therapeutic procedures and technique. While it may be useful to pay attention to the supervisor–supervisee relationship, one study, using video-recordings of supervisory sessions and relying upon trainees' evaluations as measures of outcome, showed that supervisors characterized as being outstanding were those who focused more attention on the patient and less upon the trainee (Goin and Kline, 1974).

Conventional supervision represents the trainer's selective observations on the edited account of the session presented by the trainee. Kubie (1958) argued powerfully for the greater relevance and learning potential for the trainee of tape-recordings of sessions, which offer a basis both for supervision and for self-monitoring. In training, as in therapy, there are strong arguments for a more comprehensive theoretical base and a more diverse range of training methods. There has been a recent and welcome trend in Britain towards the provision of such broad-based training programmes (Haldane *et al.*, 1979; Margison, 1980; Lieberman *et al.*, 1978).

The possible harmful effects of therapy have attracted relatively little attention. Active treatment methods are often evaded or resisted by patients, but their potential for serious harm is relatively low. Interpretive methods, on the other hand, where transference plays a large part, can leave patients worse off (see, for example, Bergin, 1966) and the ways in which such harm may be done must be borne in mind. Meares and Hobson (1977) provide a useful discussion of this issue, offering a description of the "persecutory therapist" under six headings. The distortions of the therapist's relationship they describe are often justified by theoretical beliefs. The six features of negative therapist-patient interactions which they identify are summarized as follows:

(a) *Intrusion* into the patient's personal space can occur by crude interrogation, by premature intuitive understanding, and by forcing the confession of secrets.

(b) *Derogation* is a term used to cover various ways in which a therapist can denigrate his patient, seriously damaging his self-esteem.

(c) *Invalidation* of experience occurs when the therapist does not respect everything that his patient says and responds by explaining away or categorizing, rather than by elaborating and amplifying affects, images, and memories.

(d) The *opaque therapist*, in attempting to maintain an impersonal neutrality, denies his involvement in a two-person situation with its rhythm of intimacy and distance.

(e) The *untenable situation* renders the patient helpless, confused, and unable to explore and learn; it is promoted by lack of clarity about the structure of therapy; by the imposition of impossible requirements; by giving conflicting messages; and by making conflicting demands.

(f) The *persecutory spiral* is an escalating, destructive interaction in which both therapist and patient are, or feel, persecuted. Potent factors are "all-knowing", authoritarian, rigid and sectarian attitudes and beliefs regarding psychotherapeutic theory and technique.

To these various acts of commission, Older (1977) under the title "Four Taboos That May Limit the Success of Psychotherapy" considers common rigidities whereby therapists may fail their patients. The four he considers are, firstly, the fear of any physical contact because of the dangers of sexual involvement and the general difficulty in physical expression in our culture; secondly, the avoidance of embarrassing topics; thirdly, not allowing the noisy expression of emotion; and fourthly, an unwillingness to vary durations of the patient's sessions in response to the occasional patient's need to work through a problem to its conclusion.

14
Aids to Self-scrutiny and Self-help

My work as a psychotherapist has evolved over the years in a number of directions. I have become more varied in the methods I use, I have become increasingly explicit about what I am doing, and about the ideas underlying my approach and, in talking to patients, I use the word "work" much more often. Over this period, I seem to find my patients less perplexing and less exhausting, and their changes more predictable and more rapidly achieved. While this could be the result of the accumulating illusions, rather than the skills, of greater age, I prefer to believe that it is because I am better at providing the conditions and concepts that patients need in order to change themselves. In this chapter, I want to describe some of the ways in which people can be helped to think clearly and differently about themselves and to learn new ways of acting outside the therapy situation. Some of these ways may be useful to people not in therapy, as aids to self-exploration and problem-definition.

One of the main threads running through the book has been an emphasis on the description of the aims of treatment as being the revision of self-perpetuating errors or failures in procedures. The value of these descriptions is that they direct attention away from the surface manifestations of symptoms, moods, and unwanted behaviours to the underlying modes of thought and action that perpetuate difficulty.

People do not usually reflect on their procedures in this way, and they often lack concepts with which to engage in such reflection. As I became clearer about these concepts, I found myself sharing them with many patients, and after a time I decided to give to most of my patients, during the assessment period, a "personal therapy file" which described in some detail the ideas I was operating on, and which invited them to apply these ideas to their own difficulties. In such cases, the last assessment session was devoted to a discussion of the aims and methods of treatment, based on what they, in their way, and I, in my way, had concluded over the first sessions.

Not every patient is suitable for this approach; a few make little use of the file and in some cases I do not even offer it, or I give only certain pages of the file, describing the most relevant concepts. If it makes sense to the patient to use these sheets, then the overarching framework of understanding offered by the concepts and methods suggested, and the active participation in the therapeutic work called for, provides early relief to the patient's sense of helplessness and a basis for continued self-generated work. Some other written instructions and test procedures which may also be helpful to patients and may save time to therapists will be discussed later in this chapter, after the personal therapy file has been presented in the following sections.

PERSONAL THERAPY FILE

Introduction

These sheets are offered as a way of helping you think about the problems we shall be dealing with in your therapy. People seek therapy because of a wish to stop doing or experiencing things they do not like but cannot control, or because they cannot achieve some aims or life purposes. In the former case, one needs to see what it is that prevents one learning different ways; in the latter case, one needs either to revise or abandon unrealistic aims, or learn better procedures for attaining realizable ones. In living our lives, we are continually making sense of the world around us, especially of the people in it, and are pursuing the aims and expressing the beliefs and values that are important to us. Most of this goes on without the need for us to be consciously aware of our mental processes, but when things go badly it is helpful to be able to reflect, so that we can recognize how we cause ourselves trouble or why we fail to solve our problems. In both small-scale actions (like planning the morning shopping) or large scale ones (like maintaining a relationship or pursuing a career) the basic procedures involved are similar. They can be described as eight stages; we will consider these and note (in brackets) how we may create problems for ourselves at any stage.

(1) We consider whether the situation is suitable for our purposes; sometimes our purposes are determined by the situation (problem: always looking on the dark side, not seeing things clearly).

(2) We consider our ability to influence events (problem: over- or underestimating our capacity; belief in luck or magic).

(3) We consider if the aim will produce a bad reaction from ourselves (guilt) or from others we care about (problem: overstrict criteria for self-acceptance, unreasonable self-blame; seeing others as harsh).

(4) We consider the ways in which we might pursue the aim (problem: lack of skills or experience; narrow definition or polarization of the alternatives).

(5) For each possible way, we consider whether it will work (problem: pessimistic predictions) and what will be the consequences (problem: unrealistic expectation of blame or guilt).

(6) We select a means and proceed (problem: relative incompetence).

(7) We reflect on how we did (problem: exaggerating failures; overgeneralizing from failures; not allowing our success; unrealistic fears that others are hurt or angered).

(8) We review the whole process and revise or confirm the aim, the assumptions, and the means (problem: abandonment of reasonable aims, failure to revise procedures).

With this sequence in mind, read the sheet that follow describing common patterns of difficulty; these suggest some ways of thinking about these issues, which you may find useful. You may be given one or two additional ''tests'' with the same purpose in mind.

Negative beliefs, defensiveness symptoms

Note any of the following that apply to you.

(1) Negative beliefs, e.g. undue self-criticism, guilt, unrealistically low opinion of capacities, unreasonable need for reassurance from others, unreasonable need for self proof, not seeing your ability to influence your life.

(2) Defensiveness: some problems arise because we don't know what we feel or what our life and our past mean to us. Are you someone who is liable to forget important events, or blot out unpleasant feelings? Do you tend to see in others things that are really aspects of yourself? Do you find yourself blocking or avoiding doing what you really wish to do? Do you feel as much in control of your life as other people seem to be?

(3) Symptoms: do you have any of the following?

(a) Prolonged or repeated unreasonable depression or anxiety.
(b) Physical symptoms that seem to be related to how your life is going.
(c) A tendency to avoid situations (on irrational grounds).
(d) A tendency to carry out acts that you don't really intend.

Traps (thoughts, acts, and social strategies)

Traps are what one cannot escape from. Certain kinds of thinking and acting that are self-perpetuating are called traps. An example in the realm of thinking would be depressive assumptions about one's capacity that lead to anxiety and impaired performance, followed by a negative evaluation of the performance and overgeneralization from this, leading to depressive assumptions about one's capacity (see the description of the stages on the first page). A common self-perpetuating *behaviour* is phobic avoidance: initial anxiety about entering a situation which causes anxiety is subsequently anticipated with anxiety and this leads to avoidance; avoidance relieves the fear, but does not challenge the irrational expectation of danger and, hence, maintains the avoidance behaviour.

More complex social behaviours of this sort include the following:

(a) The social isolation trap — feeling underconfident about ourselves, we fear that others will find us boring or stupid, so we avoid contact with them and do not respond to friendly moves. As a result we come to be seen as unfriendly and then are, in fact, socially isolated, from which we conclude that we are boring or stupid, and feel still less confident.

(b) The placation trap — feeling uncertain about our worth or value, or anxious about our right to be assertive, we seek to please other people by doing what they want or what they seem to want. As a result we end up being taken advantage of by others, which makes us either childishly angry or guilty or depressed; hence, our sense of uncertainty about ourselves is maintained or increased. One important issue here is concerned with the distinction between assertion and aggression. A fear of being destructive makes many people invite destruction. In the placation trap in particular, it is common for one's self-effacement to invite or allow abuse, and one's consequent resentment can lead to childish anger. Observing oneself to behave so unreasonably reinforces one's belief that aggression is impermissible. However, tantrums are neither assertive nor effectively aggressive. In being assertive we do no more than make a claim to exist. In being aggressive we give the other person less claim than we do to ourselves. In most circumstances, assertion based on mutual respect is perfectly acceptable; those few people who (aggressively) do not allow us our proper assertions must either be fought (aggressively) or avoided. The image of birdsong provides a useful metaphor here. Most birdsong serves to define territory; by singing, the bird announces its claim to its piece of ground. Most of the time, rivals respect this and fighting only occurs if the line is crossed. People often need to be instructed in the art of "singing on the boundary".

Self-monitoring

Any symptom, unwanted thought, or unwanted behaviour that comes and goes, or varies in intensity, can be better understood as a result of self-monitoring, and this can also very often help one gain control. Many of the problems listed on the previous pages may be worth studying in this way. Here is the way to proceed:

Each time you notice that one such change has occurred, think about (a) the trigger — whether it was an event outside in the world, or a thought or image in your mind; (b) the subsequent thoughts or images in your mind, or the conversation you have with yourself following the triggering event. We often fail to notice or to recall thoughts and images of this kind. It is helpful for 2 or 3 weeks to concentrate on them by spending a little time each day noting down any triggers and the following thoughts that have occured in relation to the symptoms, actions, or mood changes of which you would like to have better control. By writing them down, you will learn to recognize more clearly what causes them, and you will almost certainly find that you imagine situations or consequences much more extreme that those existing in reality. Often one's moods or acts reflect this imagined situation rather than the real one. By noting down these negative thoughts you will begin to distance yourself from them, and by learning to recognize them as they occur you will achieve much more control over them.

From time to time, take a look at the record from two points of view: first of all, note down regularities or recurrences; and secondly, evaluate the realism or otherwise of the judgements and predictions made. From the first you will probably be able to form for yourself a more general view of what causes trouble; for example, does it always occur around issues of rejection or separation, or in relation to acts of assertion? From the second, you may come to recognize a recurrent process of spiralling into catastrophic imagining. This recognition can help you thereafter to tell yourself to stop these imaginery spirals and attend to the real situation that you are in. The purpose of this exercise is to learn to recognize, and then to redefine or relabel, an aspect of your experience or action. For example, the passive experience of depression or the compulsive repetition of overeating can become recognized as your reaction to particular experiences or as the consequences of particular ways of thinking about yourself. Once you have defined situations or the thoughts associated with your unwanted experiences or acts in this way, the possibility of alternative action becomes available. At this point you may move on from monitoring and redefinition to exploring and elaborating different ways of acting, and this may be aided by developing explicit alternative self-instructions. Initially these self-instructions may be essentially negative, for example "do not dwell on catastrophic thinking" or "think about what you are feeling and do not go to the cupboard for another slice of bread". As soon as possible they should be extended to the trying out of more positive and relevant acts designed to further your real wishes and aims.

Dilemmas

We very often continue to act in certain ways, even when we don't particularly enjoy what we do, because other possible ways seem as bad or worse. Yet there may in reality be many other ways of acting; it is just that our particular personal history has given us a narrow view of what is possible, or a narrow range of strategies. Dilemmas can be described briefly as "either/or", e.g. *either* in firm control of one's feelings *or* in chaotic confusion; or as "if/then", e.g. *if* feminine, *then* submitting to others.

In the "either/or" dilemma, the choices seem to lie between two courses: A and B. Not to do A implies necessarily doing B and vice versa. Restricted by such a dilemma one may alternate between A and B or, if one of the two is worse, say B, then one will be confined only to doing the other, A. In "if/then" dilemmas, to follow a desired course, C, is seen necessarily to imply an associated unwanted quality, D; seeing it this way, one may choose to give up C altogether, even though it is otherwise an appropriate and important aim.

Some dilemmas operate to restrict the ways in which we see it possible to relate to other people. Others are to do with how we control and look after ourselves. Think about ways in which you may restrict your options in this way. It may help you to look through the list of common dilemmas on the next sheet. Note any dilemma that you think may restrict the ways in which you go about your life.

Common dilemmas

(i) *If* caring for someone, *then* giving in to them.
(ii) *If* depending on someone, *then* controlling them.
(iii) *If* caring for someone, *then* controlling them.
(iv) *If* depending on someone, *then* giving in to them.
(v) *Either* dependent and controlling *or* caring and submissive.
(vi) *Either* caring and controlling *or* dependent and submissive.
(vii) *Either* involved with someone and vulnerable *or* detached and controlling.
(viii) *If* dependent, *then* guilty.
(ix) *Either* cut off and hence lonely, *or* emotionally involved and hence scared, confused, angry.
(x) *If* loved by another, *then* feeling trapped.
(xi) *If* feminine, *then* passive.
(xii) *If* masculine, *then* unemotional.
(xiii) *If* I win people's praise or approval by trying to please them or do what they want, *then* I feel childish/guilty/trapped/resentful.
(xiv) *Either* assertive and rejected by others *or* compliant and and abused/hurt by others.
(xv) *If* competitive, *then* feeling depressed, under stress, rejected by others.
(xvi) *Either* anxiously self-reliant *or* dependent and feeling childish/trapped/resentful.
(xvii) *If* I try to be perfect, *then* I feel depressed and angry and often blocked; if I don't try to be perfect, then I feel guilty, dissatisfied, anxious.
(xviii) *If* I get what I want, *then* I feel childish and guilty; *if* I don't get what I want, *then* I feel angry and depressed.
(xix) *Either* I keep feelings bottled up and feel cut off, depressed, *or* I express feelings and risk rejection/hurting others/making a mess.
(xx) *If* I must, *then* I won't (obligations from others, or even my own plans, are sensed as oppressive and I block, postpone, evade, and do not meet them).
(xxi) *If* not structured by tasks or by relationships with others, *then* I feel anxious, out of control.
(xxii) *Either* I spoil myself and am greedy, *or* I am self-denying and self-punishing.

It is obvious from the list that many dilemmas are familiar to most of us to some extent, representing as they do inescapable paradoxes of human life. They are sources of trouble when they are extreme and unresolved.

Snags

Many people have to deny or dismantle the gains, achievements or assertions which they make in their lives, and people wanting to change themselves often find that they are unable to take advantage of the gains they make. The process underlying this is a snag, as in, "I want to get better but the snag is . . .", but snag also stands for Subtle Negative Aspects of Goals. Such prohibitions on succeeding or doing or being may have external origins, for sometimes parents, spouses, lovers, or friends resist or seem unable to cope with one's changes. Often, however, the prohibitions are more subtle and are more in our own minds, not always consciously. Such self-prohibitions often relate to the need to avoid guilt. The guilt is usually quite irrational, stemming either from misinterpretations made early in life or from the experience of external prohibitions, of the sort described above, during childhood or adolescence.

Do you think in your own case there is any tendency to avoid success, deny success, or dismantle it, or any need to restrict your pleasure or interest in life, or to pay for it? If there is, do you have any idea where this might come from, taking account of the ideas put forward above?

In considering external snags, it is helpful to list the changes you hope to achieve in yourself and to imagine the reaction such changes might provoke in those people close to you Although in principle these people are probably all in favour of you getting better and doing what you want to do, it may be the case that the response of some (most often family member, lover, or spouse) is less clear and positive. There may, in fact, be quite powerful instructions implied by some relationships, based on attributions of identity (such as "he's always been such a gentle person . . .") or upon family myths ("in our family we never . . ." or "you are the one who always . . ."). Such views often restrict our sense of ourselves and they certainly do not define all the possible ways we might be. In some cases, as we change, these others will prove more able to accommodate to the new version of us than we expect; in other cases, there will be a rearguard action, and sometimes we are confronted with such major opposition that we have to choose between the change we desire and the continuation of the relationship.

Internal snags are more difficult to locate because they are sensed as being part of our nature and are based usually upon unacknowledged and irrational guilt. If, in your life, you can trace a pattern that could be described as one of having avoided, damaged, or paid for, your successes or for your existence, or if you habitually sell yourself short, hurt or deprive yourself, then you should suspect that you are "snagged". The guilt underlying a snag is often unconscious. Common sources are the illnesses, deaths, or disasters of parents or other family members during childhood or adolescence, for which one has assumed magical responsibility; or the experience of having been actively envied, commonly by parent, brother, or sister. If you can see that such a process is at work undermining your life, or if you can see that you act *as if* you were guilty, whether or not you experience guilt, you will begin to understand that your self-sabotage is arbitrary and undeserved. You will, however, have to recognize and fight against a tendency to forget that you know this, and a continuing tendency to give away the gains you make, because snags are subtle and persistent.

THE SELF-ESTEEM SOURCES TEST

In this section I am going to describe a simple test procedure which can be self-administered and self-scored, the aim of which is to identify trap behaviours. The test investigates the sources one relies upon for the maintenance of self-esteem. The acts we perform and the things needed from others to feel good about ourselves vary from person to person, and are not all equally effective. The aim of the Self-Esteem Sources Test is to guide one's examination of one's sources and of the costs and benefits attached to them. Going through this procedure often leads to the recognition of the fact that some of the sources one relies upon bring little benefit or high costs, so that acts intended to make one feel better are persisted in and, in fact, make one feel worse.

SES Test — page 1: Description and Instructions

The purpose of this test is to explore the sources you depend on to feel good and secure in yourself. People differ greatly in this respect and there are no right or wrong answers; the answers you give should be as accurate and undefensive as possible.

Thirty-eight possible sources are listed on SES Test page 2. Go through this list (taking time over each item, as you may not have thought about yourself in these terms before) and when you recognize an item that applies to you, circle its number. You can add other sources that are important to you, in the blanks (39–42, or more if you wish).

The second part of the test is an examination of the costs and benefits of these various *sources*. First pick out the fifteen items that are most important to you. In judging importance consider how much effort you put into them, and how much it would matter to you if they ceased to operate. Now turn to SES page 3 and list the numbers of these 15 in the space indicated at the top of the page. Fourteen possible effects or *consequences* are listed, and you may add further ones if you wish. Indicate the degree to which each of these possible consequences follows upon each of the 15 *sources* by giving a rating of 1 – 5 (see rating instructions). This part of the test should be completed fairly quickly, rating all the sources on each possible consequence in turn.

SES Test — page 2: In order to feel good about myself I need, or tend, to

1. Be a helpful and caring person.
2. Feel I am competent at my work.
3. Be tolerant and forgiving.
4. Avoid close emotional involvement.
5. Make certain I am not caught out.
6. Be loved by my family (i.e. parents, brothers, sisters, children).
7. Try to do what others want.
8. Be praised for what I do.
9. Behave badly in order to be reassured by the forgiveness of others.
10. Criticize or undervalue others.
11. Be a social success.
12. Be part of a group of friends giving mutual support.

13. Feel that I am sexually attractive.
14. Be placatory, avoid arguments.
15. Try to make up for what I feel is wrong with me.
16. Look good (e.g. clothes, make-up, etc.).
17. Disarm others (e.g. by weakness, sexuality, etc.).
18. Depend upon a stronger person.
19. Assert myself in work or social situations.
20. Think about what I hope to be or achieve.
21. Get intensely involved in people or activities.
22. Deprive or punish myself.
23. Know that I can make others want me sexually and/or emotionally.
24. Identify with and/or participate in something larger than myself (e.g. politics, religion, etc.).
25. Think about where I come from (e.g. family, class, country, etc.).
26. Give myself treats (e.g. food, comforts, presents, etc.).
27. Make others envy me.
28. Show I don't have to do what others want or expect.
29. Be active and productive all the time.
30. Control those I am emotionally close to.
31. Never show angry feelings.
32. Feel expert at the things that really concern me.
33. Feel properly valued and regarded for what I do.
34. Compete successfully with others.
35. Be loved by my spouse/lover.
36. Feel self-reliant.
37. Have others grateful to or dependent on me.
38. Be rejected or disliked by most people.
39.
40.
41.
42.

(*continued overleaf*)

SES Test — page 3

Ratings: 5 applies very strongly; 4 definitely applies; 3 may or may not apply; 2 does not apply; 1 very definitely does not apply.

Consequences	*List the numbers of the SESs that matter most to you here:*														
1. I feel calm															
2. I feel trapped															
3. I feel guilty															
4. I feel strong															
5. I feel hopeful															
6. I feel free															
7. I feel depressed															
8. I get what I want															
9. I feel under stress															
10. I feel confident															
11. I feel lonely															
12. I feel happy															
13. I feel childish															
14. I feel angry															
15.															
16.															
17.															
18.															

SES Test — page 4: Scoring Instructions

Go through the list of consequences and mark those you regard as indicating positive outcomes; for most people these are those numbered 1, 4, 5, 6, 8, 10, and 12. Mark these rows regarded as positive with a pencil or magic-marker line. Now go through each source in turn, adding up for each the total positive score. Now do the same for the consequences which you regard as negative (omitting any outcome you see as neutral or unimportant).

From these two sets of figures identify those sources that yield the highest negative and/or the lowest positive total scores. On the basis of this, consider why it is that this is the case, and why it is that you still rely upon sources that, at least in present terms, are unhelpful.

INTERPRETATION OF SES TEST

Anne

Anne's SES test was completed after her second assessment session. She had neither added nor omitted any consequences but she had rated all sources as 2 on the outcome *I feel angry*, so this was not included in the scoring. (This rating suggests a difficulty in acknowledging anger.) The highest potential positive score was therefore 35 for positive, and 30 for negative outcomes. The lowest positive scores (values in brackets) were in respect to the items: *control those I am emotionally close to* (16), *feel properly valued and regarded for what I do* (16), *be loved by my family* (16), and *identify with and/or participate in something larger than myself* (14). The highest negative scores were for *be a helpful and caring person* (19), *be loved by my family* (18), and *compete successfully with others* (18). We can see that, although at that time Anne could not directly acknowledge her difficult feelings for her family and did not know how much she tended to be controlling in relationships, and although she still prized perfectionist and ambitious work attitudes, the SES test recorded her awareness in detail of the low benefit and high costs attached to these ways of pursuing her two central aims of being loved and being successful.

David

David's SES test was similarly revealing. The lowest positive scores (22) and highest negative scores (15 and 17) were recorded for *I like to feel needed in some way by certain people* and *get involved intensely in people or activities*; both these refer to issues which, it will be remembered, played an important part in his predicament.

In a study of twenty-eight patients who completed the SES test during assessment, the outcomes attached to various commonly selected sources were classified as positive, negative, or mixed (for this purpose a more complex scoring system was used but the results produced are essentially the same as those coming from the method described above). Mixed consequences were those where the outcomes included high ratings for both positive and negative effects. Self-dependent sources like *being competent, expert,* and *self-reliant* gave largely positive outcomes, although assertion was negative or mixed in effect in half the cases. Other-dependent sources such as *being praised, being properly valued,* and *feeling sexually attractive* were associated with largely positive outcomes, but *being placatory* and *avoiding arguments* were predominantly negative in effect, and *being a helpful and caring* person was negative or mixed in a third of subjects. *Being loved by family* or *being loved by spouse or lover* had unmixed positive consequences in only one third of this patient population.

The explicit recognition of the effects of acts designed to reinforce self-esteem is aided by this simple procedure; faced with high-cost or low-gain procedures, one can begin to consider whether the sources should be abandoned or whether their terms and implications should be revised.

SIMPLE BEHAVIOURAL TECHNIQUES

To complete this chapter, we will consider some simple behavioural methods. The following descriptions could serve as a bases for a self-administered programme or for a professionally supervised one.

(a) Relaxation

Relaxation requires practice. Some people can relax "all at once" by letting their whole body go limp and heavy. For others, relaxation is best achieved piecemeal, by learning to relax one part of the body at a time, either by tightening and then loosening a particular group of muscles, or by thinking of a part such as a limb or the neck and imagining it to be heavy and loose. Try out which method suits you best and practice it daily. While relaxing, breathe more slowly and deeply than usual. It may help you to memorize, or even tape-record, the self-instructions that you find most useful in achieving relaxation. The ability to achieve relaxation voluntarily can help one cope with tense situations, even if one does not achieve complete relaxation under those circumstances.

(b) Rehearsal

Some people find it helpful to imagine feared situations before entering them. To do this requires you to be good at relaxing. Try to imagine the feared situation in as vivid detail as possible, and similarly try to recreate your reaction to it. As soon as you begin to feel tense or anxious, then turn your attention to the induction of relaxation; once you are relaxed again, return once more to imagining the situation. Repeat this process several times. Rehearsal in this way can be built into programmes of graded exposure to feared situations (see below).

(c) Self-instruction

Linked with this rehearsal in imagination of a situation and your response to it, you can also rehearse ways of dealing with it. These can take the form of reassuring statements about the absence of real danger, reminders of the immediate goal and of your long-term intentions of losing symptoms, or recollections of the satisfaction of previous situations which you have coped with. Sometimes it helps to carry written reminders of these into the actual situation, or to use objects or phrases as talismans to take with you. As well as such reassurances, try to prepare effective ways of coping with the situation, and rehearse simple reminders of these ways.

(d) Paradoxical intention

The quickest way to get over a fear about having symptoms is to try to have the symptoms. This approach works very well for some people with situationally-provoked anxiety or panic. The method involves you in determining to have the symptoms as soon as you enter the situation or, if you begin to have the symptom, in attempting to have it as thoroughly as you can manage. The paradox is that this usually prevents the symptom developing; even if that is not the case, the situation is no worse than usual, so nothing has been lost. The explanation is that you cannot deliberately lose control. For symptoms which are maintained by performance anxiety (such as insomnia, impotence, inability to urinate in public toilets), the instruction is to enter the situation with the express intention of *avoiding* the performance (sleep, intercourse, urination). Increasingly prolonged and frequent exposure under these conditions leads, in the end, to the anxiety diminishing to the point at which the rule to avoid attempting the performance is broken.

(e) Overcoming avoidance behaviours

If you avoid situations because of physical symptoms, and if you have any doubt about whether the symptoms you experience are dangerous, seek medical advice. The ordinary symptoms of fear or panic, however extreme, are never dangerous to a healthy person, but could put a strain on someone with physical disease. Once you are sure on this point, proceed with a graded programme of exposure as follows. To begin with, prepare a detailed list of all the situations you avoid or have difficulty in entering, and list them in order from the least difficult to the most difficult. On the basis of this list, go through a programme of exposing yourself to increasingly difficult situations. For each exposure set a clear goal and do not proceed to a more difficult situation until that goal has been achieved. Each exposure may be preceded by rehearsal in imagination as described above, if you find that helpful. However, the essential fact is that recovery from avoidance behaviours depends upon staying in the feared situation. The more fearful the situation entered, and the longer you stay in it, the quicker the effect. To start with, however, do not be over-ambitious about the difficulty of the situation but do aim to stay in it as long as possible. Remember that you will certainly have some symptoms, remember that you can leave if you have to, but try to stay in as long as possible, preferably until you are bored, not scared. In putting yourself through such a programme, get rid of "props" such as being accompanied by other people or dogs, depending upon carrying walking-sticks or cases, or hiding behind newspapers. If you depend upon these to cope with a given situation, your next task should be to cope with the same situation without these "props". Similarly, if you use alcohol or tranquillizers you should aim to manage a situation without them before you attempt any more difficult situations. If you do use drugs, take them 2 to 3 hours before you go into the difficult situation so that the effects of the drug will wear off while you are in that situation and give you the experience of mastering your fear on your own. After each exposure, record the place and duration and some measure of how bad you felt and for how long. If you have a friend who knows about your programme, show him the record from time to time. If you have a set-back, which is likely, enter a less difficult situation as soon as possible and proceed to increase your range again from that point. Your record will show you how, over time, you do make progress and also how the intensity and duration of fear subsides, and it will prevent your becoming discouraged by inaccurate, negatively biased self-evaluations.

The above description applies particularly to phobic avoidance, but the overcoming of obsessive–compulsive behaviours is based on essentially similar methods. Rituals are ways of controlling fear, and to overcome them involves accepting exposure to fear without the magical reassurance of the ritual act. The seeking of reassurance from others can itself become a compulsion, and the co-operation of close others in withholding such reassurance and in supporting resistance to the compulsions is an important back-up to the individual's programme of graded exposure.

DISCUSSION

Interest in self-help aids has been confined to the behavioural and cognitive tradition, where it represents a logical extension of the use of specific homework assignments in therapy. Psychoanalysts, with their emphasis on unconscious mental processes and on the transference as the agent of cure, would clearly be sceptical. Little good evidence exists for the effectiveness of the behavioural self-help literature (Glasgow and Rosen 1978). I have no evidence for the effectiveness of the material described in this chapter beyond the reports of my patients, many of whom have found them useful in maintaining and extending the understandings reached during sessions.

15
Afterword

Just as a patient, in the act of telling his story to a psychotherapist, may discover that he understands more than he knew, so an author in the act of writing may clarify and extend the ideas which prompted him to write. While my original aim has been largely achieved, and while my approach has largely followed what I originally envisaged, I am aware of a number of shifts in emphasis that have resulted from the act of writing this book. These are not easily conveyed because they are somewhat paradoxical. In many respects the book makes a larger and more definite claim than I had anticipated and yet, at the same time, I have the sense that experienced practitioners will read much of it with a sense of familiarity. I think this is a reflection of the fact that therapists are often more flexible and various and less restrained in action than they are in their theoretical writing. Some of the positions I have discussed or dismissed polemically may seem to such people windmills rather than giants. The gap between acts and the accounts given of acts is, however, one that needs closing, and if I have contributed to that closure I am satisfied. I have argued throughout the book that a main function of therapy is the provision to patients of accurate, usable accounts of how they think and act, and the attempt to do the same for therapists seems appropriate.

No attempt is made to proclaim a New Therapy; I think it is unfortunate that inflated claims are nearly always made for new ideas or approaches in the field of psychotherapy; current enthusiasm for cognitive psychotherapy seems to be a contemporary example of this. In my own view, it is impossible for any one contribution in this field to dispose of all the issues, and exaggerated claims such as are expressed most baldly on the dust-jackets or in publishers' advertisements serve only to delay the evolution of a more coherent theoretical base for the field. In this book, I have offered an account of practice that is largely derived from psychoanalysis, behaviourist and cognitive therapies, and the suggested name of cognitive–analytic therapy declares this derivation; but I am aware that there are many other therapeutic methods I have not discussed that may also have their place. In the procedural sequence model, however, I have proposed a simple schematic description of the essential processes involved in human action and change, and I believe that the full range of neurotic difficulties and of psychotherapeutic methods can be understood in relation to this model. The idea that psychotherapeutic theory is at the point of a paradigm shift is commonly expressed, and the dominance of inadequate paradigms in the field can hardly be denied. If this book has contributed to the evolution of a shared, integrated account, it will have achieved its main purpose.

References

Amacher, P. (1974). The concept of the pleasure principle and infantile erogenous zones shaped by Freud's neurological education. *Psychoanal. Quarterly* **43**, 218–223

Appelbaum, S.A. (1977). The anatomy of change *In* "Menninger Foundation Report on Testing the Effects of Psychotherapy". New York and London, Plenum Press.

Ascher, L.M. and Turner, R.M. (1980). A comparison of two methods for the administration of paradoxical intention. *Behaviour Research and Therapy* **18**, 121–126.

St Augustine. (1961). "Confessions" (Tr. Pine-Coffin, R.S.) Harmondsworth, Penguin.

Bancroft, J. (1975). The behavioural approach to marital problems. *Brit. J. Med. Psychol.* **48**, 147–152.

Bandura, A. (1977a). "Social Learning Theory". Eaglewood Cliffs N.J., Prentice-Hall.

Bandura, A. (1977b). Self-Efficacy — towards a unifying theory of behavioural change. *Psychol. Review* **84**, 191–215.

Bartlett, F.C. (1954). "Remembering: A Study in Experimental and Social Psychology." Cambridge, C.U.P.

Battle, C.C., Imber, S.D., Hoehn-Saric, R., Stone, A.R., Nash, E.R. and Frank, J.D. Target complaints as criteria of improvement. *Am. J. Psychother.* **20**, 184–192.

Bayer C.A. (1972). Self-monitoring and mild aversion treatment of trichitillomania. *J. Behav. Research and Exp. Psychiat.* **3**, 139–141.

Beck, A.T. (1976). "Cognitive Therapy and the Emotional Disorders". New York, Int. Univ. Press.

Bergin, A.E. (1966): Some implications of psychotherapy research for therapeutic practice. *J. Abnorm. Psychol.* **71**, 235–246.

Bergin, A.E. and Garfield, S.L. (1971). "Handbook of Psychotherapy and Behaviour Change". New York and London, John Wiley & Sons.

Bergin, A.E. and Strupp, H.H. (1972). "Changing Frontiers in the Science of Psychotherapy" New York, Aldine and Atherton.

Blacke, Y. (1968). Psychotherapy with the more disturbed patient. *Brit. J. Med. Psychol.* **41**, 199–207.

Bower, G.H. (1978). Contacts of cognitive psychology with social learning theory. *Cognitive Ther. and Research* **2**, 123–146

Brown, D. and Pedder, J. (1979). "Introduction to Psychotherapy" London, Tavistock Publications.

Bruch, H. (1973). "Eating Disorders — Obesity, Anorexia and the Person Within". New York, Basic Books.

Bruner, J. (1966). "Toward a Theory of Instruction" Cambridge, Mass., Harvard Univ. Press.

Cade, B. (1979). The use of paradox in therapy. *In* "Family and Marital Psychotherapy" (Waldrond-Skinner S. ed.) London, Routledge & Kegan Paul.

Candy, J., Balfour, F.H.G., Cawley, R.H., Hildebrand, H.P., Malan, D.H., Marks, I.M. and Wilson, J. (1972). A feasibility study for a controlled trial of formal psychotherapy. *Psychol. Med.* **2**, 345–362

Crowe, M. (1979). The treatment of sexual dysfunction. *In* "Family and Marital Psychotherapy" (Waldrond-Skinner S. ed.) London, Routledge & Kegan Paul.

Davanloo, Ho. (Ed.) (1979). "Basic Principles and Techniques in Short-Term Dynamic Psychotherapy". New York, Spectrum Publications.

Davanloo, H. (Ed.) (1980). "Current Trends in Short-Term Dynamic Therapy" New York, Aronson.

Dockar-Drysdale, B. (1968). "Therapy in Child Care". London, Longman.

Ellis, A. (1962). "Reason and Emotion in Psychotherapy". New York, Lyle Stuart.

Emmelkamp, P.N.G. and Wessels, H. (1975). Flooding in imagination v. flooding in vivo. A comparison with agoraphobics. *Behav. Res. and Therapy* **13**, 7–15.

Epstein, S. (1973) The self concept revisited, *American Psychologist*, May issue 404–416.

Erikson, E. (1959). Identity and the Life Cycle. *Psychol. Issues* **No 1**.

Fairbairn, B.D. (1952). "Psychoanalytic Studies of the Personality" London, Tavistock Publications.

Försterling, F. (1980). Attributional aspects of cognitive behaviour modification: a theoretical approach and suggestions for techniques. *Cognitive Ther. and Research*, **4**, 27–37.

Freud, A. (1936). "The Ego and the Mechanisms of Defence". London, Hogarth Press.

Freud, S. (1933). "New Introductory Lectures on Psychoanalysis". Standard Edition, Vol. 22. London, Hogarth Press.

Freud, S. (1937). "Constructions in Analysis" Standard Edition, Vol. 23. London, Hogarth Press.

Gallwey, P.L.G. (1978). Transference utilisation in aim-restricted psychotherapy. *Brit. J. Med. Psychol.* **31**, 225–236.

Gelder, M. (1979). Behaviour therapy for neurotic disorders *Behav. Modification,* **3**, 469–495.

Gill, H. (1978). The reconstruction of childhood in psychoanalysis. *Brit. J. Med. Psychol.* **51**, 311–318.

Glasgow, R.E. and Rosen, G.M. (1978). Bibliotherapy: a review of self-help behaviour therapy manuals. *Psychol. Bulletin*, **85**, 1–23.

Goin, M.C. & Kline, F.M. (1974). Supervision observed. *J. Nerv. Ment. Diseases*, **158**, 208.

Goldfried, M.R. (1979). Anxiety reduction through cognitive/behavioural intervention. *In* "Cognitive and Behavioural Intervention: A Theory of Research Procedures". Kendall P.C. and Hollon S.D. (eds). New York and London, Academic Press.

Goldfried, M.R. and Golfried, A.P. (1975). Cognitive change methods. *In* "Helping People Change". Oxford and New York, Pergamon Press.

Green, H. (1964) "I Never Promised You a Rose-Garden" London, Gollancz.

Guntrip, H. (1961) "Personality Structure and Human Interaction". London, Hogarth Press.

Guntrip, H. (1968). "Schizoid Phenomena: Object-Relations and the Self". London, Hogarth Press.

Gurman, A.S. and Razin, A.M. (1977) "Effective Psychotherapy: A Handbook of Research". Oxford and New York, Pergamon Press.

Haan, N. (1977). "Coping and Defending. Processes of Self-Environment Organization"

New York and London, Academic Press.
Hafner, R.J. (1977). The husbands of agoraphobic women and their influence on treatment outcome. *Brit. J. Psychiat.*, **131**, 289.
Hafner, R.J. (1979). Agoraphobic women married to abnormally jealous men. *Brit. J. Med. Psychol.*, **52**, 99–104.
Haldane, J.D., Alexander A.D., Hebditch J.G. and Walker L.G. (1979). Training in psychotherapy: the Aberdeen University diploma course: Second Report. *Bulletin of the Royal College of Psychiatrists* (Sept).
Haley, J. (1963). "Strategies of Psychotherapy". New York, Grune & Stratton.
Hartmann, H. (1950). Notes on the psychoanalytic theory of the ego. *Psychoanal. Study of the Child,* **5**, 74–95.
Heppner, P.P. (1978). A review of the problem-solving literature and its relationship to the counselling process. *J. Couns. Psychol.*, **25**, 366–375.
Holzman, P.S. (1978). *In* "The Human Mind Revisited" Sidney Smith (ed.). New York, Int. Univ. Press.
Horney, K. (1937). "The Neurotic Personality of Our Time". New York, Norton.
Kaplan, H. (1974). "The New Sex Therapy". New York.
Katz, J.M. (1980). Discrepancy, arousal and labelling: towards a psycho–social theory of emotion. *Sociological Inquiry,* **50**, 147–156.
Kazdin, A. and Wilson, G.T. (1978). "Evaluation of Behaviour Therapy: Issues, Evidence and Research Strategies". Cambridge, Mass.,Bellinger.
Kelly, G.A. (1955). "The Psychology of Personal Constructs" New York, Norton.
Kennedy, H. (1971). Problems in reconstruction in child analysis. *Psychoanal. Study of the Child,* **26**, 386–402.
Kernberg, O. (1967). Borderline Personality Organization. *J. Am. Psychoanal. Assoc.*, **15**, 641–685.
Kernberg, O. (1974). Further contributions to the treatment of narcissistic personalities. *Int. J. Psychoanal.*, **55**, 215–240.
Khan, M.M.R. (1970). Towards an epistemology of the process of cure. *Brit. J. Med. Psychol.*, **43**, 363-366.
Klein, G. (1970). "Perception, Motives and Personality". New York, Knopf.
Kohut, H. and Wolf, E.S. (1978). The disorders of the self and their treatment: an outline. *Int. J. Psychoanal.*, **59**, 413–425.
Kovacs, M. (1979). Treating depressive disorders: the efficacy of behavioural and cognitive therapies. *Behav. Modification,* **3**, 496–517.
Kris, E. (1956). The recovery of childhood memories in psychoanalysis. *Psychoanal. Study of the Child,* **11**, 54–88.
Kris, A.D. (1977). Either–or dilemmas. *Psychoanal. Study of the Child,* **32**.
Kubie, L.S. (1968). Research into the Process of supervision in psychoanalysis. *Psychoanal. Quarterly,* **27**, 226–234.
Kuhn. T.S. (1962). "The Structure of Scientific Revolutions". Chicago, Univ. Chicago Press.
Laing, R. (1967). "The Politics of Experience". Harmondsworth, Penguin Press.
Lang, P.J. (1977). Imagery in therapy: an information processing analysis of fear. *Behav. Ther.*, **8**, 862–886.
Lazarus, A. (1971). "Behaviour Therapy and Beyond". New York, McGraw-Hill.
Lieberman, S., Hafner, R.J. and Crisp, A.H. (1978). Teaching psychotherapy in mental hospitals. *Brit. J. Psychiat.*, **132**, 398–402.
Loevinger, J. (1976). "Ego Development: Conception and Theories". San Francisco, Jossey Bass.

995–1008.
Mahler, M.S., Pine, F. and Bergman, A. (1975). "The Psychological Birth of the Human Infant". London, Hutchinson.
Mahoney, M.J. (1974). "Cognitive and Behaviour Modification". Cambridge, Mass., Ballinger.
Malan D.H. (1963). "A Study of Brief Psychotherapy". London, Tavistock Publications.
Malan, D.H. (1976a). "Toward the Validation of Dynamic Psychotherapy". New York and London, Plenum Medical Press.
Malan, D.H. (1976b). "The Frontiers of Brief Psychotherapy". London, Hutchinson.
Malan, D.H., Heath, E.S., Bacal, H.A., Balfour, F.H.G. (1975). Psychodynamic changes in untreated neurotic patients. *Arch. Gen. Psychiat.*, **32**, 110–126.
Mancuso, J.C. and Ceely, S.G. (1980). The self as memory processing. *Cognitive Ther. and Research,* **4**, 1–25.
Main, T.F. (1957). The ailment. *Brit. J. Med. Psychol., 30*, 129–145.
Mann, J. (1973). "Time-Limited Psychotherapy" Cambridge, Mass., Harvard Univ. Press.
Margison, F. (1980). Teaching psychotherapy skills to postgraduate psychiatrists. *Bulletin of the Royal College of Psychiatrists* (December).
Marmor, J. Woods, S.W. (Eds) (1980). "The Interface Between the Psychodynamic and Behavioural Therapies". New York, and London, Plenum Medical Books.
Masters, W.H. and Johnson, V.E. (1966). "Human Sexual Response". Boston, Little, Brown & Co.
Matarazzo, R.G. (1971). Research on the teaching and learning of psychotherapeutic skills. *In* "A Handbook of Psychotherapy and Behaviour Change" (Bergen, A.E. and Garfield, S.L. eds) New York, John Wiley & Sons.
McCoy, M. (1977). A reconstruction of emotion *In* "New Perspectives in Personal Construct Theory" (Bannister, D. ed.) London and New York, Academic Press.
Mead, G.H. (1964). "On Social Psychology". Chicago and London, Univ. Chicago Press.
Meares, R.A. and Hobson, R.F. (1977). "The Persecutory Therapist". *Brit. J. Med. Psychol.,* **50**, 349–359.
Meichenbaum, D.H. (1977). "Cognitive Behaviour Modification". New York, Plenum Press.
Miller, G.A., Galanter, E. and Pribram, F.H. (1960). "Plans and the Structure of Behaviour". New York, Holt.
Milner, M. (1969). "The Hands of the Living God" London, Hogarth Press.
Minsky, M. and Pappert, S. (1972). Artifical intelligence. *Progress Report, Massachusetts Inst. Technology.*
Mischel, W. (1973). Towards a cognitive social learning reconceptualisation of personality. *Psychol. Rev.,* **80**, 252–283.
Neisser, U. (1967). "Cognitive Psychology". New York, Appleton.
Noy, P. (1979). The psychoanalytic theory of cognitive development. *Psychoanal. Study of the Child,* **34**, 169–216.
Oatley, K. (1978). "Perceptions and Representations". London, Methuen.
Oatley, K. (1981), Representing ourselves: mental schemata, computational metaphors and the nature of consciousness. *In* "Aspects of Consciousness", Vol. II, 85–117, (Underwood, G. and Stevens, R. eds). London and New York, Academic Press.
Olds, D. (1981). Stagnation in psychotherapy and the development of active techniques. *Psychiatry* **44**, 135–140.
Older, J. (1971). Four taboos that may limit the success of psychotherapy. *Psychiatry* **40**, 197–204.
Parkes, C.M. (1975). "Bereavement: Studies of Grief in Adult Life" London and Harmondsworth, Penguin Books.
Perry, J.C. and Klerman, G.L. (1978). The borderline patient: a comparative analysis of four sets of diagnostic criteria. *Arch. Gen. Psychiatry,* **35**, 141–150.

Pine, F. (1979). On the pathology of the separation–individuation process as manifested in later clinical work: an attempt at delineation. *Int. J. Psychoanal.* **60**, 225–242.
Pines, M. (1980). What to expect in the psychotherapy of the borderline patient. ''Group Analysis'', **13**, 168–177.
Plutchik, R. (1980). A language for the emotions. *Psychology Today* (February), 68–78.
Rehm, L.P. (1977). A Self-Control Model of depression. *Behav. Ther.*, **8**, 787–804.
Roth, S. (1980), A revised model of learned helplesness in humans. *J. Personality*, **48**, 103–133.
Rotter, J.B. (1966). Generalized expectancies for internal versus external locus of control of reinforcement. *Psychol. Monograph*, No. 609.
Rotter, J.B. (1978). Generalized expectancies for problem-solving and psychotherapy. *Cognitive Therapy and Research*, **2**, 1–10
Rush, A.J., Beck, A.T., Kovacs, M. and Hollon, S. (1977). Comparative efficacy of cognitive therapy and pharmacotherapy in the treatment of depressed outpatients. *Cognitive Therapy and Research,* **11**, 17–37.
Ryle A. (1975). ''Frames and Cages''. London, Sussex Univ. Press, Chatto & Windus.
Ryle, A. (1979a). Defining goals and assessing change in brief psychotherapy: a pilot study using target ratings and the dyad grid. *Brit. J. Med. Psychol.*, **52**, 223–233.
Ryle A. (1979b). The focus in brief interpretive psychotherapy: dilemmas, traps and snags as target problems. *Brit. J. Psychiat.* **134**, 46–54.
Ryle, A. (1980). Some measures of goal attainment in focussed, integrated, active psychotherapy: a study of fifteen cases. *Brit. J. Psychiat.* **137**, 475–486.
Ryle, A. (1981). Dyad grid dilemmas in patient and control subjects. *Brit. J. Med. Psychol.* **54**, 353–358.
Ryle, G. (1979) ''On Thinking'', Oxford and London, O.U.P.
Sandler, J. and Joffe, W.G. (1970). Towards a basic psychoanalytic model. *Int. J. Psychoanal.* **51**, 183–193.
Sandler, J., Dare, C. and Holder, A. (1973). "The patient and the analyst. The basis of the psychoanalytic process." London, George Allen & Unwin.
Santostefano, S. (1980). Cognition and personality in the treatment process. *Psychoanal. Study of the Child,* **35**, 41–66.
Schachtel, E.G. (1959). ''Metamorphosis: On the Development of Affect, Perception, Attention and Memory''. New York, Basic Books.
Schachter, S. (1964). The Interaction of cognitive and physiological determinants of emotional states. *In* ''Psychological Approaches to Social Behaviour''. (Leidermann, P.D. and Shapiro, D. eds). California, Stanford Univ. Press.
Schachter, S. and Singer, J.F. (1962). Cognitive, social and psychological determinants of emotional states. *Psychol. Review,* **69**, 379–399.
Schafer, R. (1975). Psychoanalysis without psychodynamics. *Int. J. Psychoanal.*, **56**, 41–55.
Schafer, R. (1978). ''Language and Insight'' Newhaven and London, Yale Univ. Press.
Sifneous, P.E. (1972). ''Short-Term Psychotherapy and Emotional Crisis''. Cambridge, Mass., Harvard Univ. Press.
Singer, G.L. (1974). ''Imagery and Day Dream Methods in Psychotherapy and Behaviour Modification''. New York and London, Academic Press.
Skynner, A.C.R. (1976). ''One Flesh, Separate Persons: Principles of Family and Marital Psychotherapy''. London, Constable.
Slater, P. (1972). ''Notes on Ingrid '72''. London, Inst. of Psychiatry.
Slater, P. (1972). The measurement of consistency in repertory grids. *Brit. J. Psychiat.*, **121**, 45–51.
Sloane, R.B., Staples, S.R., Cristol, A.H., Yorkston, N.J. and Whipple, K. (1975). ''Psychotherapy Versus Behaviour Therapy''. Cambridge, Mass. and London, Harvard Univ. Press.

Stanton, A.H. and Schwartz, M.S. (1954). "The Mental Hospital". New York, Basic Books.

Steiner, J. (1979). The border between the paranoid schizoid and the depressive positions in the borderline patient. *Brit. J. Med. Psychol.*, **52**, 385–391.

Strachey, J. (1934). The nature of the therapeutic action of psychoanalysis. *Int. J. Psychoanal.*, **15**, 127–159.

Strupp, H.H. (1975). Psychoanalysis, "focal psychotherapy" and the nature of the psychotherapeutic influence. *Arch. Gen. Psychiatry*, **32**, 127–135.

Turner, J. (1980). "Made for Life — Coping, Competence and Cognition". London and New York, Methuen.

White, R.W. (1963). Ego and Reality in psychoanalytic theory: a proposal regarding independent ego energies. *Psychol. Issues*, III, 3, Monograph 11.

Whitehead, A. (1979). Psychological treatment of depression: A review. *Behav. Research and Therapy*, **17**, 495–509.

Wilson, G.T. (1978). *In* "Cognitive Behaviour Therapy". (Foreyt, J.D. and Rathjen, D.P. eds). New York and London, Plenum Books.

Winnicott, D.W. (1958). "Collected Papers" London, Tavistock Publications.

Winnicott, D.W. (1965). "The Maturational Process and the Facilitating Environment". London, Hogarth Press.

Wolberg, L.R. (ed.) (1965). "Short-Term Psychotherapy". New York, Grune & Stratton.

Wood, D., Bruner, J.E. and Ross, G. (1976). The role of tutoring in problem-solving. *J. Child Psychol. Psychiat.*, **17**, 89–100.

Appendix
Repertory Grid Contributions to Understanding

The repertory grid technique, evolved from the work of Kelly (1955) and related to his construct theory, was my own first direct introduction to a cognitive approach to the issues facing psychotherapists. The first 10 years of my work with this technique are summarized in Ryle (1975) and subsequent papers have reported the further uses of the method for the investigation of couples (Ryle and Lipshitz, 1975, 1976) and as the means of identifying and recording change in therapy (Ryle, 1979 and 1980)

REPERTORY GRID TECHNIQUE

The basic grid technique is relatively simple. A grid is made up of a subject's systematic ratings of a range of *elements* according to how well they are described by a range of *constructs*; in relation to psychotherapy, the elements are commonly people or, in the dyad grid (Ryle and Lunghi, 1970), the relationships between people — usually those between the subject and a range of others. Which kind of people, or relationships, may be indicated by the tester, but they will always be those of importance to the subject. The constructs are the terms by which these people or relationships are described. These terms may be wholly or partly supplied by the tester, provided they make sense to the subject, but it is usually best for at least some of them to be elicited from the subject. Elicitation involves presenting random pairs or triads of elements to the subject, and noting all the contrasts and similarities he marks between them. When the elements and constructs have been elicited and listed, the subject rates each element against each construct, usually on a 5 or 7 point scale, according to how far the construct applies.

The resulting matrix of figures represents a mathematical space in which the constructs are dispersed in the space defined by the elements, and the elements are dispersed in the space defined by the constructs. These relationships can be analysed by the use of Slater's Ingrid 72 program (Slater 1972a). A table of construct correlations provides a means of seeing how far each construct is used similarly or differently to each other construct and, hence, provides access to the individual's idiosyncratic network of meanings. A table of element distances provides similar information about the overall similarities and differences between elements in terms of the constructs used. A principal component analysis extracts the principal mathematical components of the grid and gives the loadings of each construct and each element on these components. By plotting out the distribution of elements and constructs in terms of the first two components (which commonly account for 60% or more of total variance) a "map of conceptual space" is obtained, the elements being dispersed in regions, the meanings of which are indicated by the construct loadings.

Fuller accounts of grid technique are to be found in Ryle (1976) and Fransella and Bannister (1977). For those who are scared off by the mathematical proceedings, the point of the analysis can be summarized simply in prose. It shows, for the subject tested, what goes with what: what judgements with what judgements; what people or relationships with what people or relationships; what people or relationships with what judgements.

To illustrate the use of grids and their relation to psychotherapy, I will first briefly summarize the application of dyad grids, where the elements are relationships, to outcome research; I will then consider the relationship of grid data to the issue of consciousness; and then present the dyad grid data on the patient, Anne, whom we have followed through many chapters of this book.

SPECIFYING COGNITIVE GOALS IN OUTCOME RESEARCH

Where two constructs, for example *dependent upon* and *gives in to* are highly correlated, one can say that, for this person, there is a dilemma as defined in Chapter 3, which can be expressed as "*if* dependent, *then* giving in to"; similarly, a low correlation between *looks after* and *controls* implies the dilemma "*either* looking after *or* controlling". Provided that the elements in the grid are a typical or inclusive example of the type of relationship being considered, such correlations will indicate assumptions that will be reflected in the way the person sets about his relationships, and may explain or constitute his difficulties. In this sense we are assuming that the judgements in the grid are a sample of the general construct system used by the individual. In the examples above, in the first instance *dependency*, and in the second *looking after*, are seen as risky and are likely to be avoided or to have bad consequences because they imply loss of control.

Dyad grid testing of a patient during the assessment priod can serve, therefore, to identify dilemmas and, in practice dilemmas so identified usually help illuminate the person's difficulties. In a pilot study of six cases (Ryle, 1979a) and in a second study of fifteen cases (Ryle, 1980) the resolution of such dilemmas was made one of the goals of therapy. It was predicted that successful therapy would be reflected in changes in the value of the construct correlations in the appropriate direction. These predictions of specific cognitive changes were tested at the end of treatment by repeating the repertory grid and were confirmed in the great majority of instances. The grid, therefore, helped to identify dilemmas, the revision of the dilemmas was made one of the specific goals of treatment in the manner explained earlier in this book, and retesting after treatment confirmed that the problematic cognitive features had been modified.

The recognition of psychologically significant dilemmas from grid data depends essentially upon establishing with the patient the relevance of the identified dilemma to their life problems. Some guidance as to the likely significance of such dilemmas on the grid may be provided by normative date and, having used a dyad grid with some standard supplied constructs over a series of patients, I have calculated the means and standard deviations of the correlations between the following constructs: *dependent on, looks after, gives in to, controls, gets cross with.* The values of these, expressed as angular distances (0° = a correlation of +1; 90° = a correlation of 0; 180° = a correlation of —1) are given in Table 1. Values of more than one standard deviation from the mean usually identify clinically relevant dilemmas (Ryle, 1981).

Table 1

	Is cross with	Gives in to	Controls	Is dependent on
Looks after	93 SD 30	73 SD 20	74 SD 25	73 SD 23
Is dependent on	89 SD 20	64 SD 21	83 SD 23	
Controls	79 SD 29	96 SD 24		
Gives in to	90 SD 18			

GRID DATA AND CONSCIOUSNESS

A subject, in completing his grid test, exercises a large number of discrete conscious judgments. In discussing the results of grid testing after the grids have been analysed with subjects, one is frequently faced with their surprise. The fact that one always regards people who are caring as submissive may not have struck one; the similarity of one's relationship with one's girlfriend and with one's mother may be a revelation; or the fact that one always plays the same role in relation to others may never have been realized. In terms of the PSM, this suggests that, at the "tactical" level of encounters with others, such as are described in the grid ratings, one's judgements and acts are guided by more general ("strategic") assumptions of which one is incompletely aware. Bringing these strategic assumptions to a person's awareness provides him with more accurate self-monitoring, and opens the way to greater control. While the origins of such strategies may include "dynamically unconscious" factors, e.g. the repression of forbidden anger, the recognition of the patterns is not resisted by the patient, and is frequently followed by "de-repression" in the sense of his allowing the recognition and expression of feelings and aims not previously acknowledged.

ANNE'S DYAD GRID

Anne was given a standard form of a dyad repertory grid to complete at the end of her second assessment session. The instructions attached to the form and a copy of the form are given in Fig. 1a and b. Anne amended the constructs *gets cross with* and *blames* by adding "implicitly often" and "implicitly always" to them. The relationships listed on her form were with her husband, two contemporary male friends, her brother, an older male friend, and her sister. Angular distances between

Appendix Fig. 1a Relationships Test

The purpose of this form is to help in the understanding of the patterns of your relationships with others. It is part of an ongoing research project and a similar form has proved useful in identifying difficulties and clarifying the goals of treatment. You are asked to rate a number of relationships against a number of descriptions; some descriptions are provided and some relationships named, but there are also spaces for you to add your own. First decide which relationship you are going to add, listing these people in the numbered spaces below, giving their initials, their sex, and their relationship; e.g. boyfriend; female flatmate; hated male teacher; sister, etc.

	Initials	*Sex*	*Role in your life*
1.			
2.			
3.			
4.			
5.			
6.			

Now choose at random any two of these and jot down, on scrap paper, descriptions of how they feel and act towards you, and of how you feel and act towards them, noting both similarities and differences. Repeat this with different relationships, and go on until you feel the important descriptions have been noted. Now turn to page 2 [Fig. 1b], the rating form; you will see that ten descriptions are provided and that a further 6 spaces are left blank. Write into these six spaces the six most important of your own descriptions, leaving out any that are already provided. At the top of the form you will see the numbered relationships, these numbers corresponding to your list above. Each relationship is rated against each description by allocating a score between 5 (very true) and 1 (not true at all). Fill in the form fairly quickly, rating all the relationships on each description in turn (i.e. fill row by row, not column by column). After it has been processed, we will discuss what can be deduced from the test.

Appendix Fig. 16

No.: Date: *5 = Very true 4 = True 3 = ± 2 = Not true 1 = Not true at all	Mother to Father	Father to Mother	Self to Father at age:	Father to Self	Self to Mother at age:	Mother to Self	Self to (1)	(1) to Self	Self to (2)	(2) to Self	Self to (3)	(3) to Self	Self to (4)	(4) to Self	Self to (5)	(5) to Self	Self to (6)	(6) to Self	Self to Self
1. Looks after																			
2. Is forgiving to																			
3. Respects																			
4. Controls																			
5. Feels guilty to																			
6. Is dependent on																			
7. Gets cross with																			
8. Blames																			
9. Gives in to																			
10. Confuses																			
11.																			
12.																			
13.																			
14.																			
15.																			
16.																			

* Rate each relationship on each description with a number, thus scoring according to the degree to which the description applies.

the five constructs *looks after, controls, is dependent on, is cross with,* and *gives in to* that differed by more than one standard deviation from the mean for the patient population were identified as follows: the correlation between *looks after* and *is dependent on* was low (−0.15) indicating the dilemma "*either* dependent *or* looking after"; the correlation between *is dependent on* and *gives in to* was low (−0.15) implying the dilemma "*either* dependent on *or* giving in to", and the correlation between *gives in to* and *is cross with* was high (0.38) implying the dilemma "*if* giving in to, *then* cross". The two-component graph of Anne's grid is given in Fig. 2 Going round the space defined by the graph in a clockwise direction starting from the top, we go through forgiveness, relaxed affection, respect, demanding, dependent, cross, blame, and guilt, control, gives in to, and supportive. In this graph, the reciprocal ends of each dyadic relationship are joined by a line; the most striking observation from this graph is that in her relationships, whether at the negative (left-hand) or positive (right-hand) end of the first component, Anne usually sees herself as playing the forgiving, caring role to the respecting dependence of the other; the exceptions are her relationship with her husband and tutor. The importance of this recognition will be clear to the reader who has followed her case history, and the fact that the most polarized dyad on this dimension is that of self-to-mother will come as no surprise. The restrictive "theory of relationships" identified in this grid data was incorporated in the target problems elaborated at the end of her assessment session, in particular in number 4 (the problem of compulsive caretaking).

DIFFERENT ASSUMPTIONS IN SELF–OTHER AND OTHER–SELF RELATIONSHIPS

The construct correlations derived from the analysis of a whole dyad grid are based upon all the ratings and this does not take account of the fact that the meaning system applied to self–other relationships may differ from that applied to other–self relationships. Whether this is so can be investigated by analysing two halves of the grid separately and comparing the two grids, using Slater's Coin program (Slater 1972b). In Anne's case, the self–other and other–self grids were, in fact, very dissimilar, the coefficient of convergence between them, which is a measure similar to a correlation, being only 0.30. The differences between the two grids were therefore investigated for their psychological interest. Table 2 lists all those construct correlations with the constructs *looks after, controls, is dependent on* and *gives in to,* which differed between these two grids by 35° or more of angular distance. Anne's "theory of relationships" can be understood more fully on the basis of this Table, which reveals certain special "rules" distinguishing the implication of various constructs. This can be summarized (in Anne's voice) as follows:

When I look after you I control, blame, and give in to you and I do not respect you; when you look after me you respect me, you tend to control me, and do not blame me. If I control

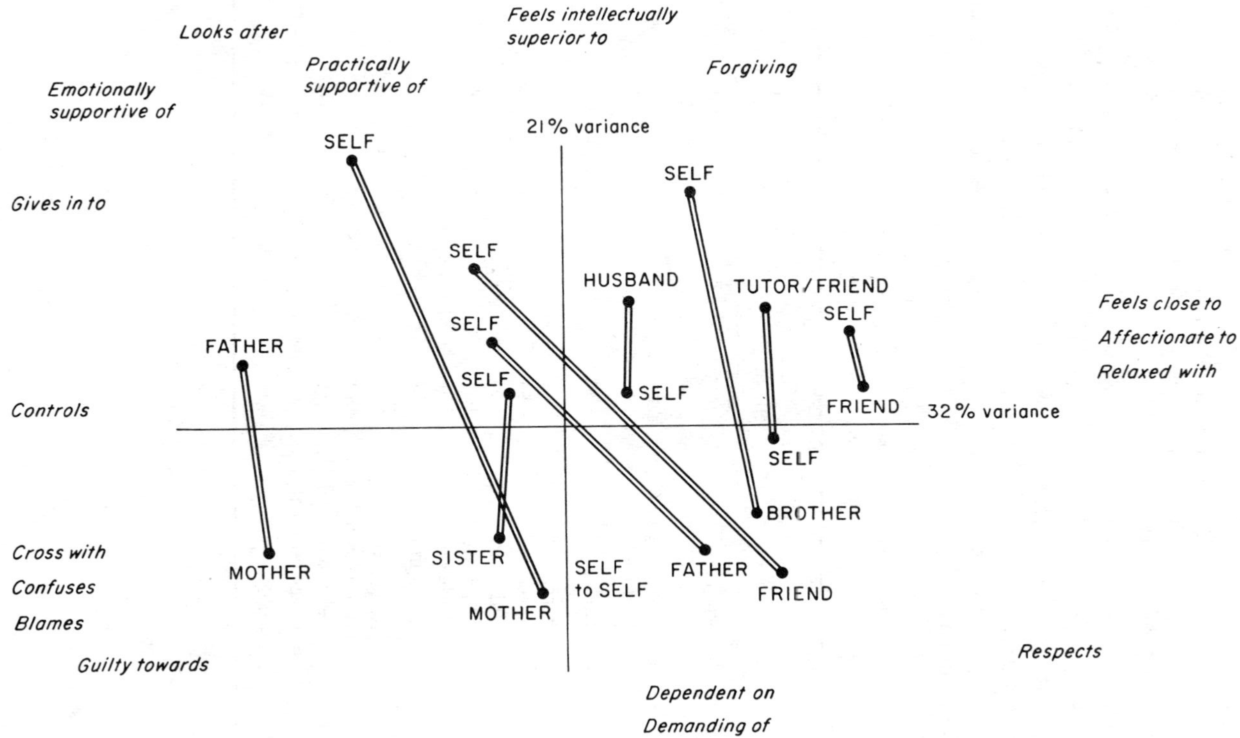

Appendix Fig. 2 Ann's dyad grid.

you I do not feel guilty but if you control me you do feel guilty; when I depend upon you it is associated with respect for you; I do not feel guilty, feel cross with, or blame, you, or give in to you, but when you depend upon me you do all those things; when I give in to you it is associated with the giving of practical support but I do not feel relaxed with you and do not respect you; if you give in to me it is associated with feeling affectionate and relaxed but not with giving me practical support.

These differences suggest that the 'theory' owes much to her relationship with her mother, showing in particular how Anne's giving of care involves blaming control of the other but how she was able to receive care from those whom she respected. The fact that dependence, for herself, did not have a negative connotation, which dependence in others had, was important in allowing her to have a good relationship with her husband and allowing her to commit herself to therapy.

Table 2 Angular distances between four constructs and all other constructs differing by 35° or more between self–other and other–self grids.

		Grid of self–to–other elements	Grid of other–to–self elements
Looks after	Respects	109	55
	Blames	56	108
	Gives in to	64	90
	Controls	31	71
Controls	Guilty	90	38
Dependent on	Forgiving to	101	62
	Respects	33	70
	Guilty to	100	62
	Cross with	102	61
	Blames	113	65
	Gives in to	128	57
Gives in to	Respects	143	96
	Affectionate to	87	38
	Relaxed with	123	67
	Gives practical support to	61	109

Appendix References

Fransella. F. and Bannister. D. (1977). "A Manual for Repertory Grid Technique". London and New York, Academic Press.

Kelly, G.A. (1955). "The Psychology of Personal Constructs". New York, Norton.

Ryle, A. (1975). "Frames and Cages". London, Sussex Univ. Press, Chatto & Windus.

Ryle, A. (1979). Defining goals and assessing change in brief psychotherapy: a pilot study using target ratings and the dyad grid. *Brit. J. Med. Psychol.* **52**, 223–233.

Ryle, A. (1980). Some measures of goal attainment in focussed, integrated, active psychotherapy, a study of fifteen cases. *Brit. J. Psychiat.* **137**, 475–486.

Ryle, A. (1981). Dyad grid dilemmas in patient and control subjects. *Brit. J. Med. Psychol.* **54**, 353–358.

Ryle, A. and Lipshitz S. (1975). Recording change in marital therapy with the reconstruction grid. *Brit. J. Med. Psychol.* **48**, 39–48.

Ryle, A. and Lipshitz, S. (1976). Repertory grid elucidation of a difficult conjoint therapy. *Brit. J. Med. Psychol.* **49**, 281–285.

Ryle, A. and Lunghi, M. (1970). The dyad grid — a modification of repertory grid technique. *Brit. J. Psychiat.* **117**, 323–327.

Slater, P. (1972a). "Notes on Ingrid '72". London, Inst. of Psychiatry.

Slater, P. (1972b). The measurement of consistency in repertory grids. *Brit. J. Psychiat.* **121**, 45–51.

Author Index

Augustine, St., 55
Amacher, P., 18
Appelbaum, S.A., 128
Ascher, L.M., 99

Bancroft, J., 53
Bandura, A., 18, 37, 78
Bannister, D., 184
Bartlett, F.C., 16, 17
Battle, C.C., 148
Bayer, C.A., 100
Beck, A.T., 6, 18, 33, 37, 52, 92, 99
Bergin, A.E., 5, 160
Blake, Y., 141
Bower, G.H., 18
Brown, D., 127
Bruch, H., 42
Bruner, J., 74

Cade, B., 99
Candy, J., 5
Ceely, S.G., 66
Crowe, M., 53

Davanloo, H., 89
Dockar-Drysdale, B., 137

Ellis, A., 99
Emmelkamp, P.N.G., 99
Epstein, S., 66
Erikson, E., 66

Fairbairn, B.D., 19
Försterling, F., 36
Fransella, F., 184
Freud, A., 37
Freud, S., 122

Gallwey, P.L.G., 116
Garfield, S.L., 5
Gelder, M., 99
Gill, H., 138
Glasgow, R.E., 174
Goin, M.C., 159
Goldfried, A.P., 18, 99
Goldfried, M.R., 18, 99
Gorman, A.S., 5, 53
Green, H., 141
Guntrip, H., 19, 141

Haan, N. 24, 37, 66
Hafner, R.J., 100
Haldane, J.D., 160
Haley, J., 99
Hartmann, H., 19
Heppner, P.P., 68
Hobson, R.F., 160
Holzman, P.S., 100
Horney, K., 56

Joffe, W.G., 19
Johnson, V.E., 53

Kaplan, H., 53
Katz, J.M., 42, 53
Kazdin, A., 5
Kelly, G.A., 8, 11, 17
Kennedy, H., 39
Kernberg, G., 141
Khan, M., 115
Klein, G., 39
Klerman, G.Z., 140
Kline, F.M., 159
Kohut, H., 56
Kovacs, M., 89

Kris, A.D., 30
Kris, E., 39
Kubie, L.S., 159
Kuhn, T., 80

Laing, R.D., 7
Lang, P.J., 74
Lazarus, A., 18
Lieberman, S., 160
Lipshitz, S., 183
Loevinger, J., 37
Lomas, P., 155
Luborsky, L., 5
Lunghi, M., 183

Mahler, M.S., 141
Mahoney, M.J., 99
Main, T., 141
Malan, D.H., 6, 88, 89, 128, 148
Mancuso, J.C., 66
Mann, J., 89, 148
Margison, F., 160
Marmor, J., 127
Masters, W.H., 53
Matarazzo, R.G., 159
McCoy, M., 52
Mead, G.H., 66
Meares, R.A., 160
Meichenbaum, D.H., 18, 99
Miller, G.A., 17
Milner, M., 141
Minsky, M., 39
Mischel, W., 99

Neisser, U., 17
Noy, P., 19

Oatley, K., 17, 20
Older, J., 160
Olds, D., 127

Pappert, S., 39
Parkes, C.M., 53
Pedder, J., 127
Perry J.C., 140
Pine, F., 141
Pines, M., 132
Plutchik, R., 53

Razin, A.M., 5
Rehm, L.P., 33, 34
Rosen, G.M., 174
Roth, S., 33, 34
Rotter, J.B., 18, 35, 37
Rush, A.J., 6
Ryle, A., 6, 17, 24, 39, 76, 88, 90, 100, 148, 183
Ryle, G., 71

Sandler, J., 19, 113, 123
Santostefano, S., 39
Schachtel, E.G., 43
Schachter, S., 42, 52
Schafer, R., 18, 41, 129
Schwartz, M.S., 141
Sifneos, P., 88, 89
Singer, G.L., 18
Singer, J.F., 42, 52
Skynner, R. 53
Slater, P., 185
Sloane, R.B., 5, 128
Stanton, A.H., 141
Steiner, J., 141
Strachey, J., 112, 114
Strupp, H.H., 5, 128

Turner, J., 67
Turner, R.M., 99

Wessels, H., 99
White, R.W., 19
Whitehead, A., 33
Wilson, G.T., 5, 100
Winnicott, D., 132, 141
Wolberg, L.R., 89
Wolf, E.S., 66, 141
Wood, D., 68
Woods, S.W., 127

Subject Index

Abandonment of aims, 22–23, 31
Anorexia nervosa, 48

Behavioural treatment, 95–100
  of sexual problems, 51
  relaxation, 172
  rehearsal, 172
Behaviourism,
  and human values, 2
  and learning, 74
  and the PSM, 33
  developments in, 18
Borderline patients, 130, 140–141
Bulimia, 28, 48, 93, 124, 143

Case histories,
  Anne, 8, 15, 30, 33, 38, 44, 57, 62, 64, 83, 86, 106, 124, 146, 171, and Appendix
  David, 10, 15, 28, 31, 32, 43, 57, 61–64, 83, 84, 105, 126, 145, 171
  Beth (regression), 139
  Bridget (phobia), 96
  Charlotte (self-monitoring, transference), 93, 108
  Cora (self-monitoring diary), 94
  Eileen (hysterical symptoms), 45
  James (psychosomatic symptoms), 46–47
  Jane (physical contact), 158
  Kate (limited therapy), 132
  Michael (self-monitoring), 92
  Nora (transference), 168
  Peter (transference), 106
  Rachel (dreams and target problem ratings), 124, 143
  Robert (phobia, obsessive-compulsive), 26
  Ronald (limited therapy), 133
  Rosa (denial), 24
  Sally (panic attacks), 95
  Win (transference), 109
Cognitive model, 2, 8, 11, 12 *et seq.*
Cognitive psychology and learning, 74
Cognitive psychotherapy,
  and the PSM, 33
Cognitive styles, 39
Consciousness, 16, 20, 98, and Appendix
Constructions, 122
Countertransference, 153, 158

Defence mechanisms
  denial, 23, 37, 38
  projective identification, 60–62, 148
  reaction formation, 37
  regression, 28
  repression, 24, 37, 38
  splitting, 60, 148
Depression
  as trap 27
  endogenous factors 27
Dilemmas, 29–30, 83–84, 124, 165
Disclaimed actions, 41
Dreams, 124

Efficacy,
  of self, 37
Emotions,
  abnormal emotional states, 42
  and "embeddedness", 43
  in cognitive terms, 41 *et seq.*
  physical changes in, 42, 44
Emotional states,
  related to loss, 48, 53
  related to sexual intimacy, 49 *et seq.*
Ending treatment (*see* Termination)

Expectancies, 34, 35

Focus,
  of psychotherapy (*see* Target problems)

Goals of therapy (*see* Target problems)

Hysterical symptoms, 45

Interpretation, 123

Learning,
  and emotion, 71
  and the PSM, 22
  and therapy, 68 *et seq.*
Locus of control, 33, 36

Memory, 16
  cognitive view of, 122
  recovery of, during psychoanalysis, 38–39
Models,
  of man, 2, 7, *et seq.*
Motivation, 41

Negative therapeutic reaction, 32

Object-relations, 59–60
Obsessive-compulsive symptoms, 25, 26, 29, 174

Panic attacks, 95, 133
Paradoxical intention, 95–96, 99, 173
Personality, 71
Personal therapy file, 82, 161 *et seq.*
Phobia, 25, 173
Primary process thought, 19
Problem-solving, 68
Procedural sequence, 12
Procedural sequence model (PSM), 12–15
  and defence mechanisms, 23
  and other theories, 17–20, 33–40, 97
Projective identification (*see* Defences)
Psychoanalysis, 2, 18
  and learning, 74
Psychosomatic symptoms, 48, 109
Psychotherapist,
  opaqueness of, 156
  research into training of, 159
  responsibility for control of, 157 *et seq.*
  training of, 150 *et seq.*, 159
Psychotherapy,
  aims of, 2, 72
  depth of, 127–128
  harmful, 160
  outcome research, 5, 184
  selection for, 76 *et seq.*, 88
  starting, 77–79
  supportive, 81
  the setting for, 81, 154

Regression (*see* Defence mechanisms)
  in the course of treatment, 136 *et seq.*

Schema, 12
Schematic mismatch,
  and emotion, 42
Schizoid patients, 130
Script, 12
Self, 54 *et seq.*
  attitude to, 59
  infantile roots of, 55–58, 62
Self-esteem sources,
  test, 167 *et seq.*
Self-help, 174
Self-monitoring, 91–95, 120, 164
Separation,
  adolescent conflicts 50
Sexual difficulties, 51
Sexual identity, 58
Snags, 31, 83–84, 166
  and family therapy 31
Social learning theory, 18, 98
Splitting (see Defences)
Symptoms,
  self-monitoring of, 120
Symptom substitution, 100

Target problems,
  of psychotherapy, 79–80, 83–84, 89, 120, 148
  rating progress on, 142 *et seq.*
Termination of therapy, 144
Therapist,
  as teacher, 70, 73
Transference, 82, 102 *et seq.*
  "cures", 148
  effect of active therapeutic methods on, 115, 127
  in terms of PSM, 111 *eq seq.*
  psychoanalytic definition of, 113–114
  sexualization of, 112
  training in use of, 155
Traps, 25, 37, 83–84, 163
  placation trap, 29
  social isolation trap, 29